LESSONS IN THE SHANGHAI DIALECT

This edition published by Lector House in 2024

ISBN: 978-93-5800-993-4

Lector House LLP
Registered Office: H. No. 96, Block C, Tomar Colony,
Burari, Delhi – 110084, India
info@lectorhouse.com
www.lectorhouse.com

LESSONS IN THE SHANGHAI DIALECT

FRANCIS LISTER HAWKS POTT

2024

LECTOR HOUSE LLP

LESSONS IN THE SHANGHAI DIALECT

BY

REV. F. L. HAWKS POTT, D.D.

REVISED EDITION

Preface

At a time when there is much discussion in China as to the desirability and possibility of the adoption of a uniform language all over the Empire, it may seem strange to put forth a book on the Shanghai Dialect.

The writer sympathizes fully with the aims of those who would make Mandarin the Medium of Communication throughout China, but at the same time feels very strongly that a great many years must pass before this can be accomplished.

Local Dialects die hard, as witness the still existing varieties of speech found in Great Britain. Even more perfect means of communication binding the parts of a country closely together, and even the introduction of a common language into the School System, are not able of themselves to do away with the speaking of the old local dialect. Men cling persistently to the speech of their forefathers.

When we reflect that the so-called Shanghai Dialect is in reality the ancient language of the Wu Kingdom, and is perhaps more closely akin to the original language of the Chinese people than Mandarin, we can understand why it will last for many years.

Further, it has a very wide range. Although local varieties occur every few miles, yet in the main the Shanghai Dialect is understood by at least 20,000,000 of people.

For the missionary working is the Kiangsu Province a knowledge of the local dialect is indispensable, and the acquisition of it would be most useful for all those whose lot is cast to this part of China. Foreigners living in Shanghai would find it a great advantage to speak the native language, and in their business relations with the Chinese would be greatly helped if they could converse is something better than the jargon known as "Pidgin" English.

It is for the purpose of making the attainment of a speaking knowledge of the language somewhat less difficult that the writing of this book has been undertaken.

It has seemed to the writer that the acquisition of a knowledge of the written characters, and of the spoken language are two distinct things. It is possible for one to learn to speak the language without being able to read the characters.

By the use of the clear and simple System of Romanization, adopted by missionaries in Shanghai, it is possible to represent approximately all the sounds employed in the dialect.

In these lessons this system is adopted, and the student is urged to master it thoroughly. If he will do so, he can use these lessons and learn to speak the language even without knowing the characters.

The characters of all the words and sentences employed are given, but they are put in the book for the benefit of the Chinese teacher. It would be unwise to trust entirely to the Romanization. The student in using the book should have a teacher by his side, who by reading the Chinese corresponding to the romanized sounds can give him a clearer idea of the pronunciation.

Although in a sense the book is a short cut to learning the spoken language, of course it is not meant to discourage the student from mastering the written language. This is however, a distinct study, and should be undertaken in a different way. The best method for this will be to use a primer in vernacular containing the most familiar characters, and then to advance from it to the reading of the New Testament or other books in the vernacular. Vernacular books should be read first, for the reading of them will be a great assistance in learning the spoken language. After the first year, books in the literary style (Wên-li) should be begun.

In using this book, the first thing to be mastered thoroughly is the introductory matter. The student must get this first, for it is the key to the rest of the book. He must also learn to distinguish the tones, and the inflections of the voice which they imply. Then he will be ready to go on with the lessons.

Although the book is divided into thirty lessons, it is not expected that the student will be able to master a lesson a day. Some of the lessons will require three or four days' work.

In putting the English sentences into Chinese, the best plan would be to write out in the Romanization what the student thinks the proper way of translating them would be. Then these sentences may be read to the teacher, who will correct them, and from the Chinese text will be able to tell the right way to say them.

At present only thirty lessons are published. The writer hopes, however, if the method proves to be useful, to extend these lessons still further in the future.

In preparing these lessons, many books have been consulted, especially the lessons by Dr. Yates, which contain a most useful collection of words and sentences, and have long been the standard book for learning the Dialect, the Grammar by Dr. Edkins which contains a mass of useful information in regard to the structure of the language, and the Mandarin Lessons by Dr. Mateer, a most exhaustive work on spoken Chinese.

The writer's thanks are due especially to Rev. J. A. Silsby for the permission to make use of his clear statement of the Shanghai System of Romanization, and to Prof. F. C. Cooper for many suggestions and the trouble he has taken in reading the proofs.

The unfailing courtesy of Rev. G. F. Fitch, D.D., Messrs. Gilbert McIntosh and C. W. Douglass has been much appreciated, in the care they have taken in seeing the book through the Press.

F. L. H. P.

January 1st, 1907.

The Revised Edition

The compiler of these lessons is gratified to find that they have proved useful to students of the Shanghai Dialect. He regrets that he has been too much occupied to prepare additional lessons.

In reprinting them care has been taken to make the necessary corrections. The copy used by the late Prof. W. O'B. Harding has been of great service in the work of revision, as in it almost all the errors in tone marks, punctuation, and typography had been noted. Dr. A. W. Tucker has very kindly compiled the vocabularies at the end of the book, and in this way has enhanced its value.

The author's thanks are due to all those who have given him suggestions and pointed out mistakes.

F. L. H. P.

April 28th, 1909.

New Edition

In preparing the new edition, the author has received most valuable help from his colleague, Prof. F. C. Cooper. The two new lessons were suggested by him, and the one containing more useful words and phrases is the result of his experience, gained through teaching the book to a class of beginners.

My thanks are also due to him for the time and care he has spent in correcting the proofs, and seeing the book through the press.

The author hopes the book will continue to be a useful stepping-stone in the acquisition of a knowledge of the Shanghai Dialect.

Inasmuch as Davis's Shanghai Dialect Exercises may be used as a second book after the completion of this, it has not been deemed necessary to add many new lessons.

F. L. H. P.

October 29th, 1913.

*　　*　　*　　*　　*

In putting out this new edition, the author has made necessary corrections, and added a few new terms. The Chinese language is changing rapidly at the present time. Some expressions and terms formerly used have become obsolete and new ones have taken their place.

The French Fathers at Siccawei, with the author's permission, have published a French edition, and it is gratifying to think that the influence of this book has in this way been further extended.

Attention is called to a very good little book, "Conversational Lessons in the Shanghai Dialect," prepared by Dr. Frank Rawlinson and Rev. J. W. Crofoot, which has as its subtitle "A Supplement to Dr. Pott's Lessons." The author would recommend it as a second book in the course on the study of the Shanghai dialect.

F. L. H. P.

November 18th, 1924.

Description of the Shanghai Romanized System

Nearly all the syllables are represented by the combination of an initial and a final, a system which has been found to be well adapted to the Chinese language.

Initials

Chinese sounds are divided into upper and lower series. The initials to represent the UPPER SERIES are—*p*, *'m*, *'v*, *t*, *ts*, *s*, *'l*, *'n*, *'ny*, *'ng*, *k*, *ky*, *kw*, *i* and *'w*. These initials are pronounced in most cases much the same as in English, but without aspiration, higher in pitch and with very little vibration of the larynx. The apostrophe before a letter indicates that the letter belongs to the "higher series." Pure vowel initials also belong to this series.

ny has a sound similar to that of *ni* in span*i*el

ky = *ch* in *ch*uk with all aspiration eliminated.

i as an initial has the sounds of *i* in dahl*i*a.

The ASPIRATES are—*ph*, *f*, *th*, *tsh*, *ky*, *ch*, *khw*, *h*, *hy*, and *hw* (*th* as in *Th*omson—not as in *th*ing).

ch = *ch* in *ch*urch.

hy is nearly like *ti* in Por*ti*a.

The other aspirates are like the corresponding initials of the higher series with the addition of a strong aspiration (indicated by *h*).

The initials to represent the LOWER SERIES are—*b*, *m*, *v*, *d*, *dz*, *z*, *l*, *n*, *ny*, *ng*, *g*, *j*, *gw*, *y*, and *w*. Their pronunciation is much the same as in English. They are lower in pitch than corresponding initials of the "higher series," and have more "voice," being pronounced with more decided vibration of the larynx. The lower vowel initials, indicated by an inverted comma (') and attended with a slight aspiration, belong to this series. It will be noted that this sign differs from that employed to indicate that a consonant initial belongs to the upper series, an apostrophe being used to denote the "upper initial." This inverted comma is used only before vowels, and if, by mistake, this sign is used before a consonant instead of the apostrophe, this need not confuse the reader, for the sign of the upper series is properly used only before the initial consonants *m*, *v*, *l*, *n*, *ny*, *ng*, *w*, and *r*.

It should be noted well that the difference between the corresponding initials of the upper and lower series is not so much a difference in consonantal quality as a difference in pitch, but there is a real consonantal difference. The higher series may be classified as *surd* and the lower as *sonant*.

Finals

1. The Vowel Endings are—*a*, *e*, *i*, *au*, *o*, *oo*, *eu*, *u*, *ui*, *ia*, *iau*, *ieu*, and *ie*.

2. The Nasal Endings are—(*a*) *an*, *en*, *ien* and *oen*, in which the *n* is not sounded, but lengthens out and imparts a nasal quality to the preceding vowel; (*b*) *ang*, *aung*, *oong*, *ung* and *iang*, in which *ng* has the value of *ng* in so*ng*; (*c*) *uin*, in which *n* is sonant and has a value varying between *n* and *ng*.

3. The Abrupt Vowel Endings are—*ak*, *ah*, *eh*, *ih*, *auh*, *ok*, *oeh*, *uh*, and *iak*, in which *h* and *k* are the signs of the *zeh-sung* (入聲), and the vowel is pronounced in a short, abrupt manner.

The sounds of the vowels are—

a as in f*a*r, except when followed by *n* or *h*, when it has the sound of *a* is m*a*n or m*a*t.

e as in pr*e*y; before *h* it has the sound of *e* as in m*e*t.

i as in capr*i*ce; before *h* or *ng* it is shortened to *i* as in m*i*t or s*i*ng.

au as in *Au*gust.

o as in s*o*.

oo as in *oo* in t*oo*.

oe as in œ G*oe*the (German ö).

eu as in French Monsi*eu*r.

u as in *oo* in f*oo*t (always preceded by an *s* sound).

ui as in fruit (or rather, French ü).

In *ia*, *iau*, *ieu* and *ie*, we have short *i* followed closely by *a*, *au*, *eu*, and *e*, as described above.

Of course it is understood that the Chinese sounds in a majority of cases vary somewhat from the English sounds which are given as the nearest equivalent. The true pronunciation of Chinese sounds should be learned from a Chinese teacher, and the student should always bear it in mind that *any Romanization used does not represent English sounds, but Chinese sounds*. This fact can not be too strongly emphasized.

The DOK-YOONG Z-MOO—"Initials *used alone*," i.e., without vowels, are—*ts*, *tsh*, *dz*, *s*, *z*, *m*, *ng*, and *r*. The first five are followed by the vowel sound in the second syllable of *able*—prolonged. Mateer and Baller use *ï* for this sound and the new Mandarin Romanized uses *i̤*. It is not written, but understood in the Shanghai system. *m* has the sound of *m* in chas*m* and *ng* the sound of *ng* in ha*ng*er. *r* is a sound between final *r* and *l*.

Tones

The tones are four in number, each occurring in the upper and lower series. As has been stated, the upper and lower series can be distinguished by the initials. Sounds in the upper series are of higher pitch and those in the lower series of a lower pitch.

The names of the tones are:—

Bing sung	=	Even sound 平聲.
Zang sung	=	Rising sound 上聲.
Chui-sung	=	Going sound 去聲.
Zeh-sung	=	Entering sound 人聲.

Tone Signs

° to the left of a word indicates the tone to be °*zang-sung*.

° to the right indicates the *chui-sung*. Final *h* or *k* indicate the *zeh-sung*. All other words are in the *bing-sung*.

Sounds of the Tones

The sounds of the tones of course can only be learnt from the Chinese teacher.

The Bing-sung is an even tone, the voice being level, with a slight falling inflection, as when we say "Come," "Hear," in our imperatives.

The Zang-sung in the upper series is a twanging sound, and sounds something like the vibration of a string of a musical instrument.

In the lower series it has a wave sound which can be symbolized to the eye by the curve ~; the voice first falls and then rises.

The Chui-sung has the same sound in both the upper and lower series. The voice rises much as it does when we ask a question.

The students should practise with the teacher on the following table of sounds, and in time will be able to distinguish the tones clearly and to make the proper inflection himself. Foreigners are seldom able to perfect themselves in the use of tones, but this is due not so much to inability as to the lack of attention paid to the matter at the beginning of the study of the language.

It should be understood that the names of the tones are those of the original tones and often bear no relation to the inflection now used, which varies in different localities.

Complete List of Initials and Finals used in the Shanghai Dialect

ZAUNG-HE LOO-MO Z

Z-MOO 字母 Initial Sounds			
P	p	不	杯
Ph	ph	潑	坏
B	b	孛	賠
’M	’m	每	螟
M	m	末	明
’V	’v	勿	
F	f	拂	°粉
V	v	物	°忿
T	t	糙	堆
Th	h	脫	推
D	d	疊	臺
Ts	ts	執	避
Tsh	tsh	出	义
Dz	dz	姪	茶
S	s	失	衰
Z	z	十	裁
’L	’l	拎	°擄
L	l	垃	°櫓

'N	'n	乃	懦°
N	n	納	怒°
'Ny	'ny	拈	°撚
Ny	ny	業	°染
'Ng	'ng	'颜	一颜
Ng	ng	丌	呆
K	k	鴿	加
Kh	kh	磕	揩
G	g	搿	茄
Ky	ky	吉	鳩
Ch	ch	怯	邱
J	j	及	求
Kw	kw	骨	規
Khw	khw	闊	奎
Gw	gw	揆	葵
I	i	一	腰
Y	y	葉	姚
'W	'w	威	彎
W	w	活	還
H	h	黑	亨
Hy	hy	歇	興
Hw	hw	忽	昏
'	'	合	恒

IUNG-YUIN 音韻
Vowel sounds and finals

A	a	挨	篩
Ang	ang	櫻	生
Ak	ak	矮	柵
An	an	俺	三
Ah	ah	押	殺
E	e	哀	衰
En	en	菴	攮

Eh	eh	齾	失
I	i	衣	西
Ien	ien	煙	先
Ing	ing	喑	心
Ih	ih	一	雪
Au	au	凹	燒
Aung	aung	盎	霜
Auh	auh	惡	朔
O	o	喔	沙
Ok	ok	屋	束
Oo	oo	烏	梭
Oong	oong	翁	松
Oe	oe	隨	雖
Oen	oen	安	酸
Oeh	oeh	曷	率
Eu	eu	謳	收
Ung	ung	恩	深
Uh	uh	厄	色
U	u	如	書
Ui	ui	餘	須
Uin	uin	雲	熏
Ia	ia	雅	斜
Iang	iang	央	廂
Iak	iak	約	削
Iau	iau	夭	小
Ieu	ieu	憂	修

DOK YOONG Z-MOO 獨用字母
Constants used as words

M	m	嘸	姆
Ts	ts	之	資
Tsh	tsh	雌	痴
Dz	dz	池	遲

S	s	思	施
Z	z	時	鰣
’R	’r	°耳	
R	r	而	兒
Ng	Ng	魚	吳

The student should practise repeating after the teacher the pronunciation of the characters in which these sounds occur.

Exercise in Tones

上平聲	Upper Bing-sung.	Tau,	刀	Pa,	叭	Si,	犀
下平聲	Lower Bing-sung.	Dau,	桃	Ba,	排	Zi,	徐
上上聲	Upper Zang-sung.	°Tau,	禱	°Pa,	擺	°Si,	死
下上聲	Lower Zang-sung.	°Dau,	道	°Ba,	罷	°Zi,	薺
上去聲	Upper Chui-sung.	Tau°,	倒	Pa°,	拜	Si°,	壻
下去聲	Lower Chui-sung.	Dau°,	導	Ba°,	敗	Zi°,	謝
上入聲	Upper Zeh-sung.	Tauh,	沰	Pah,	八	Sih,	息
下入聲	Lower Zeh-sung.	Dauh,	度	Bah,	拔	Zih,	蓆

The student should practise upon the sounds illustrating the different tones. The columns should be read from the top down. The teacher can guide him by first pronouncing the Chinese characters.

Contents

Lesson I

The Classifier

A or an is translated into Chinese by the numeral ***ih*** (一) one, and a classifier placed between the numeral and the noun. There are over forty classifiers, different nouns taking different ones, according to the class to which they belong. Nouns being generally used with classifiers accounts for the fact that in Pidgin English we have the oft recurring expression, "one piecee."

Most concrete nouns take classifiers, but not all. Exceptions will be pointed out later on. Sometimes when the object spoken of is quite definitely known, the noun is used without the classifier.

In this lesson, the two most common classifiers will be introduced, and in succeeding lessons the others will appear gradually.

It must be remarked that some nouns may take more than one classifier, sometimes one being used and sometimes another.

The most common classifier is ***kuh*** (個). "It is applied to such nouns as have no special classifier, and *may* upon occasion be applied to almost any noun as a substitute for the special classifier" (Mateer).

The classifier ***tsak*** (隻) is used with animals, birds, fowls, insects; also with articles of furniture having legs or resting on a base; also with vessels, boats, etc.

Vocabulary

A man, **ih kuh nyung** 一個人.

A woman, **ih kuh °nyui-nyung** (lit. female human being) 一個女人.

A teacher, **ih kuh sien-sang** (lit. born before) 一個先生.

A child, **ih kuh °siau-noen** 一個小囝.

An egg, **ih kuh dan°** 一個蛋.

A cash, **ih kuh doong-dien** 一個銅錢.

(See second note at end of lesson.)

A dollar, **ih kuh yang-dien** 一個洋錢.

A servant, **ih kuh yoong°-nyung** 一個用人.

A table, **ih tsak de-°ts** 一隻檯子.

A chair, **ih tsak iui°-°ts** 一隻椅子.

An orange, **ih tsak kyoeh-°ts** 一隻橘子.

A pupil, **ih kuh 'auh-sang-°ts** 一個學生子.

To want, to wish, **iau°** 要. Also used in forming the future tense of verbs, as will be explained later.

Exercises

(Translate into English)

(1) Ih kuh nyung iau° ih tsak de-°ts.

(2) Ih kuh °nyui-nyung iau° ih tsak iui°-°ts.

(3) Ih kuh °siau-noen iau° ih kuh doong-dien.

(4) Ih kuh 'auh-sang-°ts iau° ih kuh sien-sang.

(5) Ih kuh yoong°-nyung iau° ih kuh dan°.

(6) Ih kuh yoong°-nyung iau° ih kuh yang-dien.

(7) Ih kuh °siau-noen iau° ih tsak kyoeh-°ts.

(一) 一個人要一隻檯子.

(二) 一個女人要一隻椅子.

(三) 一個小囝要一個銅錢.

(四) 一個學生子要一個先生.

(五) 一個用人要一個蛋.

(六) 一個用人要一個洋錢.

(七) 一個小囝要一隻橘子.

(Translate into Chinese)

(1) A pupil wants an orange.

(2) A woman wants a dollar.

(3) A servant wants a cash.

(4) A teacher wants a table.

(5) A man wants an egg.

(6) A pupil wants a chair.

(7) A teacher wants a pupil.

(一) 一個學生子要一隻橘子.
(二) 一個女人要一個洋錢.
(三) 一個用人要一個銅錢.
(四) 一個先生要一隻檯子.
(五) 一個人要一個蛋.
(六) 一個學生子要一隻椅子.
(七) 一個先生要一個學生子.

NOTES.

(1) It is difficult to form idiomatic sentences in Chinese until a larger vocabulary has been given.

(2) With *yang-dien* (洋錢) the classifier generally used is *kwhe°* (塊), a piece or slice.

(3) It will be noticed how many words are formed from the combination of two or more words. This is a characteristic of the Chinese language; for instance the word *yoong°-nyung* (用人) is composed of the verb *yoong°* (用) use, and the word *nyung* (人) man, and means the man whom you use or employ.

(4) With *sien-sang* (先生), the classifier *we°* (位) is generally used.

(5) Nouns take no change in form for the plural, but the classifier is omitted.

(6) With *iui°-ts°* (椅子), the classifier *°po* (把) is sometimes used.

Lesson II

Demonstrative, and Personal Pronouns.

The definite article *the* is not expressed directly in Chinese, but the demonstrative pronoun takes its place.

The demonstrative pronouns are:

This or these, **di° kuh** 第個.	That or those, **i-kuh** 伊個.

The demonstrative pronouns change their forms with different nouns, being formed by the ***di°*** (第) or ***i*** (伊) and the classifier belonging to the noun. Thus "this table" is not ***di°-kuh de-°ts*** but ***di°-tsak de-°ts*** (第隻檯子).

When the demonstrative is used with a numeral it retains the form ***di°-kuh*** (第個) or ***i-kuh*** (伊個) and the classifier of the noun comes between the numeral and the noun. Thus "this one table" is ***di°-kuh ih tsak de-°ts*** (第個一隻檯子).

The personal pronouns are as follows:

SINGULAR NUMBER

Nominative and Objective	*Possessive*
I. Person: I or me, **°ngoo** 我.	I. Person: My or mine, **°ngoo-kuh** 我個.
II. Person: Thou, thee or you, **noong°** 儂.	II. Person: Thy, thine or yours, **noong°-kuh** 儂個.
III. Person: He, she, it, him, her, **yi** 伊.	III. Person: His, hers, its, **i-kuh** 伊個.

PLURAL NUMBER

Nominative and Objective	*Possessive*

I. Person: We, or us, **nyi°** or **°ngoo-nyi°** 我伲.	I. Person: Ours, **nyi°-kuh** or **°ngoo-nyi°-kuh** 伲個, 我伲個.
II. Person: You or ye, **na°** 儂	II. Person: Your, or yours, **na°-kuh** 儂個.
III. Person: They or them, **yi-la** 伊拉.	III. Person: Their, or theirs, **yi-la-kuh** 伊拉個.

The use of ***kuh*** (個) in the possessive case must be noted. ***Kuh*** (個) serves to form the possessive case of nouns as it does of pronouns. Thus to say "a man's table" would be ***ih kuh nyung kuh de-°ts*** (一個人個檯子). Exercises in possessive case formation will be found in this lesson.

Vocabulary

A son, **ih kuh 'eu-°ts** or **ih kuh nyi-°ts** 一個兒子.

A daughter, **ih kuh noen°** 一個囡.

A friend, **ih kuh bang-°yeu** 一個朋友.

A sheep, **ih tsak yang** 一隻羊.

A bird, **ih tsak °tiau** 一隻鳥.

A bed, **ih tsak zaung** 一隻牀.

°Po (把) is the classifier used with tools, instruments or articles grasped in the hand.

A knife or sword, **ih °po tau** 一把刀.

A fork, **ih °po tsho** 一把叉.

A spoon, **ih °po tshau** 一把匙.

An umbrella, **ih °po san°** 一把傘.

To have, or has, **°yeu** 有.

Exercises

(Translate into English)

(1) °Ngoo iau° ih °po tau.

(2) Di°-kuh nyung °yeu ih kuh yang-dien.

(3) Noong°-kuh bang-°yeu kuh 'eu-°ts °yeu ih tsak yang.

(4) I-kuh °nyui-nyung kuk noen° iau° ih tsak °tiau.

(5) Yi iau° ih °po san°.

(6) °Ngoo iau° ih °po tsho.

(7) Nyi° iau° ih tsak zaung.

(8) Na° °yeu ih kwhe° yang-dien.

(9) Di°-kuh sien-sang °yeu ih tsak kyoeh-°ts.

(10) I-kuh yoong°-nyung °yeu ih kuh dan°.

(一) 我要一把刀.
(二) 第個人有一個洋錢.
(三) 儂個朋友個兒子有一隻羊.
(四) 伊個女人個囡要一隻鳥.
(五) 伊要一把傘.
(六) 我要一把叉.
(七) 伲要一隻床.
(八) 㑚有一塊洋錢.
(九) 第個先生有一隻橘子.
(十) 伊個用人有一個蛋.

(Translate into Chinese)

(1) Your teacher has a table.

(2) My friend has a son.

(3) Their daughter has an umbrella.

(4) They want a bed.

(5) That servant wants a knife.

(6) This pupil's teacher has a chair.

(7) My son wants a dollar.

(8) He wants a fork.

(9) She wants a spoon.

(10) The woman's daughter has an orange.

(11) He has mine.

(12) He has yours.

(一) 儂個先生有一隻檯子.
(二) 我個朋友有一個兒子.

(三) 伊拉個囡有一把傘.

(四) 伊拉要一隻床.

(五) 伊個用人要一把刀.

(六) 第個學生子個先生有一隻椅子.

(七) 我個兒子要一塊洋錢.

(八) 伊要一把叉.

(九) 伊要一把匙.

(十) 一個女人個囡有一隻橘子.

(十一) 伊有我個.

(十二) 伊有儂個.

NOTES.

(1) Verbs undergo no change in form for the singular and plural number. Tense formation will be explained later.

(2) The verb °*yeu* is often used for the expression "there is." Thus, °*yeu ih-kuh nyung iau*° *doong-dien* (有一個人要銅錢) means, "There is a man who wants cash."

(3) °*yeu kuh* (有個) means "some." Thus °*yeu kuh nyung* (有個人) is "some men."

(4) Sometimes the *kuh* is omitted and we have °*yeu nyung*. Thus °*yeu nyung iau*° *yang-dien* (有人要洋錢) means, "some man want dollars."

Lesson III

The Numerals up to one Hundred

One, **ih** 一.

Two, **nyi°** or **°liang** 二, 两.

Three, **san** 三.

Four, **s°** 四.

Five, **°ng** 五.

Six, **lok** 六.

Seven, **tshih** 七.

Eight, **pah** 八.

Nine, **°kyeu** 九.

Ten, **zeh** 十.

From ten to twenty the numerals are formed by adding the digits after ten.

Eleven, **zeh-ih** 十一.

Twelve, **zeh-nyi°** 十二, etc.

Fifteen, **zeh-°ng**, pronounced **°se-°ng** 十五.

Twenty, **nyan°** 念. (In speaking of the day of the month **nyi°-seh** is used) 二十.

Thirty, **san-seh** 三十. (Lit. three tens. The Z sound in zeh becomes S when preceded by another word.)

Forty, **s°-seh** 四十.

Fifty, **°ng-seh** 五十.

Sixty, **lok-seh** 六十.

Seventy, **tshih-seh** 七十.

Eighty, **pah seh** 八十.

Ninety, **°kyeu-seh** 九十.

One Hundred, **ih pak** 一百.

The intervening numbers between twenty and thirty, etc., are formed regularly by adding the digits to the decimals. Thus twenty-one is ***nyan°-ih***. Thirty-one, is ***san-seh-ih***, etc.

Thirty-five is pronounced ***san-°so-°ng***.

In using the numeral with the noun, the classifier of the noun is introduced between the numeral and the noun. Thus "Four men" is ***s° kuh nyung*** (四個人) not ***s° nyung***. "Six chairs" is ***lok tsak iui°-°ts*** (六隻椅子) not ***lok iui°-°ts***.

In speaking of a thing well understood the noun is often omitted, and we have simply the numeral with the classifier, as ***lok kuh***, ***tshih tsak***, etc.

Vocabulary

A cow, **ih tsak nyeu** 一隻牛.

A native, **ih kuh °pung-di°-nyung** 一個本地人.

A foreigner, **ih kuh °nga-kok-nyung** 一個外國人. (Literally, outside kingdom man).

Children, **°siau-noen** 小囝.

A large box or trunk, **ih tsak siang-°ts** 一隻箱子.

A small box, **ih tsak 'ah-°ts** 一隻匣子.

A fan, **ih °po sen°-°ts** 一把扇子.

A broom, **ih °po °sau °tseu** 一把掃箒.

A tea pot, **ih °po dzo-'oo** 一把茶壺.

To be, is, are, **°z** 是.

Exercises

(Translate into English)

(1) °Ngoo iau° san tsak siang-°ts.

(2) °Di °po sen°-°ts °z noong°-kuh.

(3) I-kuh 'eu-°ts °yeu ih tsak 'ah-°ts.

(4) °Ngoo-kuh sien-sang iau° ih °po dzo-'oo.

(5) San-seh-ih tsak yang °z i-kuh.

(6) Nyan°-tshih tsak nyeu °z i-kuh.

(7) I-kuh °nga-kok-nyung °yeu °liang tsak iui°-°ts.

(8) San-seh, °z san kuh zeh.

(9) Ih pak, °z zeh kuh zeh.

(10) °So-°ng kuh nyung °yeu °so-°ng tsak de-°ts.

(11) Sien-sang °z °pung-di°-nyung, °ngoo °z °nga-kok-nyung.

(12) Yoong°-nyung iau° ih °po °sau-°tseu.

(一) 我要三隻箱子.
(二) 第把扇子是儂個.
(三) 伊個兒子有一隻匣子.
(四) 我個先生要一把茶壺.
(五) 三十一隻羊是伊個.
(六) 念七隻牛是伊個.
(七) 伊個外國人有两隻椅子.
(八) 三十是三個十.
(九) 一百是十個十.
(十) 十五個人有十五隻檯子.
(十一) 先生是本地人我是外國人.
(十二) 用人要一把掃箒.

(Translate into Chinese)

(1) He wants three tea pots.

(2) Four pupils want four fans.

(3) This large box is my friends.

(4) He has thirty knives.

(5) These five dollars are the pupils'.

(6) The teacher has twenty-five pupils.

(7) These two fans are his.

(8) That small box is the foreigner's.

(9) Six tens are sixty.

(10) My friend has five children, three sons and two daughters.

(一) 伊要三把茶壺.

(二) 四個學生子要四把扇子.

(三) 第隻箱子是我個朋友個.

(四) 伊有三十把刀.

(五) 第個五塊洋錢是學生子個.

(六) 先生有念五個學生子.

(七) 第個兩把扇子是伊個.

(八) 伊隻匣子是外國人個.

(九) 六個十是六十.

(十) 我個朋友有五個小囝三個兒子兩個囡.

NOTE.

'Ah-°ts is a small box in distinction from *Siang-°ts*, a large box, but as will be seen later the adjectives for large and small may also be used with both of these words.

Lesson IV

Adjectives

Certain words in Chinese are distinctly used as adjectives, but many other words, such as nouns, verbs and adverbs may be used to qualify nouns. In the expression ***dok su-nyung*** (讀書人), meaning "a scholar," we have the verb ***dok*** (讀), "to read," and the noun ***su*** (書), "book," qualifying ***nyung*** (人) "man;" the whole expression being literally "the reading-book-man."

Adjectives may be compared as follows: ***°tien*** (點) is added after the adjective to make the comparative degree, and ***°ting*** (頂) is placed before the adjective to form the superlative degree. Thus, Positive Degree, "Good," is ***°hau*** (好). Comparative Degree, "Better," is ***°hau °tien*** (好點). Superlative Degree, "Best," is ***°ting °hau*** (頂好).

There are, however, many other ways of expressing the Superlative. Thus we may have ***°hau-le-°si*** (好來死), which is literally "good-come death" that is, "good to the death." This is a very frequent expression.

We have also ***tsoe °hau*** (最好) or ***juh °hau*** (極好). Very good is usually ***'man °hau*** (蠻好). ***°Hau-tuh-juh*** (好得極) means superlatively good.

The adjective ***°hau*** (好) has a very wide use. Everything that is good, suitable, correct, or proper, may be said to be ***°hau*** (好).

Vocabulary

Good, **°hau** 好.

Bad, **cheu** (怺). More often **'veh °hau** (勿好), **'Veh** means "not."

Cold, **°lang** 冷.

Hot, **nyih** 熱.

White, **bak** 白.

Black, **huh** 黒.

Large, **doo°** 大.

Small, **°siau** 小.

A scholar, **ih kuh dok-su-nyung** 一個讀書人.

A dog, **ih tsak °keu** 一隻狗.

Water, **°s** 水, (Generally used without a classifier).

A horse, **ih tsak °mo** (一隻馬). 匹 **phih** is sometimes used as the classifier of horses.

°Pung (本) is the classifier for book.

A book, **ih °pung su** 一本書.

Diau (條) is the classifier with long, winding or limber objects.

A bridge, **ih diau jau** 一條橋.

A street, **ih diau ka** 一條街.

A road, **ih diau loo°** 一条路.

To read, to study, **dok** 讀.

To come, **le** 來.

To go, **chi°** 去.

Exercises

(Translate into English)

(1) Di°-tsak °keu °z °hau kuh.

(2) °Ngoo iau° dok su.

(3) °Ngoo iau° °lang °s.

(4) Di°-tsak yang °z huh kuh.

(5) I-tsak nyeu °z bak kuh.

(6) I-kuh °pung-di°-nyung °yeu °liang tsak huh kuh °mo.

(7) °Ngoo °yeu ih kuh bang-°yeu iau° le.

(8) Yi kuh sien-sang iau° chi°.

(9) Di°-kuh °s °z nyih kuh.

(10) Di°-diau jau °z doo° kuh.

(11) Di°-kuh ih diau ka °z °siau kuh.

(12) Di°-kuh ih diau loo° °z ’veh °hau.

(13) I-°pung su °z sien-sang kuh, di°-°pung su °z °ngoo kuh.

(14) Di°-tsak de-°ts °z °siau °tien.

(15) Di°-tsak zaung °z °ting doo°.

(一) 第隻狗是好個.

(二) 我要讀書.

(三) 我要冷水.

(四) 第隻羊是黑個.

(五) 伊隻牛是白個.

(六) 伊個本地人有兩隻黑個馬.

(七) 我有一個朋友要來.

(八) 伊個先生要去.

(九) 第個水是熱個.

(十) 第條橋是大個.

(十一) 第個一條街是小個.

(十二) 第個一條路是勿好.

(十三) 伊本書是先生個第本書是我個.

(十四) 第隻檯子是小點.

(十五) 第隻牀是頂大.

(Translate into Chinese)

(1) These five oranges are bad.

(2) The teacher wishes me to study.

(3) The native's cows are good.

(4) I have a white bird.

(5) I want warm water.

(6) The dog is very black.

(7) That bed is smaller.

(8) This box is larger.

(9) The tea pot is very white.

(10) My teacher will come.

(11) The foreigner will go.

(12) I want a large dog.

(一) 第個五隻橘子是勿好.

(二) 先生要我讀書.

(三) 本地人個牛是好個.

(四) 我有一隻白個鳥.

(五) 我要熱水.

(六) 一隻狗是黑得極.

(七) 一隻牀是小點.

(八) 第隻箱子是大點.

(九) 一把茶壺是蠻白.

(十) 我個先生要來.

(十一) 一個外國人要去.

(十二) 我要大個一隻狗.

NOTES.

(1) Adjectives generally take *kuh* after them; the kuh 個 standing between the adjective and the noun. In some cases the kuh is omitted, as in the expression °*lang* °*s* (冷水), "cold water." We do not say °*lang kuh* °*s*.

(2) *Dok-su* (讀書) is the common expression for "to study."

(3) In such a sentence as "I want warm water" the °*ngoo* (我) may be omitted. In speaking to a servant one would say *iau*° *nyih* °*s* (要熱水), "I want hot water."

Lesson V

Interrogatives, and Negatives

Va° (否) is used as the sign of a direct question, expecting the answer "yes" or "no." It is added at the end of the sentence. Thus ***di°-kuh °z noong° kuh va°?*** (第個是儂個否) means, "is this yours?" ***Di°-kuh °hau va°?*** (第個好否) means, "is this good?" (the verb ***°z*** being omitted). The Chinese do not use a rising inflection of the voice to indicate that a question is being asked.

Meh (末) is used for asking a question when the action is presumed to have been completed. Thus ***van° chuh meh?*** (飯吃末) means, "have you eaten your rice?" or "have you dined?" ***Sien-sang chi° meh?*** (先生去末) means, "has the teacher gone?"

Nyi (呢) is used for asking a question implying the alternative. Thus ***noong° chi° nyi 'veh chi°?*** (儂去呢勿去) means, "are you going or not going?" ***noong° le nyi 'veh le?*** (儂來呢勿來) means, "are you coming or not coming?"

Nyi (呢) is also used in a question expecting a negative answer, but the explanation of this must be reserved until later.

"Who" is ***sa°*** (啥). In this sense it is always joined to the noun ***nyung*** (人). Thus ***sa° nyung?*** (啥人) means, "who?" Pidgin English, "who man?"

Sa° (啥) is also used in the sense of "what." It sometimes precedes the noun as ***sa° sang-i°?*** (啥生意). "what business?" In a sentence like "what do you want," it follows the verb. Thus ***noong° iau° sa°*** (儂要啥). Literally, "you want what?"

Sa° is also used with ***va°*** in the sense of "any," in asking a question, Thus ***noong° iau° sa° va°?*** (儂要啥否) means, "do you want anything?" ***°Yeu sa° nyung iau° chi° va°?*** (有啥人要去否) means, "does any one wish to go?" ***Noong° °yeu sa° doong-dien va°?*** (儂有啥銅錢否) means, "have you any cash?"

Which is ***°'a-°li*** (那裏). It is always used with numeral and classifier. Thus

°*'a-°li ih kuh nyung?* (那裏一個人) means, "which man?" °*'A-°li ih diau loo°?* (那裏一條路) means, "which road?" °*'A-°li ih °pung su?* (那裏一本書) means, "which book?" °*'A-°li °liang °po tau?* (那裏兩把刀) means, "which two knives?" When the subject is understood about which you are conversing, the noun may be omitted, and °*'a-°li* with the numeral and the classifier are sufficient. Thus in speaking of roads °*'a-°li ih diao?* would be enough.

"No" or "not", is expressed by **'veh** (勿). Thus *yi 'veh iau° chi°* (伊勿要去) means, "he does not wish to go."

M-meh (無末) is used in the sense of "not any" in answering a question asking whether you have any, thus ***noong° °yeu sa° yang-dien va°?*** (儂有啥洋錢否) "have you any dollars?", the answer might be ***m-meh***.

Sometimes ***m-sa°*** (無啥) is used in answering questions in the negative. Thus ***noong° °yeu sa° tsoo° va°?*** (儂有啥做否) "have you anything to do?" (Have you any employment?) The answer might be ***m-sa° tsoo°*** (無啥做) "not anything to do."

No one is ***m-sa°-nyung*** (無啥人). Thus ***°yeu sa° nyung le va°?*** (有啥人來否), "has any one come?" The answer might be ***m-sa° nyung*** (無啥人).

Vocabulary

Rice (growing), **°dau** 稻.

Rice (uncooked), **°mi** 米.

Rice (cooked), **van°** 飯.

A hat, cap or bonnet. **ih °ting mau°-°ts** 一頂帽子 or **ih tsak mau°-°ts** 一隻帽子.

A carpenter, **ih kuh mok-ziang°** 一個木匠. Lit. Wood worker.

A hand, **ih tsak °seu** 一隻手.

A foot, **ih tsak kyak** 一隻脚.

Kung (根) Is the classifier denoting objects long and generally stiff.

A cane or stick, **ih kung °baung** 一根棒.

Zoo° (座) is the classifier for hills and buildings.

A house, **ih zoo° vaung-°ts** 一座房子. (Sometimes **ih zak vaung-°ts** 一宅)

Sen° (扇) is the classifier for broad objects.

A door, **ih sen° mung** 一扇門.

To eat, eats, eat, **chuh** 吃.

To invite, invites, invite, **°tshing** 請. (Also used in the sense of please, when making a request of any one).

To take, **tan** (擔) or **nau** (拿).

To call, calls, call, **kyau°** 叫.

To open, opens, open, **khe** 開.

To shut, shuts, shut, **kwan** 關.

To do, does, perform, make, **tsoo°** 做.

To enter, enters, come in, **tsing°** 進.

Exercises

(Translated into English)

(1) I-kuh sien-sang van° chuh meh?

(2) °Ngoo iau° °tshing ih we° sien-sang.

(3) Khe khe mung.

(4) Di°-kuh kyau° sa°?

(5) Kwan mung.

(6) Di°-°pung su sa° nyung tan-le kuh?

(7) °'A-°li kung °baung °z noong°-kuh?

(8) °'A-°li ih zoo° vaung-°ts °z i-kuh?

(9) Sa° nyung tan-chi° kuh?

(10) Nyung °yeu °liang tsak °seu, °liang tsak kyak.

(11) Noong° °yeu sa° sang-i° tsoo° va°?

(12) Ngoo m-sa° sang-i° tsoo°.

(13) Noong° kyau° sa°?

(14) °Yeu sa° nyung tsing°-le va°? M-sa° nyung.

(15) Noong° mau°-°ts °yeu va°? M-meh.

(一) 伊個先生飯吃末?

(二) 我要請一位先生.

(三) 開開門.

(四) 第個叫啥?

(五) 關門.

(六) 第本書啥人担來個?

(七) 那裡一根棒是儂個?
(八) 那裡一座房子是伊個?
(九) 啥人擔去個?
(十) 人有兩隻手兩隻脚.
(十一) 儂有啥生意做否?
(十二) 我無啥生意做.
(十三) 儂叫啥?
(十四) 有啥人進來啥?無啥人.
(十五) 儂帽子有否?無末.

(Translated into Chinese)

(1) Have the children eaten their rice?
(2) Which cow is yours?
(3) Which bird is black?
(4) Bring the hot water.
(5) Bring the boiling water.
(6) Please come in.
(7) Who did it?
(8) Who brought it?
(9) Who took it away?
(10) Who wants it?
(11) Who entered?
(12) Who opened the door?
(13) Who shut the door?
(14) Which table is yours?
(15) What do you want?
(16) Have you anything to eat?
(17) I have nothing to eat.
(18) Have you any oranges?
(19) I have.
(20) I have none.

(一) 小囝飯吃末?
(二) 那裡一隻牛是儂個?
(三) 那裡一隻鳥是黑個?
(四) 担熱水來.
(五) 担開水來.
(六) 請進來.
(七) 啥人做個?
(八) 啥人擔來個?
(九) 啥人擔去個?
(十) 啥人要個?
(十一) 啥人進來個?
(十二) 啥人開門?
(十三) 啥人關門?
(十四) 那裡一隻檯子是儂個?
(十五) 儂要啥?
(十六) 儂有啥吃否?
(十七) 無啥吃
(十八) 儂有啥橘子否?
(十九) 有個
(二十) 無末

NOTES.

(1) Note the difference between °*tshing* (請), *kyau*° (叫) and *han*° (喊). °*Tshing* is used in speaking to an equal or to a superior. *Kyau*° in speaking to a servant. *Han*° in even more curt than *kyau*°. Thus °*tshing yi le* (請伊來) means, "invite him to come," and is the polite form of speech if you wish an equal to come to you. *Kyau*° *yi le* (叫伊來) or *han*° *yi le* (喊伊來) would be used if you tell some one to call your servant or a workman to you.

(2) Notice the repetition of the *khe* (開) in the third sentence of the first exercise. This makes it more emphatic.

(3) The verbs *tan* (擔) "take" and *le* (來) "come" are often used together in the sense of "bring." Literally "take-come." So also with *tan* (擔) and *chi*° (去); this means, "Take away." Literally "Take-go." Sometimes the *tan* and the *le*, and the *tan*

and the *chi°* are separated from one another by other words in the sentence. Thus *tan su le* (擔書來) means "bring the books." The above remarks also hold true of *nau*.

(4) In the sixth sentence of the first exercise the words *°di-°pung su* stand first. This is because they are emphatic. It is difficult to give any hard and fast rule in regard to the order of words in a Chinese sentence, but generally speaking, we may say that the most emphatic word is placed first. In this sentence it is the *book* which is being talked about, and so it occurs first.

(5) The words in the thirteenth sentence of the first exercise would only be addressed to a servant or to a child. "What are you called?" means, "what is your name?" not "what is your surname?"

(5) In polite phraseology, in speaking to a person the pronoun *noong°* is never employed. The third person is used instead of the second. To ask your teacher his name, you would say *Tsung sing°?* (尊姓), which means, "what is your honorable name?" (surname). If you wish to inquire further as to his other name, you would say *°tshing kyau° da° 'au?* (請叫大號) which means, "please tell me your great official name?" The requirements of etiquette as to the use of words will be explained later somewhat fully.

(6) In the fifth sentence of the second exercise, the expression boiling water is used. For this the words *khe* (開) "open," and *°s* (水) "water" are used. It signifies that boiling water is open water on account of the bubbles which proceed from it.

Lesson VI

Some Remarks on the Verb

In a monosyllabic language like the Chinese the words themselves are never inflected, and therefore the Moods and Tenses of the Verbs are formed by the addition of auxiliary words to mark the change of meaning.

We will take the verb ***chuh*** (吃) to illustrate.

Indicative Mood

Present Tense, Simple Form, I eat, **°ngoo chuh** 我吃.

Present Tense, Continuous, I am eating, **°ngoo leh-°li chuh** 我拉裏吃, **°ngoo la° chuh** 我拉吃.

Past Tense, Simple Form, I ate, **°ngoo chuh kuh** 我吃個.

Past Tense, Continuous, I was eating, **°ngoo leh-la° chuh** 我拉拉吃.

Past Tense, Emphatic Form, I did eat, **°ngoo °z chuh kuh** 我是吃個.

Perfect Tense, I have eaten, **°ngoo chuh tse** 我吃哉. **°ngoo chuh° la° tse** 我吃拉哉, **°ngoo chuh koo° tse** 我吃過哉.

Past Perfect, I had eaten. **°ngoo °i-kyung chuh tse** 我已經吃哉, **°ngoo °i-kyung chuh la° tse** 我已經吃拉哉, **°ngoo °i-kyung chuh koo° hyih tse** 我已經吃過歇哉.

Future Tense, I will or shall eat, **°ngoo iau° chuh** 我要吃.

The *Future Perfect Tense* cannot be expressed directly.

The only change for the different persons is the above will be in the use of the pronouns of the different persons.

Imperative Mood

Eat, **chuh** (吃), **chuh meh tse** (吃末哉).

Participles

Present, Eating, **chuh** (吃), *Past*, Having eaten, **chuh-°ts** (吃仔).

A few words of explanation are necessary. The use of ***leh-°li*** and ***leh-la°*** are a little difficult to understand at first. As stated ***°ngoo leh-°li chuh*** (我拉裏吃) means, "I am eating." If, however, a third person asked your servant ***Sien-sang van° chuh meh?*** (先生飯吃 末), "Has the Teacher eaten his rice?", the servant would answer, if you were still eating, ***yi leh-la° chuh*** (伊拉拉吃) meaning "he is eating." If you yourself said ***°ngoo leh-la° chuh***, it would mean, "I was eating." In the Perfect Tense the word ***koo°*** (過) means literally "to pass over." In the Past Perfect the words ***°i-kyung*** (已經) mean "already."

The real force of ***leh-°li*** (拉裏) is "here," and the real force of ***leh-la°*** (拉拉) is "there."

There are a great many ways of expressing completed action in Chinese. These will be explained later. In this lesson one of the most common will be explained. It is by the use of the adjective ***°hau*** after the verb. Thus ***chuh °hau tse*** (吃好哉) means, "I have finished eating." ***Dok °hau tse*** (讀好哉) means, "I have finished reading."

°Hau (好), "good," is also used before the verb to qualify it. Thus we have the expressions ***°hau chuh kuh*** (好吃個) meaning "good to eat." ***°Hau dok kuh*** (好讀個), "Easy to read." ***°Hau tsoo° kuh*** (好做個), "Easy to do," etc.

Vocabulary

To arrive, **tau°** 到.

To give by hand, **peh** 撥.

To buy, **°ma** 買.

To speak, **wo°** 話.

To burn or cook, **sau** 燒.

To learn, **'auh** 學.

A table boy, **ih kuh si°-tse°** 一個細崽.

A horse boy or coachman, **ih kuh °mo-foo** 一個馬夫.

A pear, **ih tsak sang-li** 一隻生梨.

A peach, **ih tsak dau-°ts** 一隻桃子.

A tailor, **ih kuh ze-voong** 一個裁縫.

China or Chinese, **Tsoong-kok** (中國), Lit. Middle Kingdom.

Shanghai, **°Zaung-°he** 上海.

Jien° is the classifier denoting garments, pieces of baggage and merchandize, and also an affair.

A garment, **ih jien° i-zaung** 一件衣裳.

Saung (雙) is the classifier denoting pairs.

A pair of shoes, **ih saung 'a-°ts** 一雙鞋子.

A pair of socks or stockings, **ih saung mah** 一雙襪.

New, **sing** 新.

Old, **°jeu** 舊, or **°lau** 老. (Of persons, only **°lau** is used.) **°Lau** is old as to time. **°Jeu** generally means worn out, in bad condition. (**°Lau** is often used as a title of respect, meaning venerable).

Exercises

(Translate into English)

(1) °Ngoo iau° 'auh wo° tsoong-kok wo°.

(2) °Ngoo iau° 'auh dok tsoong-kok su.

(3) Noong° iau° dok su va°?

(4) I-tsak siang-°ts tan-chi° meh?

(5) Kyau° yi chi° meh tse.

(6) I-kuh °mo-foo iau° °ma san tsak °mo.

(7) °Ngoo peh yi °ng kwhe° yang-dien kyau° yi chi° °ma ih tsak yang.

(8) °Ngoo °i-kyung wo° koo° tse.

(9) °Zaung-°he tau° koo° hyih meh?

(10) Tau° koo° hyih tse.

(11) °Ngoo-kuh i-zaung ze-voong tsoo° °hau meh?

(12) Yi leh-la° tsoo°.

(13) Noong° chuh-°hau-°ts van° iau° tsoo° sa°?

(14) Chuh-°hau-°ts van° iau° dok su.

(15) °Ngoo iau° chi° °ma ih saung sing kuh 'a-°ts.

(16) Van° sau °hau meh?

(17) Sau °hau tse.

(18) °Lau sien-sang kyau° si°-tse° chi° °ma sang-li.

(19) Kyau° yi le tsoo° meh tse.

(20) Di°-kuh tsoo° koo° hyih meh? Tsoo° koo° hyih tse.

(一) 我要學話中國話.

(二) 我要學讀中國書.

(三) 儂要讀書否?

(四) 伊隻箱子擔去末?

(五) 叫伊去末哉.

(六) 伊個馬夫要買三隻馬.

(七) 我撥伊五塊洋錢叫伊去買一隻羊.

(八) 我已經話過哉.

(九) 上海到過歇末?

(十) 到過歇哉.

(十一) 我個衣裳裁縫做好末?

(十二) 伊拉拉做.

(十三) 儂吃好之飯要做啥?

(十四) 吃好之飯要讀書.

(十五) 我要去買一雙新個鞋子.

(十六) 飯燒好末?

(十七) 燒好哉.

(十八) 老先生叫細崽去買生梨.

(十九) 叫伊來做末哉.

(二十) 第個做過歇末?做過歇哉.

(Translate into Chinese)

(1) I have already read this book.

(2) Do you want to buy a dog?

(3) When I arrive at Shanghai, I wish to buy an umbrella.

(4) Has my friend come?

(5) I gave him four dollars and told him to buy a table.

(6) The teacher is eating his dinner.

(7) I have already given him ten dollars.

(8) Come along.

(9) When the teacher has come, call me.

(10) Have you ever eaten Chinese peaches?

(11) I have eaten them.

(12) Those pupils are studying Chinese.

(13) The foreign teacher is learning to speak Chinese.

(一) 第本書我已輕讀過哉.

(二) 一隻狗要買否?

(三) 到之上海我要買把洋傘.

(四) 我個朋友來末?

(五) 我撥伊四塊洋錢叫伊去買一隻擡子.

(六) 先生垃拉吃飯.

(七) 我已經撥伊十塊洋錢.

(八) 來末哉.

(九) 先生來之末來叫我.

(十) 中國桃子儂吃過歇末?

(十一) 吃過歇哉.

(十二) 伊個學生子拉拉讀中國書.

(十三) 外國先生拉拉學中國話.

NOTES.

(1) China is known by many different names. The most common is *Tsoong-kok* (中國). We also have *Da° tshing kok* (大清國), "the great pure kingdom," *Tsoong-wo* (中華), "the middle civilized kingdom," and *Zeh pah °sang* (十八省) "the eighteen provinces" (used of China Proper, without its dependencies). A modern name is *Ts-na* (支那). It represents the sound of China, and was much used by the reform party. The name adopted for The Republic of China is *Tsoong-wo ming kok* (中國民國) "The middle civilized people's kingdom."

(2) In the ninth sentence of the first exercise the force of the *Tau°* (到) is visiting the place for the first time.

(3) In the twentieth sentence of the first exercise the meaning

is, "Have you ever done this before?"

(4) In the ninth sentence of the second exercise, you use the past participle, *le-°ts* (來仔). After it *meh* (末) is often used for euphony, thus the sentence would be *Sien-sang le-ts meh, le kyau° °ngoo* (先生來之末來叫我).

(5) In the twelfth sentence of the second exercise *su* (書) is added after *tsoong-kok* (中國). The meaning is "The pupils are studying Chinese books."

(6) In the thirteenth sentence of the second exercise, the foreign teacher would be *nga°-kok sien sang* (外國先生). *Nga°-kok* is used as an adjective.

Lesson VII

Prepositions and Postpositions, and Common Connectives

The words expressing the relations of nouns to one another are placed, some of them before and some of them after the governed substantive. 'At' or 'to' is expressed by ***la°*** (拉). Thus ***°ngoo peh la° yi*** (我撥拉伊), "I gave it to him."

'To' or 'towards' in the sense of direction is expressed by ***tau°*** (到). Thus: ***°ngoo iau° tau° °Zaung-°he chi°*** (我要到上海去), "I wish to go to Shanghai." 'To' or 'towards' is also expressed by ***te°*** (對), as in the expression to speak to a person. Thus: ***°ngoo te° yi wo°*** (我對伊話), "I said to him." 'From' is expressed by ***dzoong*** (從). Thus: ***°ngoo dzoong °Zaung-°he le*** (我從上海來), "I came from Shanghai."

'With' is expressed by ***tah*** 搭 or ***doong*** 同. Thus: ***°ngoo tah yi bak wo°*** (我搭伊白話) or ***°ngoo doong yi bak wo°*** (我同伊白話), "I talked with him."

'Instead of' is ***thi°*** (替) or ***°de thi°*** (代替). Thus: ***°ngoo °de thi° yi tsoo°*** (我代替伊做), "I do it instead of him." The idea of doing it for a person is expressed by ***theh*** (忒). Thus: ***°ngoo theh yi tsoo°*** (我忒伊做), "I will do it for him."

'In' is expressed by placing ***la°*** (拉) or ***leh-la°*** (拉拉) before the noun and ***°li*** (裏) or ***°li-hyang°*** (裏向) after the noun. Thus: ***la° vaung-°ts °li*** (拉房子裏) means, "In the house." ***La° siang-°ts °li*** (拉箱子裏) means "In the box."

'On' is expressed by placing ***la°*** or ***leh-la°*** before the noun and ***laung°*** (上) after it. Thus: ***la° loo° laung°*** (拉路上) means, "On the road." ***La° de-°ts laung°*** (拉檯子上) means, "On the table."

Nga° (外) means "out." The usual expression is ***nga°-deu*** (外頭) "outside." It follows the noun.

Other prepositions will be introduced later.

The most common connective is °*lau* (佬) and corresponds quite closely to our use of "and." Thus °*ngoo iau*° °*ma 'a-°ts* °*lau mah* (我要買鞋子佬襪) means, "I wish to buy shoes and stockings." Nouns are often placed beside one another without any connective between them. *Tah-ts* (搭之) is used much in the same sense as °*lau* (佬).

'Also' is °*'a-°z* (也是) or °*'a* (也). Thus: *di°-kuh* °*'a-°z hau kuh* (第個也是好個) means, "This also is good." °*Ngoo* °*'a iau*° °*ma* (我也要買) means, "I also wish to buy." °*Ngoo wan iau*° °*ma* (我還要買) means, "I still wish to buy."

Vocabulary

A city, **ih zoo° dzung** 一座城.

A school, **ih kuh 'auh-daung** 一個學堂.

A hat, **ih °ting mau°-°ts** 一頂帽子.

A head, **ih kuh deu** 一個頭.

A foot, **ih tsak kyak** 一隻脚.

A hand, **ih tsak °seu** 一隻手.

A heart, **ih kuh sing** 一個心.

Father, **ya** 爺.

Mother, **nyang** 娘.

A body, **ih kuh sung-°thi** 一個身體.

Home, **ok-°li** 屋裏.

To sit, **°zoo** 坐.

To live, dwell, **dzu°** 住.

To wear, **tsak** 着.

To place, **faung°** 放, **°pa** 擺.

To use, **yoong°** 用.

To wear on the head, **ta°** 戴.

Exercises

(Translate into English)

(1) Sa° nyung peh la° yi kuh?

(2) I-kuh ya peh la° yi kuh.

(3) Di°-kuh iau° tan tau° ok-°li chi°.

(4) Mau°-°ts iau° ta° la° deu laung°.

(5) ‘A-°ts iau° tsak la° kyak laung°.

(6) I-zaung iau° tsak la° sung laung°.

(7) Sien-sang dzu° la° dzung° °li va°?

(8) ‘Auh-sang-°ts iau° tau° ‘auh-daung °li chi°.

(9) °Ngoo kyau° si°-tse° °pa °ngoo-kuh i-zaung la° siang-°ts °li.

(10) Sien-sang dzoong nga°-kok tau° Tsoong-kok le.

(11) Sien-sang kyau° °siau-noen yoong° sing dok su.

(12) ’Veh iau° °zoo la° zaung laung°, iau° °zoo la° iui°-°ts laung°.

(13) Su faung° la° de-°ts laung°.

(14) Bang-°yeu i°-kyung le koo°-°ts °lau chi° tse.

(15) Sang-li °z °hau chuh kuh, dau-°ts °‘a-°z °hau chuh kuh.

(16) Di°-kuh °siau noen ’m ya nyang kuh.

(17), Sa° nyung la° ‘auh-daung °li? Sien-sang tah-ts ‘auh-sang-°ts.

(18) Noong° wan iau° °ma sa° va°? ’Veh iau°.

(一) 啥人撥拉伊個?

(二) 伊個爺撥拉伊個.

(三) 第個要擔到屋裏去.

(四) 帽子要戴拉頭上.

(五) 鞋子要着拉脚上.

(六) 衣裳要着拉身上.

(七) 先生住拉城裏否?

(八) 學生子要到學堂裏去.

(九) 我叫細崽擺我個衣裳拉箱子裏.

(十) 先生從外國到中國來.

(十一) 先生叫小囡用心讀書.

(十二) 勿要坐拉床上要坐拉椅子上.

(十三) 書放拉檯子上.

(十四) 朋友已經來過之佬去哉.

(十五) 生梨是好吃個桃子也是好吃個.

(十六) 第個小囝無爺娘個.

(十七) 啥人拉學堂裏?先生搭之學生子.

(十八) 儂還要買啥否?勿要.

(Translate into Chinese)

(1) I placed the knives and the forks on the table.

(2) Who lives in this house? Mr. Tsang.

(3) The father and mother wish the child to study.

(4) Do you live in the city or out of the city?

(5) The cat is on the table.

(6) Take it in your hand.

(7) Keep it in mind (place it on your heart).

(8) The heart is in the body.

(9) That child has no shoes on his feet

(10) That man has no hat on his head.

(11) To whom do the cows and sheep belong?

(12) When you have put on your clothes, come and eat.

(13) The horse boy wishes to feed the horse also.

(14) You and I are friends.

(15) Have you ever been to foreign countries?

(一) 刀叉我放拉檯子上.

(二) 啥人住拉第個房子裏?張先生.

(三) 爺娘要第個小囡讀書.

(四) 儂住拉城裏呢城外?

(五) 貓拉檯子上.

(六) 擔拉手裏.

(七) 放拉心上.

(八) 心拉拉身體裏.

(九) 伊個小囝脚上無沒鞋子.

(十) 伊個人頭上無末帽子.

(十一) 牛佬羊是啥人個?

(十二) 着好之衣裳佬來吃.

(十三) 馬夫也要撥馬吃.

(十四) 儂搭之我是朋友.

(十五) 外國去過歇末.

NOTES.

(1) There are many different ways of saying “father” and “mother,” but these will have to be explained later.

(2) *Laung°* is really the character *°Zaung*. It has the latter sound when used in the adverb “above,” which is *°Zaung-deu*, 上頭.

(3) The seventh sentence of the first exercise is correct grammatically, but would not be used in polite speech. The usual way of asking a gentleman where he lives is to say *Sien-sang °foo laung° la° °‘a-°li*, 先生府上拉那裏.

(4) In the eleventh sentence of the first exercise the expression *yoong° sing* means “to be diligent” or “to pay attention.”

(5) In the second sentence of the second exercise Mr. Tsang is translated *Tsang Sien-sang*. *Tsang* is a common surname in Chinese. The *Sien-sang* follows the surname.

(6) Doong (同) is generally used with *ih-dau* (一淘), *Doong* coming before the noun, and *ih-dau* after it. Thus *°Ngoo doong °ngoo kuh bang-yeu ih-dau tau° °Zaung-°he chi°*.

Lesson VIII

Potential and Subjunctive Moods, and some Interrogative Adverbs

"May" or "can" is expressed by ***°khau-°i*** (可以). Thus "I may or can eat" is ***°ngoo °khau-°i chuh*** (我可以吃). When physical ability is implied ***nung-keu°*** (能穀) is frequently used. Thus "I have the physical ability to do," is ***°ngoo nung-keu° tsoo°*** (我能穀做). When acquired ability is to be expressed ***we°*** (會) is generally used. Thus: "I have the ability to speak Chinese" is ***°ngoo we° wo° Tsoong-kok wo°*** (我會話中國話).

The Subjunctive Mood is expressed exactly like the Indicative Mood except that some word meaning "If" is placed at the beginning of the clause, and that the particle ***meh*** (末) is generally placed at the end of the clause.

"If" is ***zak*** (若), ***zak-s°*** (若使), ***zak-zen*** (若然), ***°thaung-zen*** (倘然), ***°thaung-s°*** (倘使). Thus "If I go, I will call you," is expressed ***zak-zen °ngoo chi° meh, °ngoo iau° kyau° noong°*** (若然我去末我要叫儂).

Very often the word implying "If" is omitted at the beginning of the clause, and the condition is implied simply by the use of the ***meh*** (末) the end of the clause. Thus: "When he has finished it, come and tell me" is ***yi tsoo° °hau meh, le te° °ngoo wo°*** (伊做好末來對我話).

"How" is ***°na-nung*** (那能). Thus "How do you know", is ***noong° °na-nung °hyau-tuh?*** (儂那能曉得).

"When?" is ***°kyi-z*** (幾時). Thus "When did you come?" is ***noong° °kyi-z le kuh?*** (儂幾時來個). "When did you arrive?", is ***noong° kyi-z tau°?*** (儂幾時到). Beginners in Chinese often make the mistake of using ***°kyi-z*** as the ordinary adverb of time. To express such a sentence as "When I come he will go," we say ***°ngoo le-°ts meh yi iau° chi°*** (我來仔末伊要去), the past participle being used, and ***meh*** implying that it is conditional. It is incorrect to say ***°ngoo °kyi-z***

le, yi iau° chi°. Let it be remembered that ***°kyi-z*** is only used in asking a question.

We have the ***°kyi-z*** used after the verb in such a sentence as ***noong° tau°-ts °kyi-z tse?*** (儂到仔幾時哉) meaning, "How long since you arrived?" or ***yi chi°-°ts °kyi-z tse?*** (伊去仔幾時哉) meaning, "How long since he went?"

Vocabulary.

To sell, **ma°** 賣 or **ma°-theh** 賣脫.

To see, **khoen°** 看 or **khoen°-kyien°** seen 看見.

To walk, **°tseu** 走.

To run, **bau** 跑.

To know, **°hyau-tuh** 曉得.

To know a person, **nyung°-tuh** 認得.

To understand, **°toong** 懂 or **ming-bak** 明白.

A pagoda, **ih zoo° thah** 一座塔.

A sedan chair, **ih °ting jau°-°ts** 一頂轎子.

A visitor or guest, **ih we° khak-nyung** 一位客人.

A doctor, **ih we° laung tsoong** 一位郎中 or **ih we° i-sung** 一位醫生.

A grave mound, **ih kuh °vung-san** 一個墳山.

A mouth, **ih kuh °kheu** 一個口 or **ih tsang °ts** 一張嘴.

A doorway, **ih kuh mung-°kheu** (Mouth of the door) 一個門口 or **mung-°kheu-deu** 一個門口頭.

An ear, **ih tsak °nyi-°too** 一隻耳朵.

A nose, **ih kuh bih-deu** 一個鼻頭.

An eye, **ih tsak °ngan-tsing** 一隻眼睛.

A face, **ih kuh mien°-khoong** 一個面孔.

Boo (部) is the classifier used with carriages, and vehicles on wheels.

A carriage, **ih boo °mo-tsho** 一部馬車.

A ricsha, **ih boo toong-yang-tsho** 一部東洋車. (Lit. East of the Ocean carriage.) Japan is known as the land East of the Ocean, and ricshas were first used there.

A wheelbarrow, **ih boo tsho-°ts** 一部車子 or **°siau-tsho** 小車.

Short, **°toen** 短.

Long, **dzang** 長.

Fast, **kwha°** 快.

Slow, **man°** 慢.

To-morrow, **ming-tsau** 明朝.

Exercises

(Translate into English)

(1) Noong° ming-bak va°? 'Veh ming-bak.

(2) Tsoong-kok wo°, noong° we° wo° va°? °Ngoo 'veh we° wo°.

(3) Tsoong-kok su noong° we° dok va°? °Ngoo 'veh we° dok.

(4) °Tshing sien-sang ming-tsau le.

(5) Noong° °kyi-z khau-°i chi°? °Ngoo ming-tsau khau-°i chi°.

(6) Di°-tsak °mo 'veh nung-keu° bau le kwha°.

(7) Zak-zen sien-sang le meh, noong° te° yi wo° °ngoo °Zaung-°he chi° tse.

(8) Chi° kyau° ih boo toong-yang-tsho.

(9) Di°-zoo° thah noong° khoen°-kyien° hyih meh?

(10) Mok-ziang° °zoo-ts °siau-tsho-°ts tau° °Zaung-°he chi° tse.

(11) Di-°kuh nyung noong° nyung°-tuh va°? 'Veh nyung°-tuh.

(12) Noong° °na-nung chi° kuh? °Ngoo °zoo-ts °mo-tsho chi kuh.

(13) Iau° noong° chi° °tshing i-sung le.

(14) °Tshing sien-sang wo° le man° °tien.

(15) Zah-zen sien-sang wo° le kwha° meh, °ngoo 'veh °toong.

(16) Di°-kung °baung °z dzang kuh, di°-°po tau °z °toen kuh.

(17) Khak-nyung tau°-°ts mung-°kheu-deu iau° °tshing yi °li-hyang° °zoo.

(18) I-kuh °siau-noen kuh mien°-°khoong 'man °hau khoen°.

(19) Nyung °yeu °liang tsak °nyi-°too, °liang tsak °ngan-tsing, ih kuh bih-deu, °lau ih tsang-°ts.

(20) Di°-zoo° vaung-°ts °i-kyung ma°-theh tse.

(一) 儂明白否?勿明白.

(二) 中國話儂會話否?我勿會話.

(三) 中國書儂會讀否?我勿會讀.

(四) 請先生明朝來.

(五) 儂幾時可以去?我明朝可以去.

(六) 第隻馬勿能彀跑來快.

(七) 若然先生來末儂對伊話我上海去哉.

(八) 去叫一部東洋車.

(九) 第座塔儂看見歇末?

(十) 木匠坐之小車子到上海去哉.

(十一) 第個人儂認得否?勿認得.

(十二) 儂那能去個?我坐馬車去個.

(十三) 要儂去請醫生來.

(十四) 請先生話來慢點.

(十五) 若然先生話來快末我勿懂.

(十六) 第根棒是長個,第把刀是短個.

(十七) 客人到之門口頭請伊裏向坐.

(十八) 伊個小囝個面孔蠻好看.

(十九) 人有兩隻耳朵,兩隻眼睛,一個鼻頭佬一張嘴.

(二十) 第座房子已經賣脫哉.

(Translate into Chinese)

(l) Please take a seat.

(2) When will that teacher come?

(3) He said he will come to-morrow.

(4) Have you seen my dog?

(5) Ask the visitor to come in.

(6) The sheep is on the grave mound.

(7) I wish to ride in a sedan chair, and go into the city.

(8) When the doctor comes, come and call me.

(9) Call two ricshas.

(10) How long have you been in China?

(11) If men had no eyes they would not be able to see.

(12) If the pupil is not diligent he will not be able to learn Chinese.

(13) I do not know how to say this.

(14) When will the doctor come?

(15) To-morrow he will come.

(16) The road to Shanghai is very long.

(17) If you do not understand you can ask the teacher to speak more slowly.

(18) The ears of that dog are very long.

(19) The child runs very fast.

(20) Do you know my friend? I do not.

(一) 請坐.

(二) 伊個先生幾時要來?

(三) 伊話伊明朝要來.

(四) 我個一隻狗儂看見歇末?

(五) 請客人進來.

(六) 第隻羊拉墳山上.

(七) 我要坐轎子到城裏去.

(八) 醫生來之末來叫我.

(九) 去叫兩部東洋車.

(十) 儂到之中國幾時哉?

(十一) 若然人無沒眼睛伊拉勿能彀看見.

(十二) 苦然學生子勿用心伊勿會學中國話.

(十三) 第個我勿曉得那能話個.

(十四) 醫生幾時要來?

(十五) 伊明朝要來.

(十六) 到上海路是蠻長.

(十七) 若然儂勿懂末儂可以請先生話來慢點.

(十八) 伊隻狗個耳朵是蠻長.

(十九) 第個小囝跑來蠻快.

(二十) 我個朋友儂認得否?勿認得.

NOTES.

(1) In the sixth sentence of the first exercise, notice that the adjective *kwha°* is turned into an adverb by the *le* coming before it. Adjectives are often used with verbs in this way.

(2) In the twelfth sentence of the first exercise, notice the expression for travelling in a carriage. In Chinese you "sit a

carriage."

(3) In the first sentence of the second exercise we have the usual polite expression for asking one to be seated °*Tshing* °*zoo*. This should be said as soon as a guest or stranger enters the room, but of course is not used in speaking to inferiors, In such cases it is enough to say °*zoo*-°*zoo* (坐坐).

(4) Notice the difference between °*ma* (買) to buy, and *ma*° (賣) to sell. To our ears the sounds are hard to distinguish. The only difference is in the tones.

(5) The new term for ricsha is *ih boo waung bau tsho* 黃跑車, a yellow running carriage.

Lesson IX

The Use of Dzak, Reduplication of Verbs, Reflexive Pronouns

In expressing the carrying of the action of the verb into effect ***dzak*** (着) is often used after it. Thus: ***zing-dzak*** (尋着) means that a thing has been actually found. ***Zing*** means 'to find'. There are a great many active verbs which can take the ***dzak*** after them. For example we have ***tuh-dzak*** (得着), meaning a thing has been obtained. ***Tuh*** means 'to get'. ***Bang°-dzak*** (掽着) means a person or thing has been met. ***Bang°*** (掽) means 'to strike against'.

Verbs are often repeated for emphasis. We have had an example of this in the expression ***°zoo °zoo***, meaning "sit down" Thus ***khoen° khoen°*** (看看) means "Look, look."

In many cases ***ih*** (一) is inserted between the verbs, as ***khoen° ih khoen°***. In such cases the last verb is changed into a verbal noun. Literally it would be "Look a look."

The Reflexive Personal Pronouns hardly require any explanation. They are formed by adding ***z°-ka*** (自家) after the Personal Pronouns. Thus "I myself" would be ***°ngoo z°- ka*** (我自家). "You yourself" would be ***noong° z°-ka*** (儂自家) and so on for the rest.

Vocabulary

To teach, **kau°** 教.

To write, **°sia** 寫.

To ask, **mung°** 問.

To pay, **foo°** 付.

To build, °**zau** 造.

To look for, **zing** 尋.

To hear, **thing** 聽 or **thing kyien°** (heard) 聽見.

To know a Chinese character, **suh** 識.

To strike against, **bang°** 掽.

To get, **tuh** 得.

A mason, **ih kuh nyi-°s ziang°** 一個泥水匠.

A water buffalo, **ih tsak °s-nyeu** 一隻水牛.

An apple, **ih tsak bing °koo** 一隻蘋果.

A dining table, **ih tsak chuh-van°-de-°ts** 一隻吃飯檯子.

An office desk, **ih tsak °sia-z°-de-°ts** 一隻寫字檯子.

A Chinese character, **ih kuh z°** 一個字.

A drawer of a table, **ih tsak tsheu-thi** 一隻抽屜; **ih tsak tsheu-teu** 一隻抽斗.

An unmarried woman, **ih kuh °siau-°tsia** 一個小姐.

Tea, **dzo** 茶.

Now, **yien°-°dze** 現在.

Not yet, **'veh zung** 勿曾.

Still not yet, **wan 'veh zung** 還勿曾.

Why? **we°-sa°** 爲啥 or **we°-sa°-°lau** 爲啥佬.

Because, **iung-we°** 因爲 or **we°-ts** 爲之.

In using ***iung-we°*** the particle °***lau*** (佬) is generally added at the end of the clause. Thus: "Why did you not go? Because I did not want to go" is ***noong° we°-°sa 'veh chi°? Iung we° °ngoo 'veh iau° chi° °lau*** (儂爲啥勿去？因爲我勿要去佬.)

Exercises

(Translate into English)

(1) °Tshing sien-sang kau° °ngoo dok Tsoong-kok su.

(2) Yien°-°dze °ngoo iau° 'auh °sia Tsoong-kok z°.

(3) Noong° °ma-°ts ih tsak °sia-z°-de, doong-dien foo° meh? 'Veh zung.

(4) Di°-kuh z° °ngoo 'veh suh.

(5) Zak-zen noong° 'veh suh meh °khau-°i mung° sien-sang.

(6) Vaung-°ts °zau °hau meh? Wan ’veh zung.

(7) °Ngoo kuh sen°-°ts °tshing noong° theh °ngoo zing zing-khoen°.

(8) Sen°-°ts °i-kyung zing-dzak tse.

(9) Noong° we°-sa°-°lau ’veh zung chi°? Iung-we° °ngoo iau° dok su °lau.

(10) °Tshing sien-sang chuh dzo.

(11) °Tshing sien-sang yoong° dzo.

(12) Zak-zen nyung m-meh °nyi-°too, yi-la ’veh nung-keu° thing.

(13) °Ngoo ’veh zung tau° Tsoong-kok le, °s-nyeu ’veh zung khoen°-kyien° hyih.

(14) Nyi-°s-ziang° bang°-dzak hyih meh? ’Veh zung.

(15) °Sia-°z-de-°ts laung° kuh su °z sa° nyung kuh? °Z °ngoo-z°-ka kuh.

(16) °Ngoo kyau° noong° faung° °ngoo-kuh i-zaung la° tsheu-thi °li, noong° we°-sa° ’veh zung faung° kuh?

(17) Chi° khoen° khoen° sien-sang le meh.

(18) °Ngoo kuh san° noong° zing-dzak meh? Zing-’veh-dzak.

(19) Zak-zen m-meh sien-sang meh, noong° z°-ka °khau-°i dok su.

(20) Iau° °ngoo foo° doong-dien meh, kyau° yi-la z°-ka le nau.

(一) 請先生教我讀中國書.

(二) 現在我要學寫中國字.

(三) 儂買之一隻寫字檯銅錢付末?勿曾.

(四) 第個字我勿識.

(五) 若然儂勿識末可以問先生.

(六) 房子造好末?還勿曾.

(七) 我個扇子請儂忒我尋尋看.

(八) 扇子已經尋着哉.

(九) 儂爲啥佬勿曾去?因爲我要讀書佬.

(十) 請先生吃茶.

(十一) 請先生用茶.

(十二) 若然人無沒耳朵,伊拉勿能彀聽?

(十三) 我勿曾到中國來,水牛勿曾看見歇.

(十四) 泥水匠擁着歇末?勿曾.

(十五) 寫字檯子上個書是啥人個?是我自家個.

(十六) 我叫儂放我個衣裳拉抽屜裏,儂爲啥勿曾放個?

(十七) 去看看先生來末?

(十八) 我個傘儂尋着末?尋勿着.

(十九) 若然無沒先生末,儂自家可以讀書.

(二十) 要我付銅錢末,叫伊拉自家來拿.

(Translate into Chinese)

(1) Why don't you pay it?

(2) Why do you do this?

(3) When will you do it?

(4) I don't want it now.

(5) When did you go?

(6) I do not want to go now, but I will go to-morrow.

(7) Does the teacher teach well?

(8) Does the pupil write well?

(9) Why do you not look for my fan? Because I have already found it.

(10) This carpenter can make a dining table.

(11) Go, see if the doctor has come.

(12) They themselves said they wished to build a new house.

(13) I told the table boy to go to the city and buy me four chairs, a trunk, a bed, and an office desk.

(14) When the teacher comes, ask him please to be seated and to take some tea.

(15) If one does not study he is unable to know characters.

(16) My office desk has three drawers.

(17) This unmarried girl also wishes to study.

(18) Have you bought the apples? They cannot be obtained.

(19) Do you know whether the guest has already arrived? I do not know.

(20) Can you obtain these? They are unobtainable.

(一) 儂爲啥勿付個?

(二) 第個儂爲啥做個?

(三) 儂幾時要做個?

(四) 現在勿要.

(五) 儂幾時去個?

(六) 現在勿要去,明朝要去.

(七) 先生教來好否?

(八) 學生子寫來好否?

(九) 儂爲啥佬勿尋我個扇子?因爲已經尋着哉.

(十) 第個木匠可以做一隻吃飯檯.

(十一) 去看看醫生來末.

(十二) 伊拉自家話,伊拉要造新個房子.

(十三) 我叫細崽到城裏去, 買四把椅子, 一隻箱子, 一隻牀佬一隻寫字檯.

(十四) 先生來仔末請伊坐坐佬吃茶.

(十五) 若然一個人勿讀書,伊勿會識字.

(十六) 我個寫字檯有三隻柚屜.

(十七) 第個小姐也要讀書.

(十八) 苹果買好末?買勿着.

(十九) 客人已經到儂曉得否?我勿曉得.

(二十) 第個儂可以得着否?得勿着.

NOTES.

(1) In the seventh sentence of the first exercise notice the *khoen°* after the reduplicated verb *zing*. This gives the force of try to look for it. "Look, look, see." *Khoen°* is used after many verbs in this way. Thus: *Tsoo° tsoo° khoen°* 做做看 means "try to do it." *°Sia °sia khoen°* 寫寫看 means "try to write it." *Wo° wo° khoen°* 話話看 means, "try to say it." *S° S° khoen°* 試試看 means "try to do it."

(2) In the tenth and eleventh sentences of the first exercise we have two ways of asking a person to drink tea. The second is the polite form. Literally it means that you ask a person "to use tea."

(3) In the nineteenth sentence of the first exercise, notice the use of *meh* for euphony after *sien-sang*, and so also in the twentieth after *doong-dien*.

(4) In the eighteenth sentence of the first exercise, notice the way in which *'veh* comes between the *zing* and the *dzak*.

This means "seek not find" or "it can not be found." So also in the second exercise in the eighteenth sentence "They cannot be obtained" should be translated *°ma- 'veh dzak?* and in the twentieth sentence "They are unobtainable" should be *tuh- 'veh-dzak*.

Lesson X

Divisions of Time. More Adverbs

"An hour" in Chinese is ***ih °tien tsoong*** (一點鐘) or ***ih kuh tsoong-deu*** (一個鐘頭). Literally "one point of the clock." This is a foreign division of time. The Chinese divide the day into twelve periods of two hours each, known as *z-zung* (時辰). Now, the divisions into hours has become very familiar.

Ih °tien tsoong may also mean "one o'clock," and the other hours are indicated in the same way by the change of the numeral. Thus "Two o'clock" is ***°liang °tien tsoong*** (兩點鐘). Two hours would be ***°liang kuh tsoong deu*** (兩個鐘頭) or ***°liang °tien tsoong koong foo*** (兩點鐘功夫). "Three o'clock" is ***san °tien tsoong*** (三點鐘), etc.

"A day" is usually ***ih nyih*** 一日. The character ***nyih*** literally means "sun." In speaking of the heavenly body, in the colloquial, ***deu*** is added to the ***nyih***, making the expression ***nyih-deu*** (日頭). Sometimes the word ***thien*** (天), meaning "Heaven," is used for "day." Thus ***san thien*** means "three days." No classifier is introduced between the numeral and the ***nyih*** or the ***thien***. Thus we have for "four days" ***s° nyih*** (四日) or ***s° thien*** (四天).

"A week" is ***ih kuh °li-pa°*** (一個禮拜) or ***ih °li-pa°*** (一禮拜). This, of course, is a foreign division of time which has been adopted into Chinese. It takes its name from the name of Sunday, which is usually ***°li-pa°-nyih*** (禮拜日). Lit. "the day of ceremonial worship." ***°Li*** means ceremony, ***pa°*** is to worship. The other days of the week are formed with the addition of the numerals as follows: Monday is ***°li-pa°-ih*** (禮拜一). Tuesday is ***°li-pa°-nyi°***. Wednesday is ***°li-pa°-san***. Thursday ***°li-pa°-s°***. Friday ***°li-pa°-°ng*** and Saturday ***°li-pa°-lok***.

A new way of expressing the days of the week is by the use of the words ***sing-ji*** (星期) meaning the star period. Thus: Sunday is ***sing-ji nyih*** (星期日), Monday, ***sing-ji ih*** (星期一), Tuesday, ***sing-ji nyi°*** (星期二), and so on for the other days.

"A month" is ***ih kuh nyoeh*** (一個月). Lit. "a moon." The Chinese year is made up of twelve lunar months. The first month is called ***tsung nyoeh*** (正月), the second, ***nyi° nyoeh*** (二月), the third, ***san nyoeh*** (三月) and so forth.

"A year" is ***ih nyien*** (一年). No classifier is used between the numeral and the word "year", ***nyien***.

"How many?" or "How much?" is ***°kyi-hau°?*** (幾化). Thus ***°kyi-hau° nyung le?*** (幾化人來) means "How many men came?" ***°Kyi-hau° °s*** (幾化水) means "How much water?"

°Kyi is often used without the ***hau°***. In such cases it is followed by the classifier of the noun. Thus "How many men came?" might be ***°kyi kuh nyung le?*** (幾個人來). "How many horses have you?" ***noong° °yeu °kyi tsak °mo?*** (儂有幾隻馬).

"Where?" is ***°'a-°li*** (那裏). Thus "Where are you going?" is ***noong° tau° °'a-°li chi°?*** (儂到那裏去). "Where are you?" is ***noong° la°-°'a-°li?*** (儂拉那裏).

Sa° meaning "what" with ***di°-faung*** meaning "place" also expresses "Where?" Thus ***sa° di°-faung?*** (啥地方). We also have ***sa° dzang-hau°?*** (啥場化) meaning "What place?" or "Where?" but this refers to a more circumscribed area than ***di°- faung***. We also have ***sa° °'oo-daung°*** (啥戶蕩) used much in the same way as ***sa° dzang-hau°***.

Vocabulary

A fish, **ih diau ng** 一條魚.

To return, **°tsen-le** 轉來, Lit. To come back; **°tsen-chi°** 轉去, Lit. To go back.

To come out or forth, **tsheh-le** 出來.

To go out, **tsheh chi°** 出去.

To thank, **zia°** 謝.

Near, **°jung** 近.

To-day, **kyung-tsau** 今朝.

Yesterday, **zau-nyih** 昨日.

A painter, **ih kuh tshih-ziang°** 一個漆匠.

Thus, **zeh-ke°** 實蓋 or **zeh-ke°-nung** 實蓋能.

Then (used as a conjunction), **nan-meh** 難末.

Only, **pi-koo°** 必過.

South, **nen** 南.

Immediately, **zieu°** 就.

Time, **z-'eu°** 時候, **zung-kwaung** 辰光 or **koong-foo** 工夫.

But, **dan°-°z** 但是, **dok-°z** 獨是.

Exercises

(Translate into English)

(1) °Tshing sien-sang ming-tsau °kyeu °tien-tsoong le.

(2) Kyung-tsau °z °li-pa°-ih, ming-tsau °z °li-pa°-nyi°.

(3) Di°-kuk nyoeh °yeu san-seh nyih.

(4) Ih °li-pa° °yeu tshih nyih.

(5) Noong°-kuh bang-°yeu dzu° la° sa° di°-faung? La° dzung °li. La° dzung °li, sa° dzang-hau°? °Jung nen mung.

(6) °Ngoo-kuh tau noong° faung° la°-°'a-°li?

(7) Zau-nyih °ngoo dok-ts °ng °tien-tsoong su, nan-meh tsheh-chi° °tseu loo°.

(8) °Kyi °pung su °z noong°-kuh °lau °kyi °pung °z yi-kuh?

(9) I-kuh nyung °yeu °kyi-kuh 'eu-°ts? Yi pih-koo° °yeu ih-kuh.

(10) Noong° tau°-ts Tsoong-kok °kyi-kuh nyoeh tse? °Ngoo le-ts san kuh nyoeh.

(11) Noong° °kyi-z iau° °tsen-chi°? °Li-pa°-san iau° °tsen-chi°.

(12) °Zaung-°he °kyi-z °tsen-le kuh? Zau-nyih °tsen-le kuh.

(13) Noong° we°-sa°-°lau 'veh tsheh-chi° °tseu °tseu? °Iung-we° m-meh koong-foo °lau.

(14) Zia° zia° noong° chi° °tshing i-sung le.

(15) °Ngoo dok-°hau-ts su zieu° iau° chuh van.

(16) °Z zeh-ke° va°? °Z zeh-ke° kuh.

(一) 請先生明朝九點鐘來.

(二) 今朝是禮拜一,明朝是禮拜二.

(三) 第個月有三十日.

(四) 一禮拜有七日.

(五) 儂個朋友住拉啥地方?拉城裏.拉城裏啥場化?近南門.

(六) 我個刀儂放拉那裏?

(七) 昨日我讀之五點鐘書,難末出去走路.

(八) 幾本書是儂個佬幾本是伊個?

(九) 伊個人有幾個兒子?伊必過有一個.

(十) 儂到之中國幾個月哉?我來之三個月.

(十一) 儂幾時要轉去?禮拜三要轉去.

(十二) 上海幾時轉來個?昨日轉來個.

(十三) 儂爲啥佬勿出去走走?因爲無沒工夫佬.

(十四) 謝謝儂去請醫生來.

(十五) 我讀好之書就要吃飯.

(十六) 是實蓋否?是實蓋個.

(Translate into Chinese)

(1) Where have you put my shoes?

(2) I put them in the box.

(3) I do not want to study on Sunday, but I will study on Monday.

(4) How many weeks are there in a month?

(5) How many peaches have you eaten?

(6) How many dollars did you give your servant?

(7) What time is it now?

(8) Where do you live?

(9) When you have bought the fish, return immediately.

(10) The guest will stay here four months, and then will return.

(11) Please tell the painter to come.

(12) The teacher, having taught for three hours, left immediately.

(13) Why do you do it this way? Because the teacher told me to do it thus.

(14) I wish to do it, but I have no time to do it.

(15) Go see what time it is now.

(一) 我個鞋子儂放拉那裏?

(二) 我放拉箱子裏.

(三) 禮拜日勿要讀書,禮拜一佬讀個.

(四) 一個月有幾個禮拜?

(五) 儂吃之幾隻桃子?

(六) 儂撥之儂個用人幾塊洋錢?

(七) 現在是幾點鐘?

(八) 儂住拉啥地方?

(九) 買好之魚就轉來.

(十) 客人要住四個月,難末轉去哉.

(十一) 謝謝儂叫漆匠來.

(十二) 先生教之三點鐘工夫,就轉去.

(十三) 儂爲啥實蓋做?因爲先生教我實蓋做.

(十四) 我要做個,但是無沒工夫.

(十五) 去看現在幾點鐘.

NOTES.

(1) "Thank you" is expressed by repeating the *Zia°*. Thus "Thank you" is *Zia°-zia° noong°*. In speaking to an equal or superior, the *Noong°* would be dropped. Often in Chinese when you ask a person to do a thing for you, you preface the request by thanking the person. Thus *Zia°-zia° noong chi° tan °ngoo-kuh san° le* (謝謝儂去擔我個傘來) means "Thank you, go bring my umbrella."

(2) *Koong-foo* has the double sense of "work" or "time." Thus: *Tsoo° koong-foo* means to do work. But *M-meh koong-foo* means "I have no time." You never say *Sa° koong-foo*, meaning "What time?" but *Sa s-'eu°?* or *Sa° zung-kwaung?* In asking what time it is by the clock the usual expression is *°Kyi °tien-tsoong?*

(3) The force of the question in the third sentence of the First Exercise is due to the fact that some Chinese months have thirty days and some have twenty-nine. A month of thirty days is called *Doo° nyoeh* (大月), "a large month," and one with twenty-nine days is called a small month *°Siau nyoeh* (小月). In order to make the seasons come right, an intercalary month is put in about every three years. This in Chinese is called *Nyung° nyoeh* (閏月).

(4) Notice the elliptical form of expression in the seventh sentence of the First Exercise. Literally it means "Yesterday I read five hours' book."

(5) In the third sentence of the Second Exercise the Chinese idiom is peculiar. You say *°Li-pa° nyih 'veh iau° dok su, °li-pa°-ih °lau dok kuh*. Literally "Sunday not want to study, Monday and study."

(6) In the eleventh sentence of the Second Exercise, the "please" should be translated *Zia°-zia° noong°*.

Lesson XI

The Passive Voice, and Adverbs of Place and Time

Peh (撥) (Mandarin 被) is used to form the Passive, and is the regular and proper form of the Passive. Thus: the verb ***°tang*** (打) means to "Strike." ***°Ngoo °tang yi*** (我打伊) means "I strike him." To put this into the Passive we would say ***°ngoo peh yi °tang*** (我撥伊打). Literally "I gave him strike," or "I was struck by him."

"Here" is expressed by ***leh-°li*** or ***°tsh-di°*** (垃裏, 此地) or ***di°-deu*** (第頭). ***°Tsh-di°*** means literally "this place."

"There" is ***leh-la°*** (垃拉) or ***i-deu*** (伊頭) or ***i-kwhe°*** (伊塊). "I am here" is ***°ngoo leh-li°*** (我垃裏). "I am there" is ***°ngoo leh-la°*** (我垃拉).

These adverbs are often used as adverbial nouns and may take prepositions before them. Thus ***Tau° °di-deu le*** (到第頭來) means "Come here." Lit. "To here come." ***Tau° i-deu chi°*** (到伊頭去) means "Go there." Lit. "To there go." ***°Pa la° °tsh-di°*** (擺拉此地) means "Place it here," Lit. "Place it at here." ***°Pa la° i-kwhe°*** (擺拉伊塊) means "Place it there." Lit. "Place it at there."

Vocabulary

Half an hour, **pen° °tien-tsoong** 半點鐘, (**pen°** means half).

Quarter of an hour, **ih khuh** 一刻.

A minute, **ih fung** 一分.

In the morning, **°zaung-pen°-nyih** 上半日. Lit. Above half day.

In the afternoon, **°'au-pen°-nyih** 下半日. Lit. Lower half day.

Night, **ya°** 夜.

At night, **ya°-deu** 夜頭 or **ya°-°li** 夜裏.

Day before yesterday, **koo°-nyih-°ts** 過日子, **zien-nyih-°ts** 前日子, **i-nyih-°ts** 伊日子.

Day after to-morrow, **°'eu nyih** 後日.

Early in the morning, **°tsau-zung-deu** 早晨頭. **°Tsau** is early.

In the evening, **ya°-kwha°** 夜快. Lit. Night coming fast.

In the middle of the day or noon, **nyih-tsoong** 日中.

To cook, **sau** 燒.

To strike, **°tang** 打.

To wait, **°tung** 等. **°Tung-ih-°tung** means "Wait a little."

To rest, **hyih** 歇. **Hyih-ih-hyih** means "Wait a little." We also have **°tung-ih-hyih**.

To remember, **kyi°** 記 or **kyi°-tuh** 記得.

To forget, **maung°-kyi°** 忘記.

An affair (abstract), **ih °jien z°-°thi** or **ih tsaung z°-thi** 一椿事體.

A thing or object (concrete), **ih-kuh meh-z°** 一個物事.

Wind, **foong** 風.

A loaf of bread, **ih-kuh men-deu** 一個饅頭.

A mosquito, **ih tsak mung-°ts** 一個蚊子 or **ih kuh mung-°ts**.

A boat, **ih tsak zen** 一隻船.

Many, much, **too-hau°** 多化, or **too** 多.

To sting, **ting** 叮.

To bite, **°ngau** 咬.

To spoil, **wa°** 壞, or **wa°-theh** 壞脫 (completely spoil).

A snake, **ih diau zo** 一條蛇.

Exercises

(Translate into English)

(1) Van° sau °hau meh? Sau °hau tse.

(2) °Ngoo-kuh i-zaung tan tau° °tsh-di° le.

(3) I-zaung tsoo° °hau meh? 'Veh zung, iau° hyih °liang nyih tsoo° °hau.

(4) °Tshing sien-sang ming-tsau °zaung-pen°-nyih zeh °tien-tsoong le.

(5) Van° sau-°hau-ts meh zieu° iau° chuh.

(6) °Ngoo nyih-°li dok tsoong-kok su, ya°-°li dok nga°-kok su.

(7) I-tsak °mo we°-ts °tseu le man° °lau peh la °mo-foo °tang.

(8) Zien-nyih-°ts °ngoo la° °Zaung-°he °ma-ts too-hau° meh-z°.

(9) °Di tsaung z°-°thi °ngoo theh noong° wo°, dan°-°z 'veh iau° peh i-kuh nyung °hyau-tuh.

(10) °Tsau-zung-deu °z °ting °hau dok su kuh zung-kwaung.

(11) °Tung-ih-hyih °ngoo zieu° iau° le.

(12) Noong° dok koo° hyih kuh su kyi°-tuh va?

(13) Ih pen° kyi°-tuh, ih pen° maung°-kyi°.

(14) °Ngoo peh la° mung-°ts ting.

(15) Men-deu peh la° °siau-noen chuh theh tse.

(16) °Ngoo-kuh kyak peh la° zo °ngau-°ts ih °kheu.

(17) Zen peh la° doo° foong °tang wa°.

(18) °Tshing sien-sang di°-deu °zoo.

(一) 飯燒好末？燒好哉.

(二) 我個衣裳擔到此地來.

(三) 衣裳做好末？勿曾，要歇兩日做好.

(四) 請先生明朝上半日十點鐘來.

(五) 飯燒好之末就要吃.

(六) 我日裏讀中國書，夜裏讀外國書.

(七) 伊隻馬爲之走來慢咾撥拉馬夫打.

(八) 前日子我拉上海買之多化物事.

(九) 第樁事體我對儂話，但是勿要撥伊個人曉得.

(十) 早晨頭是頂好讀書個辰光.

(十一) 等一歇我就要來.

(十二) 儂讀過歇個書記得否？

(十三) 一半記得一半忘記.

(十四) 我撥拉蚊子叮.

(十五) 饅頭撥拉小囝吃脫哉.

(十六) 我個脚撥拉蛇咬仔一口.

(十七) 船撥拉大風打壞.

(十八) 請先生第頭坐.

(Translate into Chinese)

(1) When will you come, in the morning or in the afternoon?

(2) I do not know; if I have no affairs to attend to, I will come in the morning.

(3) Has the carpenter finished making the table? If so, I will come and look at it.

(4) Place the bed here and the table there.

(5) These fish are cooked badly.

(6) The day after to-morrow I have invited some guests to dinner.

(7) It is already twenty minutes past ten, and my teacher has not yet come.

(8) Do you remember what I told you yesterday? I have forgotten it.

(9) In studying Chinese, you must not forget what you have already learnt.

(10) Please sit down a little while; there are many things I want to say to you.

(11) How did you come? I came in a carriage.

(12) My child was struck by your child.

(13) My face and hands were bitten by mosquitoes.

(一) 儂幾時要來,上半日呢下半日?

(二) 我勿曉得,若然嘸沒事體,要上半日來.

(三) 檯子木匠做好未?若然做好之末,我要來看看.

(四) 牀棑拉第頭,檯子擺拉伊頭.

(五) 魚燒來勿好.

(六) 後日我請幾個客人來吃飯.

(七) 已經十點過廿分哉,先生還勿曾來.

(八) 我昨日對儂話個儂記得否?我忘記脫哉.

(九) 讀中國書已經學過拉個,勿要忘記.

(十) 請坐一歇,有多化事體要對儂話.

(十一) 儂那能來個,我坐馬車來個.

(十二) 我個小囝撥儂個小囝打.

(十三) 我個面孔伲手撥拉蚊子叮.

NOTES.

(1) It will have been noticed that in Lesson VI. *Leh-li°* was used in the Present Tense Continuous of the Verb, and that *Leh-la°* was used for the Past Continuous. It was pointed out then that these words really signify "Here" and "There." The literal sense would be "I am here eating," and "I was there eating."

(2) It is very important that beginners should distinguish clearly between *meh-z°* and *z°-°thi*. Any concrete object may be called a *meh-z°*. But an abstract action or affair is always *z°-°thi*.

(2) In mandarin-speaking districts *toong-si* 東西 (Lit. "East-West") is often used for *meh-z°*, and sometimes it is heard in the Shanghai District.

(3) In the fifth sentence of the First Exercise, notice how the *°ts* is tacked on to the *°hau*, and not to the *sau*.

(4) In the tenth sentence of First Exercise notice how the *dok su* has become a verbal adjective. Lit. "Reading book time."

(5) In the fifteenth sentence of the First Exercise the force of the *theh* after *chuh* is that it has been entirely eaten up. *Theh* often comes after verbs to express completed action.

(6) In the sixteenth sentence of the First Exercise, *°Ngau-°ts ih °kheu* means literally "Bitten a mouthful."

(7) In the seventeenth sentence we have two verbs used together—*°tang* and *wa°*. Literally "Beat" or "strike spoil."

(8) In the seventh sentence of the Second Exercise twenty minutes past ten is expressed *zeh °tien koo° nyan° fung*. *°Tien* is a shortened form for *°tien-tsoong*. *Koo°* means "passed over" or "beyond."

(9) In the twelfth sentence of the First Exercise notice the use of *kuh*, It has the force of the relative pronoun, and the translation would be "the books which you have read."

(10) In the sixth sentence of the Second Exercise "some" may be translated by *°kyi-kuh*.

Lesson XII

Some Verbal Idioms

We have already explained the use of ***°khau-°i***, ***nung-keu°***, and ***we°***. There are other ways of expressing the possibility and impossibility of doing things in Chinese. For instance one way is by the addition of ***tuh le*** or ***'veh le*** after the verb. Thus: ***Dok-tuh-le*** (讀得來) means "Able to read." ***Dok-'veh-le*** (讀勿來) means "Unable to read it." Many verbs of one character admit of this construction. Thus: ***Wo°-tuh-le*** means "Able to speak." ***Wo°-'veh-le*** means "Unable to speak." ***Tsoo°-tuh-le*** (做得來), "Able to do." ***Tsoo°-'veh-le*** (做勿來), "Unable to do."

Verbs made up of two characters do not take ***tuh-le*** and ***'veh-le*** after them. Thus we do not hear ***°hyau-tuh-'veh-le*** for "Unable to know," but ***'veh we° °hyau-tuh*** (勿會曉得).

The literal meaning of ***tuh-le*** is "Obtain, come," and the literal meaning of ***'veh-le*** is "Not come."

We also have the use of ***tuh-kuh*** after verbs, expressing possibility, and ***'veh-tuh***, expressing impossibility. Thus we have ***tsoo°-tuh-kuh*** (做得個), meaning "it is possible to do a thing," and ***tsoo°-'veh-tuh*** (做勿得), meaning "it is impossible to do a thing." With verbs of physical action, we have ***tuh-°doong*** (得動) and ***'veh-°doong*** (勿動) used after the verb implying possibility and impossibility. Thus we have ***°tseu-tuh-°doong*** (走得動), meaning "I have the physical ability to walk," and ***°tseu-'veh-°doong*** (走勿動), meaning "I have not the physical ability to walk." In the same way we have ***tsoo°-tuh-°doong*** (做得動) and ***tsoo°-'veh-°doong*** (做勿動). ***'Veh-°doong*** literally means "Not move."

Strange to say we have ***°zoo-'veh-°doong*** (坐勿動), meaning "I have not the physical ability to sit up," and ***°zoo-tuh-°doong*** (坐得動), meaning "I have the physical ability to sit up."

°Ma-tuh-°doong (買得動) means "Possible to buy." ***°Ma-'veh-°doong*** (買勿動) means "Impossible to buy."

With verbs of hearing and seeing impossibility is expressed in still another way. Thus we have ***khoen°-tuh-kyien°*** (看得見), meaning "It is possible to see," and ***khoen°-'veh-kyien°*** (看勿見) meaning "It is impossible to see it." Literally translated these expressions are "See, obtain, behold," and "See, not behold." We also have ***khoen°-tuh-tsheh*** (看得出), meaning to see a thing clearly. Literally "See, obtain, come forth," and ***khoen°-'veh-tsheh*** (看勿出), meaning not to be able to see, or literally "See, not come forth."

In the same way we have ***thing-tuh-tsheh*** (聽得出) and ***thing-'veh-tsheh*** (聽勿出) in regard to hearing. Instead of ***thing-tuh-kyien°*** and ***thing-'veh-kyien°*** we have ***thing-tuh-dzak*** (聽得着) and ***thing-'veh-dzak*** (聽勿着). Literally "Hear, obtain" and "Hear, not obtain."

We have already explained the use of ***°hau*** after verbs expressing completed action. We also have other words used much in the same way. Thus ***dok-°hau-tse*** (讀好哉), ***dok-wen-tse*** (讀完哉) or ***dok-°ba-tse*** (讀罷哉) all mean the same thing. The verb ***wen*** means "to finish." Accordingly in asking a question ***tsoo°-°hau-meh*** (做好末), ***tsoo°-wen-meh*** (做完末) and ***tsoo°-°ba-meh*** (做罷末), all mean "Have you finished it?"

Verbal nouns are often formed by the addition of ***deu*** (頭) or ***fah*** (法) after the verb. Thus ***tsoo°-deu*** (做頭) or ***tsoo°-fah*** (做法) means the manner of doing a thing.

Vocabulary

To move, to excite, **°doong** 動.

To hear, **thing** (聽). Heard, **thing-kyien°** 聽見

To knock, to strike, **khau** 敲.

To finish, **wen** 完.

Kan (間) is the classifier used with rooms.

A room, **ih kan** 一間.

A bed room, **ih kan vaung-kan** 一間房間.

A guest room, **ih kan khak-daung-kan** 一間客堂間.

An office, **ih kan °sia-z°-kan** 一間寫字間.

A shroff's room, **ih kan tsang°-vaung-kan** 一間帳房間.

A study, **ih kan su-vaung** 一間書房.

A dining room, **ih kan chuh-van°-kan** 一間吃飯間.

A kitchen, **ih kan sau-van°-kan** 一間燒飯間 or **dzu-vaung** 廚房 or **tsau°-kan** 灶間.

All, °**loong-°tsoong** 攏總 or **koong°-°tsoong** 共總.

All in general, most, **da-ke** 大概.

Few, °**sau** 少.

Each, °**me** 每.

Every, **kauh** 各.

Other, **bih** 別.

High, **kau** 高.

Low, **ti** 低.

Broad, **khweh** 闊.

Narrow, **'ah** 狹.

Deep, **sung** 深.

Shallow, °**tshien** 淺

Too (denoting excess), **thuh** 忒.

Above, °**zaung-deu** 上頭.

Below, °**'au-deu** 下頭, °**'au-°ti-deu** 下底]頭, °**'au-°ti** 下底.

Under, beneath, °**ti-°'au** 底下.

Outside, **nga°-deu** 外頭.

After, °**'eu** 後.

Behind, °**'eu-°ti** 後底, °**'eu-°ti-deu**, 後底頭 °**'eu-deu** 後頭.

Before, **zien** 前, **zien-deu** 前頭.

Earth, **di°** 地 or **di°-jeu** 地球.

Exercises

(Translate into English)

(1) °Zaung-deu °yeu thien, °'au-deu °yeu di°.

(2) °Yeu too-hau° z° °ngoo °sia-'veh-le.

(3) Noong° we°-sa°-°lau °tseu le man°-le-°si? Iung-we° °ngoo °tseu 'veh-°doong °lau.

(4) Tsoong-kok wo° zak-zen nyung wo° le kwha° meh, °ngoo thing-'veh-tsheh.

(5) °Yeu-kuh su °ngoo dok 'veh le.

(6) Di°-zak vaung-°ts °kyi-hau° kau, °kyi-hau° kwheh?

(7) Di°-zak vaung-°ts °yeu °kyi kan?

(8) °Yeu ih kan khak-daung, ih kan °sia-z°-kan, ih kan chuh-van°-kan, °lau s° kan vaung-kan.

(9) Di°-kuh meh-z° °yeu sa° yoong°-deu va? ’M-sa° yoong°-deu.

(10) Sa° nyung la° khau mung? °Ngoo ’veh zung thing-kyien° °yeu sa° nyung la° khau mung.

(11) Di° diau loo° thuh ‘ah, °ting °hau noong° °tseu la° zien-deu, °ngoo °tseu la° °‘eu-deu.

(12) °Tshing khak-nyung khak-daung °li °zoo.

(13) Dzoong °Zaung-°he tau° °tsh di° °yeu °kyi-hau° loo°?

(14) Vaung-°ts nga°-deu °z °lang °tien, vaung-°ts °li-hyang° °z nyih °tien.

(15) Di°-diau ‘oo °yeu-kuh di°-faung °z sung °tien, °yeu-kuh di°-faung °z °tshien °tien.

(16) Noong° na°-nung °hyau-tuh di° tsaung z°-thi? Iung-we° °ngoo thing-tuh °yeu nyung wo° °lau.

(17) Ze-voong tsoo° le ’veh °hau, °loong-°tsoong kuh i-zaung thuh doo°.

(18) Kauh nyung °yeu kauh nyung kuh z°-°thi.

(一) 上頭有天,下頭有地.

(二) 有多化字我寫勿來.

(三) 儂爲啥佬走來慢來死?因爲我走勿動佬.

(四) 中國話若然人話來快末,我聽勿出.

(五) 有個書我讀勿來.

(六) 第宅房子幾化高,幾化闊.

(七) 第宅房子有幾間.

(八) 有一間客堂,一間寫字間,一間吃飯間,佬四間房間.

(九) 第個物事有啥用頭否?嘸啥用頭.

(十) 啥人拉敲門?我勿曾聽見有啥人拉敲門.

(十一) 第條路忒狹,頂好儂走拉前頭,我走拉後頭.

(十二) 請客人客堂裏坐.

(十三) 從上海到此地有幾化路?

(十四) 房子外頭是冷點,房子裏向是熱點

(十五) 第條河有個地方是深點,有個地方是淺點.

(十六) 儂那能曉得第椿事體?因爲我聽得有人話佬.

(十七) 裁縫做來勿好,攏總個衣裳忒大.
(十八) 各人有各人個事體.

(Translate into Chinese)

(1) Where is your teacher? He is in the study writing.
(2) Did you tell the table boy to bring the tea?
(3) If the carpenter does not make it well, I shall call another man.
(4) This manner of doing it is bad; I want you to do it better.
(5) I walked to Shanghai, and then I could walk no further.
(6) Then what did you do? I called a ricsha and came back.
(7) Is the Master in? He has gone out.
(8) Three days ago I went to see the pagoda.
(9) There is water beneath the earth.
(10) The cat is under the chair.
(11) When I have finished reading the book, I want to learn to write characters.
(12) Tell him to come inside.
(13) This table is too low; I cannot write characters on it.
(14) May I come in? Come right in.

(一) 儂個先生拉啥地方?拉寫字間裏寫字.
(二) 担茶來,儂對細崽話否?
(三) 若然木匠做來勿好,我要叫別人來做.
(四) 實蓋做頭是勿好,我要儂做來好點.
(五) 我走到上海難末走勿動哉.
(六) 難末儂那能做頭?我叫之東洋車佬轉來.
(七) 先生垃拉否?出去拉.
(八) 三日前頭我去看第座塔.
(九) 地底下有水.
(十) 貓拉椅子底下.
(十一) 我讀罷之書要學寫字.
(十二) 叫伊到裏向來.
(十三) 第隻檯子忒低,勿好寫字.
(十四) 我可以進來否?進來末哉.

NOTES.

(1) In regard to °*sau*, meaning "few," it should be noted that it never occurs before a noun. If you wish to say a few men the idiomatic expression would be °*yeu 'veh too* °*kyi-kuh nyung* (有勿多幾個人) or *m-meh* °*kyi-hau*° *nyung* (無沒幾化人). The men are few would be *nyung* °*sau* (人少). °*Sau* is often used to qualify verbs. Thus we have °*sau dok kuh*, meaning "to read less."

(2) As already pointed out in a previous lesson what correspond to prepositions in English are really postpositions in Chinese, as they come after the nouns instead of before them. When used as adverbs, however, they generally precede the verbs. Thus we have °*li-hyang*° °*zoo* for "Sit inside," °*zaung-deu* °*zoo* (上頭坐) for "take a higher seat." This is the usual polite phrase said to a guest when he enters your guest room. He will take a seat near the door, and you ask him "to be seated higher."

(3) The first sentence of the First Exercise is really an oath, and is used when one is calling Heaven and Earth to witness that his words are true.

(4) Note the impersonal use of °*yeu* in the second sentence of the First Exercise. Literally it is "There are many characters."

(5) In the seventh sentence of the Second Exercise you have the usual form of inquiring whether the gentleman you wish to see is at home. You say *Sien-sang leh-la*° *va*°*?* "is the master there?" The answer is *leh-la*°, if he is at home, meaning "He is there." If he is not at home, the answer may be *tsheh chi*° *la*°, "he has gone out," or *'veh leh-la*°, "he is not there."

Lesson XIII

Auxiliary Verbs

The verb °***chi*** (起) is often used as an auxiliary verb after the principal verb to express the idea of *inception*. Thus ***dok-°chi*** (讀起) means "Begin to read." °***Chi*** also expresses the idea of *erectness*, but when used in this sense, ***le*** (來) follows the °***chi***. Thus ***Lih-°chi-le*** (立起來) means "Stand up." ***Lok-°chi-le*** (睩起來) means "Get up." It also has a *progressive* meaning, as when you say ***Doh-°chi-le*** (讀起來) it means "read on," "go on reading."

We have the °***chi***, also used in combination with ***tuh*** (得). Thus ***Lok-tuh-°chi*** (睩得起) means "Able to get up." ***Lok-'veh-°chi*** (睩勿起) means "Unable to get up." °***Ma-tuh-°chi*** (買得起) means "Can afford to buy it." °***Ma-'veh-°chi*** (買勿起) means "Cannot afford to buy it." ***Kwhung°-'veh-°chi*** (睏勿起) means "unable to sleep." ***Khoen°-'veh-°chi*** (看勿起) means "to look down upon," "to disdain."

°***Zaung*** (上) and °'***Au*** (下) are used both as principal verbs and as auxiliaries. Thus we have the expressions °***Zaung san*** (上山), meaning "to go up hill." °'***Au san*** (下山), "to go down hill." °'***Au zen*** (下船), "to go on board a boat," °***Zaung su*** (上書), "to take an advanced lesson in a book," etc. In these cases they are used as principal verbs.

As auxiliary verbs, they express motion upwards and motion downwards.

They are not confined to verbs of motion, but are used freely with other verbs. To both of them ***le*** (來) and ***chi°*** (去) are frequently added.

Thus we have ***dok-°'au-chi°*** (讀下去), meaning "Read on down." ***Tsoo°-°'au-chi°*** (做下去), meaning "Go on doing it." ***Thiau°-°'au-le*** (跳下來), meaning "Jump down." ***Thiau°-°zaung-chi°*** (跳上去), meaning "Jump up to that place." ***Thiau°-°zaung-le*** (跳上來) "Jump up to this place."

Although the Chinese language is, strictly speaking, a monosyllabic language, yet as has already been noticed there is a strong tendency to use two or more words together forming as it were disyllables or trisyllables. In this lesson some verbs are used, composed of two characters occurring together.

Vocabulary

To like, to enjoy, **hwen-°hyi** 歡喜.

To play, take recreation, **beh-siang°** 孛相.

To converse, **bak-wo°** or **dan-dan** 白話, 談談.

To believe, **siang-sing°** 相信.

To fall, **lauh** 落 (of things) or **tih** 跌 (of men or animals).

To stand up, **lih** 立.

To get up, **lok** 趢.

To be willing, **°khung** 肯.

To back the book, **pe°** 背

To think, **°siang** 想.

To sleep, **kwhung°** 睏

To wipe, **kha** 揩.

To fly, **fi** 飛.

To reckon, **soen°** 算.

To build, **°zau** 造.

A stove, **ih kuh °hoo-loo** 一個火爐, or **ih tsak °hoo-loo**.

A rat, **ih tsak °lau-°ts** 一隻老鼠, or **ih tsak °lau dzoong** 一隻老蟲.

A washstand, **ih tsak kha-mien°-de-°ts** 一隻揩面檯子.

A temple, **ih zoo° miau°** 一座廟.

A window, **ih sen° tshaung** 一扇窗.

Ban (爿) is the Classifier for firms, shops, etc.

A tea shop, **ih ban dzo-kwen°** 一爿茶館.

A pair of chop-sticks, **ih saung kwhan** 一雙筷.

Words, **seh-wo°** 說話 or **wo°-deu** or 話頭.

A sentence, **ih kyui° seh-wo°** 一句說話.

Only, **pih-koo°** 必過, or **dok-°z** 獨自, or **tsuh-tuh** 只得.

Not only, **'veh-dan°-°z** 勿但是, or **'veh-dan°** 勿但, or **'veh-°ba** 勿罷.

Heavy, **°dzoong** 重.

Light (in weight), **chung** 輕.

Cheap, **jang** 強

Dear (in price), **kyui°** 貴.

Happy, **kha°-weh** 快活.

Clear or distinct, **tshing-°saung** 清爽.

Soochow, **Soo-tseu** 蘇州.

Therefore, **°soo-°i** 所以 or **keh-°lau** 蓋佬.

First, **sien** 先.

Together **ih-dau** 一淘, ih-doong 一同.

Exercises

(Translate into English)

(1) Di°-kuh °liang we° bang-°yeu hwen-°hyi ih-dau bak-wo°.

(2) °Ngoo dok-ba°-ts su iau° tsheh-chi° beh-siang°.

(3) Zak-zen yi °khung ma° meh, noong° °ma-meh-tse.

(4) Di° zoo° vaung-°ts °zau-°chi-le ’man kwha°.

(5) °Ngoo kyau° i-kuh °siau-noen lih-°chi-le pe° su.

(6) °Ngoo °siang di°-kuh ‘auh-sang-°ts kyung-tsau ’veh zung kha mien°.

(7) Tsoong-kok nyung chuh van° yoong° ih saung kwhan, nga°-kok nyung yoong° tau °lau tsho.

(8) Zauh ya°-deu la° vaung-kan-°li °ngoo thing-tuh ih tsak °lau-°ts leh-la° kyau°.

(9) Zak-zen yi wo° yi ’veh zung tan meh, i-kuh seh-wo° °ngoo °khung siang-sing°.

(10) Thien °hau meh °ngoo iau° tau° dzo-kwen°-°li chi° °zoo-°zoo dan-dan chuh dzo.

(11) °Yeu bih saung-°‘a-°ts va°? °Ngoo pih-koo° °yeu di°-saung.

(12) Zauh-ya°-deu °ngoo kwhung°-’veh-dzak, °soo-°i kyung-tsau lok-’veh-°chi.

(13) Thien nyih kuh zung-kwaung iau° khe tshaung °lau mung, °lang meh iau° kwan.

(14) Tsoong-kok wo°, wo° le ’veh tshing-°saung meh bih nyung ’veh °toong kuh.

(15) Di°-tsak kha-mien°-de-°ts noong° °ma le jang va°? ’Veh °hau soen° jang, °ngoo °siang ’man kyui°.

(16) Noong° °kyi kwhe° yang-dien °ma le kuh? Zeh kwhe° yang-dien la°.

(17) Noong° we°-sa°-°lau °ma le zeh-ke° kyui°? Iung-we° tsuh-tuh di°-kuh ih tsak.

(18) °Ngoo tsheh-chi° bau loo° ’veh-dan° khoen°-kyien° ih zoo° miau°, miau° mung zien ‘a °yeu ih zoo° thah.

(19) Di°-tsak °hoo-loo °z °dzoong kuh nyi chung kuh? °Z ’man °dzoong kuh.

(20) °Tshing sien-sang °zoo °zaung chi°.

(21) Sien-sang kyau° ‘auh-sang-°ts dok-°‘au-chi°.

(22) °I-°pung su dzoong de-°ts laung° lauh-°‘au-le.

(23) °Siau-noen dzoong iui°-°ts laung° tih-°‘au-le.

(24) °Ngoo khoen°-kyien° ih tsak °tiau dzoong thien laung° fi-°‘au-le.

(25) °Ngoo ming-tsau iau° °‘au zen tau° Soo-tseu chi°.

(一) 第個兩位朋友歡喜一淘白話.

(二) 我讀罷之書要出去勃相.

(三) 若然伊肯賣末儂買末哉.

(四) 第座房子造起來蠻快.

(五) 我叫伊個小囝立起來背書.

(六) 我想第個學生子今朝勿曾揩面.

(七) 中國人吃飯用一雙筷外國人用刀咾叉.

(八) 昨夜頭拉房間裏我聽得一隻老鼠垃拉叫.

(九) 若然伊話伊勿曾担末伊個說話我肯相信.

(十) 天好末我要到茶館裏去坐坐談談吃茶.

(十一) 有別雙鞋子否?我必過有第雙.

(十二) 昨夜頭我睏勿着所以今朝睩勿起.

(十三) 天熱個辰光要開窗咾門冷末要關.

(十四) 中國話話來勿清爽末別人勿懂個.

(十五) 第隻揩面檯子儂買來強否?勿好算強我想蠻貴.

(十六) 儂幾塊洋錢買來個?十塊洋錢拉.

(十七) 儂爲啥咾買來實蓋貴?因爲只得第個一隻.

(十八) 我出去跑路勿但看見一座廟廟門前也有一座塔.

(十九) 第隻火爐是重個呢輕個?是蠻重個.

(二十) 請先生坐上去.

(二十一) 先生叫學生子讀下去.

(二十二) 伊本書從檯子上落下來.

(二十三) 小囝從椅子上跌下來.

(二十四) 我看見一隻鳥從天上飛下來.

(二十五) 我明朝要下船到蘇州去.

(Translate into Chinese)

(1) Do you like to eat this?

(2) In the day time men work, in the night time they sleep.

(3) The cat came in by the window and the rat ran out by the door.

(4) I conversed with him, and he taught me many words in Chinese.

(5) I want you to wipe the windows.

(6) Last night I only slept four hours.

(7) I not only bought a washstand, I also bought a stove and three chairs.

(8) Children like to play, men like to study.

(9) Why do you go to the tea shop? Because there I can hear many men conversing, and so learn many Chinese words.

(10) Are you willing to go with me to see the temple?

(11) To-day I am very happy, because I have finished the book.

(12) The child jumped down from the table.

(13) Please write on down.

(14), When will you go up the hill with me to take a look?

(15) The teacher first hears the scholars back the book, and then gives them an advanced lesson.

(一) 第樣物事儂歡喜吃否?

(二) 日裏個辰光人做工夫拉夜裏末睏.

(三) 貓是從窗裏進來老鼠從門裏跑出去.

(四) 我對伊白話佬伊教我多化中國話.

(五) 要儂去揩揩窗.

(六) 昨夜頭我必過睏之四點鐘工夫.

(七) 我勿但買之一隻楷面檯子也買之一隻火爐佬三把椅子.

(八) 小囝歡喜勃相大人歡喜讀書.

(九) 儂爲啥佬到茶館裏去? 因爲伊頭我可以聽得多化人白話佬學中國話.

(十) 儂肯搭我一淘到廟裏去看看否?

(十一) 今朝我蠻快活因爲一本書讀完哉.

(十二) 小囝從檯子上跳下來.

(十三) 請寫下去.

(十四) 儂幾時搭我一淘上山去看看?

(十五) 先生先聽學生子背書難末對伊拉上書.

NOTES.

(1) Note that *siang-sing°* means "to like" as well as to believe. *°Ngoo siang-sing° ih kuh nyung* (我相信一個人) means, "I like him."

(2) The expression "to back the book" arises from the old Chinese custom of the pupil turning his back upon the teacher when he recites his lesson.

(3) Notice the order of the words in the eleventh sentence of the First Exercise. The verb *°Yeu* comes first in the sentence.

(4) The word *la°* is added at the end of the sixteenth sentence of the First Exercise merely for euphony.

(5) In the twentieth sentence of the First Exercise we have another polite way of asking a person to take a higher seat in the guest room.

(6) In sentences twenty-two and twenty-three of the First Exercise we have the use of *lauh* and *tih* for "fall". It is difficult to distinguish between the two, but *tih* is used always when we speak of a person falling down.

(7) The correct way of translating the first sentence of the Second Exercise is *Di°-yang meh-z° nong° hwen°-hyi chuh va°*? *Di°-yang* means "this sort."

(8) The thirteenth sentence of the Second Exercise of course refers to the fact that the Chinese write from the top down and not across the page.

(9) The last clause of the fifteenth sentence of the Second

Exercise should be *nan-meh theh yi-la °zaung su*. "Then for them, advances in the book."

Lesson XIV

Causality, and Necessity

The idea of causality, in the sense of causing a person to do a thing, is expressed in Chinese by the use of the auxiliary verbs ***kau*** (教) and ***tsha*** (差). Thus "I caused him to do it," would be ***°ngoo kao yi tsoo°*** (我教伊做). "I caused him to go," would be ***°ngoo tsha yi chi*** (我差伊去). The word ***tsha*** literally means "to send." The word ***kau*** is the same as ***kyau°***, but used with different pronunciation and different tone. When one of higher rank causes a person of lower rank to do a thing the word ***s°*** (使) is used. Thus ***S° °ngoo ieu-mung***, "Caused me to sorrow."

"Must" is expressed by the expressions ***tsoong-iau°*** (總要), ***pih-ding° iau°*** (必定要), ***ih-ding° iau°*** (一定要).

"It must be" is ***tsoong °z*** (總是). Thus "It must be so" is ***tsoong-°z zeh-ke°*** (總是實蓋).

"Ought" implying obligation, is expressed by ***iung-ke*** (應該). Thus "You ought to do it" is ***noong° iung-ke tsoo° kuh*** (儂應該做個).

Vocabulary

Perhaps, **khoong-pho°** 恐怕.

Just now, a little while ago, **khan khan** 纔纔, or **'veh too °kyi-z** 勿多幾時.

Quickly, **'au-sau°** 豪燥, or **kwha°-kwha°** 快快.

Moreover, **°ping-°tshia** 并且, or **r-°tshia** 而且, or **hwaung-°tshia** 况且.

Although, **soe-zen** 雖然, or **soe-°z** 雖是.

Yet, **zen-r** 然而.

Still (in the sense of in addition), **wan** 還, or **wan-iau°** 還要. **°ngoo wan-iau° °ma** 我還要買, "I still wish to buy more."

On the contrary, or on the other hand, °**tau** 倒.

To complete, **dzung-koong** 成功.

To light (a lamp or candle), °**tien** 點.

To light (a fire), **sang** 生.

To take with you, **ta° chi** 帶去.

To bring with you, **ta° le** 帶來.

To kill, **sah** 殺, or **sah-theh** 殺脫.

To kill with a blow, °**tang sah** 打殺.

To die, °**si** 死, or °**si-theh** 死脫.

To live, **weh** 活.

A lamp, **ih °tsan tung** 一盞燈.

To tell, narrate, **kau°-soo°** 告訴.

To sweep the ground (floor), °**sau-di°** 掃地.

Foong (封) is the classifier used for letters and other sealed parcels.

A letter, **ih foong sing°** 一封信.

An envelope, **ih foong sing° khauh** 一封信殼, or **ih foong sing° foong** 一封信封.

A candle, **ih kung lah tsok** 一根臘燭**.**

Fire, °**hoo** 火.

Tsang (張) is the classifier denoting sheets.

A sheet of paper, **ih tsang °ts** or **ih tsang °ts-deu** 一張紙頭.

A fowl, **ih tsak kyi** 一隻鷄.

Exercises

(Translate into English)

(1) °Ngoo-nyi° iung-ke tsoo°-kuh z°-°thi, °tau 'veh tsoo°.

(2) Thien °lang-°ts meh pih-ding° iau° sang °hoo.

(3) Ya°-deu iau° dok su meh, tsoong-iau° °tien tung.

(4) °Ngoo 'veh °hyau-tuh na°-nung tsoo°-deu, °ngoo-kuh bang-°yeu °i-kyung °si-theh tse.

(5) Tan ih tsang °ts-deu le, °ngoo iau° °sia ih foong sing°.

(6) °Ngoo la° su-vaung °li zing °ngoo-kuh mau-°ts, soe-zen °tien-ts lah-tsok

°‘a zing-’veh-dzak kuh.

(7) °Ngoo iau° ‘auh dok tsoong-kok z° °ping °tshia iau° ‘auh °sia tsoong-kok z°

(8) Soe-zen noong° wo° ’veh zung tan tsheh chi° zen-r °ngoo ’veh °khung siang-sing°.

(9) Kwha°-tien chi° kyau° i-sung le, °khoong pho° yi iau° °si tse.

(10) Sien-sang leh-la° va°? Yi khan-khan leh-°li, yien-dze ’veh °hyau-tuh °a-°li chi° tse.

(11) Zak-zen yi wan ’veh zung le,°ngoo °tung yi ’veh tuh.

(12) °Ngoo kyau° yoong°-nyung sah ih tsak kyi, la° chuh van° kuh zung-kwaung iau° chuh kuh.

(13) Di°-tsak de-°ts mok-ziang° tsoo° le wan °hau.

(14) °Ngoo ’man kha°-weh thing-tuh noong° wo° °ngoo °yeu ih foong sing° le, °khoong-pho° °z °ngoo-kuh bang-°yeu °sia le kuh.

(15) Nyung iau° sien tsoo° dzung-koong ih tsaung z°-°thi, nan-meh °khau-°i tsoo° bih yang°.

(16) M-meh ih kuh nyung hwen-°hyi °si.

(一) 我伲應該做個事體倒勿做.

(二) 天冷之末必定要生火.

(三) 夜頭要讀書末總要點燈.

(四) 我勿曉得那能做頭我個朋友已經死脫哉.

(五) 担一張紙頭來我要寫一封信.

(六) 我拉書房裏尋我個帽子雖然點之臘燭也尋勿着個.

(七) 我要學讀中國字并且要學寫中國字.

(八) 雖然儂話勿曾担出去然而我勿肯相信.

(九) 快點去叫醫生來恐怕伊要死哉.

(十) 先生垃拉否?伊纔纔垃裏現在勿曉得那裏去哉.

(十一) 若然伊還勿曾來我等伊勿得.

(十二) 我叫用人殺一隻雞拉吃飯個辰光要吃個.

(十三) 第把檯子木匠做來還好.

(十四) 我蠻快活聽得儂話我有一封信來恐怕是我個朋友寫來個.

(十五) 人要先做成功一樁事體難末可以做別樣.

(十六) 嘸沒一個人歡喜死.

(Translate into Chinese)

(1) I told you a little while ago that I did not want you to open the window; why do you not listen to me?

(2) Light the lamp and put it on the table in the study.

(3) If a guest comes, I want you to light the fire in the reception room.

(4) Do not strike the dog; perhaps you will kill him.

(5) You must study diligently, and then you can learn to speak Chinese.

(6) How many hours a day ought I to study? I think you should study at least four hours a day: two in the morning and two is the afternoon.

(7) If your letter has been written, I will send the servant to take it.

(8) Early in the morning I want you to sweep the floor and wipe the table and chairs.

(9) Although the carpenter works quickly, he cannot finish it in a week.

(10) When you have finished this do not think there is nothing more to do, but come and tell me.

(11) I did not tell you to take it away, but on the contrary told you to put it in the office.

(12) If the doctor does not come immediately, this man cannot live.

(13) Who caused you to do it? He caused me to do it.

(一) 纔纔我叫儂勿要開窗儂爲啥勿聽說話?

(二) 要點燈拉書房裏擺拉檯子上.

(三) 客人來末拉客堂間裏要儂生火.

(四) 勿要打狗恐怕要打殺哉.

(五) 儂總要用心讀書難末可以學讀中國話.

(六) 一日我應該讀幾點鐘工夫? 我想頂少要讀四點鐘工夫拉上半日兩點鐘佬下半日兩點鐘.

(七) 信寫好之末我差用人担去個.

(八) 早晨頭要儂掃掃地揩揩檯子佬椅子.

(九) 木匠雖然做來快一禮拜工夫勿能做好.

(十) 第個做好之來告訴我勿要想無啥做.

(十一) 我勿曾叫儂帶出去倒叫儂放拉寫字間裏.

(十二) 醫生勿就來末第個人勿能殼活.

(十三) 啥人教儂做個?伊教我做個.

NOTES.

(1) Wan is sometimes used to qualify adjectives. Thus *Wan °hau* (還好) means "fairly good" or "pretty good."

(2) *Soe-zen* and *Zen-r* are generally used together; the first introducing the first clause, and the second, the second clause.

(3) In the first sentence of the First Exercise notice the formation of the verbal noun, "the things which we ought to do."

(4) In the ninth sentence of the First Exercise notice that *kwha° °tien* does not mean "faster," but is used for "quickly."

(5) In the eleventh sentence of the First Exercise *°Tung yi 'veh tuh* means lit., "Wait him not get;" that is, "I cannot wait for him."

(6) In the fourteenth sentence of the First Exercise notice the use of *le*. *Le* and *chi* are frequently used with other verbs to make the direction of the action clear. Thus *°Sia le* is, "Write come to me"; *°Sia chi°* is, "Write send away," or "Write go."

(7) In the fifth sentence of the Second Exercise, Diligently can be expressed by *Yoong° sing*, "Use heart or mind."

(8) In this lesson frequent use has been made of the verb *°Si* (死). In speaking of a person dying the more euphonious expression is *Koo°-s°* 故世.

Lesson XV

Further Remarks on Numerals, the Relative Pronoun

Numbers above one hundred are expressed as follows: One hundred and one, is ***ih pak ling ih,*** and so on to ***ih pak ling °kyeu;*** then the ***ling*** is dropped, and we have ***ih pah zeh*** (一百十), ***ih pak zeh ih, ih pak zeh nyi°, ih pak zeh san,*** etc. ***Ling*** really means "in addition."

The hundreds are expressed simply by ***nyi pak*** (二百), "two hundred," ***san pak*** (三百), "three hundred," etc. "One thousand" is ***ih tshien*** (一千). In expressing "one hundred and one," we say ***ih pak ling ih*** (一百零一). In expressing "one thousand and one," we say ***ih tshien ling ling ih***.

"Ten thousand" is ***ih man°*** (一萬). "One million" is ***ih pak man°*** (一百萬). The ordinal numerals are expressed in Chinese by prefixing ***di°*** (第) before the cardinal. Thus "the first" is ***di° ih*** (第一) or ***deu-ih*** (頭一), "the second" ***di° nyi°*** (第二), and so forth.

°Soo 所 (lit. a place) is often used as a relative pronoun. It translates the English "who," "which," "what," "that," and "the things which." The clause it introduces usually comes before the subject of the sentence. Thus "All which you do, I am able to do also," would be ***noong° °soo tsoo° kuh z°-°thi °ngoo °'a nung-keu° tsoo° kuh.*** As has already been pointed out ***kuh*** often has the force of the relative.

Vocabulary.

To wonder, be surprised, **hyi-ji** 希奇.

To wear, **tsak** 著.

To take off, **thoeh** 脫 or **thoeh-theh** 脫脫.

To wear a hat, **ta°** 戴.

To take off a hat, **dzu** 除.

To laugh, **siau°** 笑.

To ridicule, **°lang-siau°** (Lit. Cold laugh) 冷笑, or **hyi°-siau°** 戲笑.

Laughable, **°hau-siau°** 好笑.

Very laughable, **siau°-sah-tse** 笑殺哉.

By the side of, **pien-deu** 邊頭, or **baung-pien** 傍邊.

Place, **han deu** 壗頭.

My place, **°ngoo han-deu** 我壗頭.

Right (Direction), **yeu°** 右.

Right hand, **yeu° °seu** 右手.

Left, **tsoo°** 左. (Sometimes pronounced **tsi°**.)

Left hand, **tsi° °seu** 左手.

Right side, **yeu° pien** (右邊), **yeu° pan-pan** (右板爿).

Early, **°tsau** 早.

Late, **an°** 晚.

Sharp, **kwha°** 快. (Same character as that used for fast.)

Dull, **dung°** 鈍.

Sweet, **dien** 甜.

Bitter, **°khoo** 苦.

Ugly, **pho°** 怕. (Same character as that used for fear.)

Pretty, **tshui°** 趣.

A shop, **ih ban tien°** 一爿店.

Take care, **°taung-sing** 當心, or **°siau-sing** 小心.

Take great care, **too°-°taung-sing** 多當心.

Tools, implements, **ka-sang** 傢生.

Furniture, **ka-°hoo** 傢伙.

A tea pot, **ih °po dzo-‘oo** 一把茶壺.

A class (in a school), **ih pan** 一班.

To sing, **ts’aung** 唱.

Exercises

(Translate into English)

(1) °Ngoo tau° tien° °li chi° khoen°-kyien° too-hau° meh-z°, dan°-°z °ma-’veh-°chi kuh.

(2) °Taung sing °tseu °hau.

(3) °Taung sing di°-kuh° yang-dien, faung° °hau la° siang-°ts °li.

(4) Zung-kwaung an° tse, zieu° chi° kwhung°.

(5) Kyung-tsau °ngoo ’m-sa° °hau, lok-’veh-°chi.

(6) °Ngoo °soo kau°-soo° noong° kuh ih tsaung z°-°thi ’veh iau° te° bih nyung wo°.

(7) Yoong°-nyung wan ’veh zung le °z peh °ngoo hyi-ji.

(8) °Taung-sing° di°-°po tau °z ’man kwha° kuh.

(9) Yi te° °ngoo wo° kuh z°-°thi °z °hau-siau° kuh.

(10) °Ngoo loo° °laung bang yi ’veh dzak, ’veh °hyau-tuh tau° °‘a-°li chi° tse.

(11) Di°-°po dzo-‘oo tan tau° sien-sang han-deu chi°.

(12) I-kuh nyung tsi° °seu °sia z°, da°-ke nyung yeu° °seu °sia kuh.

(13) Nyih-°li °soo tsak kuh i-zaung, ya°-°li kwhung° kuh z-eu° iau° thoeh-theh kuh.

(14) Nga-kok sien-sang tsing° mung-kheu thoeh-theh mau°-°ts, tsoong-kok nyung ’veh thoeh-theh kuh.

(15) I-tsak mau ’man °hau khoen°, dan°-°z °i tsak °keu °z pho°-le-°si.

(16) Too-hau° nyung hwen-°hyi chuh dien kuh meh-z°, ’m-nyung hwen-°hyi chuh °khoo kuh.

(17) Dzung °li °yeu °kyi-hau° nyung? Khoong-pho° °yeu zeh man°.

(18) Di°-kuh ‘auh-sang-°ts, ’man yoong° sing dok su, la° ih pan °li °z deu ih.

(19) Ih kuh nyung tan le ih pak ling san kuh doong-dien.

(一) 我到店裡去看見多化物事但是買勿起個.

(二) 當心走好.

(三) 當心第個洋錢放好拉箱子裏.

(四) 辰光晚哉就去睏.

(五) 今朝我無啥好碌勿起.

(六) 我所告訴儂個一莊事體勿要對別人話.

(七) 用人還勿曾來是撥我希奇.

(八) 當心第把刀是蠻快個.

(九) 伊對我話個事體是好笑個.

(十) 我路上�伊勿着勿曉得到那裏去哉.

(十一) 第把茶壺担到先生墻頭去.

(十二) 伊個人左手寫字大槩人右手寫個.

(十三) 日裏所著個衣裳夜裏睏個時候要脫脫個.

(十四) 外國先生進門口脫脫帽子中國人勿脫脫個.

(十五) 一隻猫蠻好看但是一隻狗是怕來死.

(十六) 多化人歡喜吃甜個物事嘸人歡喜吃苦個.

(十七) 城裏有幾化人?恐怕有十萬.

(十八) 第個學生子蠻用心讀書拉一班裏是頭一.

(十九) 一個人担來一百零三個銅錢.

(Translate into Chinese)

(1) When I was in the carriage, I told the coachman to take care.

(2) The clothes which that maiden wears are very pretty.

(3) The boat is by the side of the river.

(4) Yesterday I met a man who told me that he saw a carpenter kill a man with a sharp knife.

(5) Although I do not speak Chinese well, please do not laugh at me.

(6) I asked a man which road to take; he told me to go to the right.

(7) I did not meet a single person on the road.

(8) This bird is very beautiful; can it sing?

(9) When it is warm you do not want to wear many clothes.

(10) This tea is bitter and not good to drink.

(11) Yesterday I walked very far, and so could not get up to-day.

(12) Take this letter to the teacher.

(一) 我拉馬車裏個辰光叫馬夫當心.

(二) 伊個小姐着個衣裳蠻趣.

(三) 一隻船拉河邊上.

(四) 昨日我�着一個人告訴我話伊看見一個木匠担之快個刀殺一個人.

(五) 我雖然中國話話來勿好請儂勿要笑我.

(六) 我問一個人走那裏一條路伊話右手一條.

(七) 我路上一個人也撞勿着.

(八) 第隻鷹蠻趣會唱否?

(九) 天熱末儂勿要着多化衣裳.

(十) 第個茶苦個勿好吃個.

(十一) 昨日我走之多化路所以今朝睩勿起哉.

(十二) 第封信担到先生墻頭去.

NOTES.

(1) *Han-deu* is very frequently used with persons and personal pronouns. Thus you do not say *Tan tau° yi* for take it to him, but *Tan tau° yi han-deu chi°*. "Leave it with me" would be *°Pa la° °ngoo han-deu.*

(2) The second sentence of the First Exercise is often used in speaking to a guest when he is departing. When he is about to go, he announces the fact by saying *Chi° tse* (去哉), meaning "I am going." You say *Man° chi°* (慢去), meaning "Go slowly," and then when he is walking away, *°Taung sing °tseu °hau* (當心走好).

(3) In the fifth sentence of the First Exercise *M-sa° °hau* means "not at all well."

(4) In the tenth sentence of the First Exercise notice how the object *yi* splits up the verb into two parts.

(5) In the sixth sentence of the Second Exercise "to the right" is expressed by *yeu° °seu* (右手).

Lesson XVI

Verbal Idioms

The idea of there being time to accomplish a thing is expressed by adding the words ***tuh-ji°*** (得及) after the principal verb. If there is not sufficient time to do a thing you add ***'veh-ji°*** (勿及) after the principal verb. Thus, ***Tsoo°-tuh-ji°*** (做得及) means "there is time to do a thing." ***Tsoo°-'veh-ji°*** (做勿及) means "there is not time."

This expression is used most frequently with the verb ***le*** (來). ***Le-tuh-ji*** means "there is time," and ***le-'veh-ji*** means "there is not time."

The idea of a thing being important is expressed by the words ***iau°-°kyung kuh*** (要緊個). "Not being important," by the words ***'veh iau° °kyung*** (勿要緊), or ***'veh nge° sa°*** (勿礙啥). "Is it important?" or "Does it make any difference?" would be ***nge° sa° va°*** (礙啥否).

'Veh lauh is often used after verbs giving the idea of inability to do a thing. Thus ***Chuh 'veh lauh*** (吃勿落) means "unable to eat." ***°Zoo 'veh lauh*** (坐勿落) "Unable to sit because of lack of room." We also have the affirmative forms ***°zoo tuh lauh*** (坐得落) and ***chuh tuh lauh*** (吃得落).

Vocabulary

Lest, **°sang-ts** 省之.

Either, or, **ok-°z** 或是, **ok-tse** 或者.

Difficult, **van-nan** 煩難, or **nan** 難.

Easy, **yoong-yi°** 容易.

Slowly, gently, **man°-man°-nung** 慢慢能.

Walk slowly, **man°-man°-ts °tseu** 慢慢之走.

Besides, in addition, **ling°-nga°** 另外, **dze-nga°** 在外, or **wan** 還.

How much more, **'oo-°hwaung** 何況 (with **nyi** at the end of the clause).

Still more, **kung°-°ka** 更加, **yoeh°-ka** 越加.

To start (on a journey), **°doong-sung** 動身. (Lit. to move the body.)

To become ill, **sang bing°** 生病.

To heal, **i-°hau** 醫好, or **khoen°-°hau** 看好.

To welcome (a guest), **nyung-tsih** 迎接.

To return (a debt or thing borrowed), **wan** 還.

To cry, **khok** 哭.

To lead, **°ling** 領.

To borrow or to lend, **tsia°** 借. (See Note).

To wash, **zing°** 淨.

Illness, **mau-bing°** 毛病.

A sedan coolie, **ih kuh jau°-pan** 一個轎班, or **ih kuh jau°-foo** 一個轎夫.

A star, **ih kuh sing** 一個星.

A grave mound, **ih kuh vung-san** 一個墳山.

A goat, **ih tsak san-yang** 一隻山羊.

A hog or pig, **ih tsak ts-loo** 一隻猪玀.

A stool, **ih tsak ngeh-°ts** 一隻杌子.

A chest of drawers, **ih tsak tsheu-deu** 一隻抽頭.

A drawer, **ih tsak tsheu thi** 一隻抽屜.

A wash bowl, **ih tsak mien°-bung** 一隻面盆.

A plate, **ih tsak bung-°ts** 一隻盆子.

A Chinese eating bowl, **ih tsak °wen** 一隻碗.

A farmer, **ih kuh tsoong°-dien nyung** 一個種田人.

°Kwen (管) is the classifier for tubular things.

A Chinese or foreign pen, **ih °kwen pih** 一管筆.

A Chinese ink tablet, **ih kuh nyien°-°ts** 一個硯子, or **nyien°-de** 硯台.

A piece of ink, **ih khwe° muh** 一塊墨.

Foreign ink, **muh-°s** 墨水.

Clean, **koen-zing°** 乾淨.

Stop, **ding** 停.

Moon, **nyoeh-liang°** 月亮.

Precious, **°pau-pe°** 寶貝.

Exercises

(Translate into English)

(1) Di°-kuh °z iau° °kyung kuh, °tshing noong° 'veh iau° maung-kyi°.

(2) Di°-kuh °siau-noen van° chuh 'veh lauh, °khoong-pho° °yeu mau-bing°.

(3) Kyung-tsau le-'veh-ji°, ming-tsau °lau tsoo°.

(4) °Liang kuh nyung ih tsak iui°-°ts laung° °zoo-'veh-lauh.

(5) 'Auh-sang-°ts mung° sien-sang °'a-°li-deu dok °chi °lau °'a-°li-deu ding.

(6) Tshau zing°-°hau-°ts meh, faung° la° tsheu-thi °li.

(7) Tsoong°-dien-nyung °i-kyung °ma-°ts san tsak san-yang, i-kuh bang-°yeu ling°-nga° wan iau° °ma s° tsak.

(8) Noong° iung-ke °de loong-tsoong nyung °hau, 'oo-°hwaung °de z°-ka nyung °hau nyi.

(9) Bung-°ts °lau °wen iau° kung°-ka koen-zing°.

(10) Noong° iung-ke °tsau-zung-deu °doong-sung, °'au-pen°-nyih °doong-sung le-'veh-ji° tau° kuh.

(11) Noong° °kyi-z wan peh la° °ngoo? Ok-tse kyung-tsau °'au-pen°-nyih, ok-tse ming-tsau °tsau-zung-deu.

(12) °Ngoo-kuh bang-°yeu sang-bing° °soo-°i iau° °tshing i-sung khoen° khoen°.

(13) Ya°-°li la° thien laung° °khau-°i khoen° too-°hau sing °lau nyoeh-liang°, nyih-°li pih-koo° khoen°-kyien° nyih-deu.

(14) Di°-kuh °siau-noen nyih-°li 'veh khok, dan°-°z ya°-deu doo° khok.

(15) °Ngoo tsia°-peh yi san-seh kwhe° yang-dien, 'veh hyau° tuh yi °kyi-z wan.

(16) Kyau° jau°-foo man°-man°-°ts °tseu iung-we° °di-diau ka 'ah °lau.

(17) Iung-we° loo° 'veh nyung tuh °soo-°i °ngoo °tshing bih nyung °ling loo°.

(18) °Ngoo la° bang-°yeu han-deu tsia°-°ts nyan° kwhe° yang-dien iung-we° iau° °ma ih tsak kha-mien°-de °lau s° tsak ngeh-°ts.

(19) Kha °hau-ts mien°, mien°-bung iau° faung° °hau.

(20) °Ngoo °tseu tau° mung-°kheu-deu nyung-tsih khak-nyung.

(21) °Ngoo mung° i-sung °di-kuh mau-bing° i-tuh-°hau va°, yi wo° man°-man° nung we° °hau kuh.

(22) °Ts-deu, muh, pih, nyien°-de, tsoong-kok nyung soen° dok-su-nyung kuh s° yang °pau-pe°.

(一) 第個是要緊個請儂勿要忘記.

(二) 第個小囝飯吃勿落恐怕有毛病.

(三) 今朝來勿及明朝佬做.

(四) 兩個人一隻椅子上坐勿落.

(五) 學生子問先生那裏頭讀起佬那裏頭停.

(六) 抄淨好之末放拉抽屜裏.

(七) 種田人已經買之三隻山羊伊個朋友另外還要買四隻.

(八) 儂應該待攏總人好何況待自家人好呢.

(九) 盆子佬碗要更加乾淨.

(十) 儂應該早晨頭動身下半日動身來勿及到個.

(十一) 儂幾時還撥拉我?或者今朝下半日或者明朝早晨頭.

(十二) 我個朋友生病所以要請醫生看看.

(十三) 夜裏拉天上可以看多化星佬月亮日裏必過看見日頭.

(十四) 第個小囝日裏勿哭但是夜頭大哭.

(十五) 我借撥伊三十塊洋錢勿曉得伊幾時還.

(十六) 叫轎夫慢慢之走因爲第條街狹佬.

(十七) 因爲路勿認得所以我請別人領路.

(十八) 我拉朋友墻頭借之廿塊洋錢因爲要買一隻揩面檯佬四隻杌子.

(十九) 揩好之面面盆要放好.

(廿)我走到門口頭迎接客人.

(廿一) 我問醫生第個毛病醫得好否,伊話慢慢能會好個.

(廿二) 紙頭,墨,筆,硯台,中國人算讀書人個四樣寶貝.

(Translate into Chinese)

(1) Which is easier, to learn to read Chinese or to learn to write Chinese?

(2) I told you there was not time to do it; why do you still want to do it?

(3) Why do you cry? Because I have heard that my friend is dead.

(4) We will go early to-morrow morning to meet our friends, who have come

from abroad.

(5) Goats like to stand on the tops of the grave mounds.

(6) You say that this temple is so fine to see, that I want to go more than ever to see it.

(7) Please, teacher, do not speak so fast. If you will speak more slowly, I can understand.

(8) If you do not return it immediately, no matter, I can wait two or three days.

(9) Why did not the pupil come to school? Because he was sick.

(10) I told the servant to put my clothes in the drawer.

(11) The Chinese when they eat, use bowls; the foreigners use plates.

(12) This fan belongs either to the teacher or to the pupil.

(13) If you want to learn to write you must buy a pen, a piece of ink, and an ink tablet.

(14) If you borrow money from another person, and do not return it, he will be unhappy.

(15) I told the driver to stop the carriage at my friend's house.

(一) 那裏一樣容易點學讀中國書呢還是學寫中國字.

(二) 我對儂話來勿及做儂爲啥佬仍舊要做?

(三) 儂爲啥佬哭?因爲我聽得我個朋友已經過世哉.

(四) 明朝早晨頭我伲要去迎接外國來個朋友.

(五) 山羊歡喜立拉坟山上.

(六) 儂話第座廟是實蓋好看所以我更加要去看.

(七) 請先生勿要話來實蓋快, 若然先生話來慢點, 我可以聽得出.

(八) 若然儂勿是就還勿礙啥,我可以等兩三日.

(九) 學生子爲啥佬勿到學堂裏來?因爲伊生病佬.

(十) 我叫用人放我個衣裳拉抽屜裏.

(十一) 中國人吃飯個辰光用碗外國人用盆子.

(十二) 第把扇子或者是先生個或者是學生子個.

(十三) 若然儂要學寫字儂總要買一管筆一塊墨佬一個硯台.

(十四) 若然儂拉別人壗頭借銅錢佬勿還個伊要勿快活.

(十五) 我叫馬夫停馬車拉我個朋友屋裏.

Notes.

(1) The word for "to borrow" and "to lend" is exactly the same in Chinese. The only way you can distinguish between them is by auxiliary words used in connection with them. Thus *Tsia° peh* (借撥) means "to lend." *Tsia° le* (借來) means "to borrow." Again *Tsia° chi°* (借去) means "to lend." But we have such constructions as *°Ngoo tsia° la° yi* (我借拉伊), meaning "I lend to him," and *°Ngoo la° yi han-deu tsia° kuh* (我拉伊壗頭借個), meaning "I borrowed it from him."

(2) In the fifth sentence of the First Exercise *Dok° °chi* means "read begin," and *ding* means "stop." This is an ordinary form for asking where to begin the lesson and where to end it.

(3) In the fourteenth sentence of the First Exercise notice how *doo°* qualifies the verb *khok.*

(4) The twenty-second sentence of the First Exercise is a paraphrase of a Chinese proverb.

Lesson XVII

More Verbal Idioms

In asking questions *°yeu tuh?* (有得) sometimes precedes a verb with the sense, "is there to be had?" Thus ***°Yeu-tuh °ma va°?*** (有得買否) means, "Is there to be bought?" ***°Yeu-tuh chuh va°?*** (有得吃否) means, "Is there anything to eat?" The answers to these questions would be ***°yeu-tuh °ma kuh*** (有得買個), ***°yeu tuh chuh kuh*** (有得吃個), "It can be bought." "There is something to eat."

'Veh pih (勿必) means "It is not necessary." Thus ***'Veh pih khok*** (勿必哭), "It is not necessary to cry." ***'Veh pih chi°*** (勿必去), "It is not necessary to go."

Ih ngan 'veh (一顏勿) before the verbs means, "Not at all." Thus ***°Ngoo ih ngan 'veh °hyau-tuh*** (我一顏勿曉得) means, "I do not know at all." ***Ih ngan 'veh zung khoen°-kyien° hyih*** (一顏勿曾看見歇) means, "I have not seen it at all." ***Ih ngan 'veh iau° khoen°*** (一顏勿要看) means, "I do not want to see it at all."

Vocabulary

To visit, to pay respects to, **maung°** 望, or **pa° maung°** 拜望.

To worship, **pa°** 拜.

To pay a ceremonial visit, **pa° khak** 拜客.

To bathe, **zing° yok** 淨浴.

To catch, seize, arrest, **tsauh** 捉.

To prepare, to provide, **yui°-be°** 預備.

To move a thing, **°doong** 動.

Loose, unstable, **°doong °lau °doong** 動佬動.

Immovable, **°doong-°'a 'veh-°doong** 動也勿動.

To remove (a residence), **pen** 搬, or **pen-dzang** 搬場.

To commence work, **°doong °seu** 動手, or **khe koong** 開工.

To open school, **khe 'auh** 開學.

To dismiss school, **faung° 'auh** 放學.

A finger, **ih tsak tsih-deu** 一隻指頭.

A toe, **ih tsak kyak-tsih-deu** 一隻脚指頭.

A cup, **ih tsak pe-°ts** 一隻杯子.

A clock, **ih tsak z°-ming-tsoong** 一隻自鳴鐘.

A watch, **ih tsak piau** 一隻表.

A well, **ih tsak °tsing** 一隻井.

A basket, **ih tsak lan** 一隻籃.

An apple, **ih tsak bing-°koo** 一隻平菓.

A crab apple, **ih tsak hwo-'oong** 一隻花紅.

A towel, **ih diau °seu-kyung** 一條手巾.

A life, **ih diau sing°-ming°** 一條性命.

A hill, mountain, **ih zoo° san** 一座山.

A board, **ih kwhe° °pan** 一塊板.

Fok (幅) is the classifier of paintings or engravings.

A painting, **ih fok wo°** 一幅畫.

A chart or map, **ih fok doo** 一幅圖, or **ih fok di°-°li-doo** 一幅地理圖.

A picture, **ih fok wo° doo** 一幅畫圖.

One time, **ih we** 一回, **ih thaung°** 一盪.

Two times, twice, **°liang we** 兩回, or **°liang thaung°** 兩盪.

Whosoever, **van-i°** 凡係.

No matter who, **'veh lung° sa° nyung** 勿論啥人.

Whatsoever, no matter what, **'veh lung° sa°** 勿論啥, **dzoe-bien°-sa°** 隨便啥, or **'veh kyui-sa°** 勿拘啥.

Whichever, **dzoe-bien°** 隨便.

Whatever time you please, **dzoe-bien° °kyi-z** 隨便幾時.

Wet, **sak** 濕.

Dry, **koen** 乾.

Always, **dzang-tsaung** 常庄, or **dzang-dzang** 常常.

Exercises

(Translate into English)

(1) Z°-ming-tsoong kuh yoong°-deu °z peh nyung hyau°-tuh zung-kwaung.

(2) I-tsak mau 'm-sa° yoong°-deu, ih ngan 'veh we° tsauh lau-°ts.

(3) Ming-tsau °ngoo iau° tsheh chi° maung° bang-°yeu.

(4) °Ngoo thing-tuh sien-sang 'm-sa° °hau °soo-°i le maung° maung°.

(5) °Ngoo mung° mok-ziang° °zau vaung-°ts °kyi-z iau° °doong-°seu.

(6) °Liang tsak °seu °yeu zeh tsak tsih deu, °liang tsak kyak °yeu zeh tsak kyak-tsih-deu.

(7) Sang bing° meh tsoong-iau° °tshing i-sung we°-ts nyung kuh sing°-ming° °z iau° °kyung kuh.

(8) °Zaung san °z van-nan, °'au san °z yoong-yi°.

(9) Di°-foong sing° iau° sa° nyung tan chi°? 'Veh lung° sa° nyung °khau-i tan chi°.

(10) Kyung-ya°-deu iau° yui° be° °hau, we°-ts ming-tsau °tsau-zung-deu iau° °doong-sung.

(11) Yien°-°dze chi° ok-tse ming-tsau chi°, dzoe-bien° noong° meh tso.

(12) °Tsing °li °s °i-kyung koen tse, 'veh hyau°-tuh na°-nung tsoo°-deu.

(13) Zing°-ts yok iau° yoong° °seu-°kyung kha koen sung-°thi.

(14) Khan-khan °ngoo faung° nyan tsak bing-°koo la °lan °li, yien°-°dze pih-koo° °yeu °so-°ng tsak, 'veh hyau°-tuh sa° nyung tan-theh kuh.

(15) °Tsh-di° piau °yeu-tuh °ma va°? °Tsh-di° yang° yang° °yeu tuh °ma kuh.

(16) °Loong-°tsoong kuh z°-°thi °ngoo °i-°kyung hyau°-tuh, noong° 'veh pih te° °ngoo wo°.

(17) Di°-°pung su ih ngan m-meh wo°-doo.

(18) I-tsak pe-°ts °li °yeu sa° meh-z°? Pih-koo° °lang °s.

(19) Tsoo° di°-tsak de-°ts iau° yoong° °kyi kwhe° °pan?

(20) Di° sen tshaung tsoo° le ih ngan 'veh °hau, dzang-tsaung °doong-°lau °doong.

(21) Chi° koo° hyih meh? Chi° koo°-°ts °liang we.

(22) Sien-sang wo° ming-tsau 'veh °hau le, we°-ts iau° pen-dzang °lau.

(23) Van-i° nyung yoong° sing meh °khau-°i dzung-koong z°-°thi.

(一) 自鳴鐘個用頭是撥人曉得辰光.

(二) 伊隻貓無啥用頭一顏勿會捉老鼠.

(三) 明朝我要出去望朋友.

(四) 我聽得先生無啥好所以來望望

(五) 我問木匠造房子幾時要動手.

(六) 兩隻手有十隻指頭兩隻脚有十隻脚指頭.

(七) 生病末總要請醫生爲之人個性命是要緊個.

(八) 上山是煩難下山是容易.

(九) 第封信要啥人担去?勿論啥人可以担去.

(十) 今夜頭要預備好爲之明朝早辰頭要動身.

(十一) 現在去或者明朝去隨便儂末哉.

(十二) 井裏水已經乾哉勿曉得那能做頭.

(十三) 淨之浴要用手巾揩乾身體.

(十四) 纔纔我放廿隻平菓拉籃裏現在不過有十五隻勿曉得啥人担脫個.

(十五) 此地錶有得賣否?此地樣樣有得賣個.

(十六) 攏總個事體我已經曉得儂勿必對我話.

(十七) 第本書一顏無沒畫圖.

(十八) 伊隻杯子裏有啥物事?必過冷水.

(十九) 做第隻檯子要用幾塊板.

(二十) 第扇窗做來一顏勿好常庄動佬動.

(廿一) 去過歇末?去過之兩回.

(廿二) 先生話明朝勿好來爲之要搬場佬.

(廿三) 凡係人用心末可以成功事體.

(Translate into Chinese)

(1) When I have finished studying, I shall go to visit my friends.

(2) No matter who comes; tell him I am busy (have affairs).

(3) When the weather is wet I cannot go out to walk.

(4) The pupils should not eat apples in the school room.

(5) Children like to play the game of catching men.

(6) The pupils read badly to-day; I think they did not prepare.

(7) At what time does the school open, and at what time does it close?

(8) I shall be pleased to have a conversation with you whenever you come.

(9) This child does not want to study a bit; I think it would be best for him to go and do business.

(10) I have already told you two or three times; do not forget.

(11) Next month we shall remove our residence.

(12) Near Shanghai there are no high hills, only grave mounds.

(13) I cannot open this window; it is immovable.

(14) Has the clock already struck?

(15) How many eggs are there in the basket?

(一) 我讀罷之書要出去望朋友.

(二) 勿論啥人來對伊話我有事體.

(三) 天濕末我勿能彀出去跑路.

(四) 拉學堂間裏學生子勿應該吃平菓.

(五) 小囝歡喜做捉人個勃相.

(六) 今朝學生子讀來勿好我想伊拉勿曾預備.

(七) 啥辰光開學,啥辰光放學?

(八) 儂隨便幾時來我蠻歡喜對儂白話.

(九) 第個小囝一顏勿歡喜讀書我想頂好伊出去做生意.

(十) 我已輕對儂話兩三回勿要忘記.

(十一) 下個月我伲要搬場.

(十二) 近上海無沒高山必過坟山.

(十三) 第扇窗開勿來個動也勿動.

(十四) 鐘已輕敲過末.

(十五) 籃裏有幾個蛋?

NOTES.

(1) In the fourth sentence of the First Exercise *'m-sa° °hau* means "not at all well."

(2) In the eleventh sentence of the First Exercise the expression *Dzoe-bien° noong° meh tse* is one very frequently used. It implies, "do it whenever and however you please"

(3) In the fourteenth sentence of the First Exercise *Tan theh* means "take away." We have already had the use of *Theh* after verbs, as *Thoeh-theh*, "to take off clothes." It can be used with

almost any verb of motion. We have *Peh theh,* "to give away." *Chuh-theh,* "to eat up." *Chi°-theh,* "to cast off, disown." *Ma°-theh,* "to sell away, etc."

(4) In the fifteenth sentence of the First Exercise *Yang° yang°* repeated means, "Things of every sort."

(5) Note that the usual expression in Chinese to say you are busy is *°Ngoo °yeu z°-°thi*. It is never very polite to tell any one that you are busy. A person asking whether you were busy would say *maung va°*? "Are you busy?"

(6) In the fifth sentence of the Second Exercise the game *Tsauh nyung*, frequently played by Chinese children, is referred to.

(7) In the eighth sentence of the Second Exercise the clauses should be reversed. *Noong° dzoe-bien° °kyi-z-le* should come first.

(8) In the ninth sentence of the Second Exercise "to go and do business" is *Chi° tsoo° sang-i°*.

(9) In the fourteenth sentence of the Second Exercise *Tsoong khau koo° meh* is the usual way of asking the question. *Tsoong* is shortened form of *Z°-ming tsoong*.

Lesson XVIII

More Verbal Idioms

Siang (相) is often placed before transitive verbs and usually gives the idea of mutual or reciprocal. In some cases it is reflexive. As instances of reciprocal action we have ***siang-°tang*** (相打), "to fight with one another." ***Siang-mo°*** (相罵), "to revile one another." ***siang-lien*** (相聯), "to be connected together." ***Siang-paung*** (相幫), "to help one another."

Khe (開) or ***Khe-le*** (開來) is used with many verbs to give the idea of spreading wide open. Thus ***Than-khe-le*** (攤開來) means "to unroll a bundle." ***Hyih-khe-le*** (揭開來) means "to open a box." ***Fung-khe*** (分開), "to divide," ***san°-khe*** (散開), "to scatter wide cast." ***Tshih-khe*** (切開) or ***tshih-khe-le*** (切開來) means "to cut open, etc."

Not inclined to do a thing is expressed by the phrase ***'veh kau-hyung°*** (勿高興). Thus ***'Veh kau-hyung° chi°*** (勿高興去), "not inclined to go."

Vocabulary

To follow, **kung** 跟.

To tie, **vok** 縛.

To tie firmly, **vok-lau** 縛牢, or **vok lau-dzu°** 縛牢住.

To desire, to expect, **maung°** 望, or **po-maung°** 把望.

To bite, **°ngau** 咬.

To bark, **kyau** 叫.

To blow, **tsh** 吹.

To blow out, to extinguish, **tsh °iung** 吹隱.

To blow into a blaze or flame, **tsh yaung°** 吹旺.

To fly, **fi** 飛.

To explain, °**ka-seh** 解釋.

To forsake, desert, depart from, **li-khe** 離開.

To permit, °**hyui** 許.

To allow, **nyang°** 讓.

Colour, **ngan-suh** 顔色.

Variegated colours, °**ng-ngan-loh-suh** 五顔六色.

Thought or meaning, **i°-s°** 意思.

A thief, **ih kuh zuk** 一個賊.

Mien° (面) is used as the classifier for flat objects.

A drum, **ih mien° koo** 一面鼓.

Hope, **maung°-deu** 望頭.

Wind, **foong** 風.

Wine, °**tsieu** 酒.

Rope, **ih diau zung**, 一條繩 or **ih kung zung** 一根繩.

Tsung (尊) is the classifier denoting idols or cannon.

A Buddhist idol, **ih tsung veh** 一尊佛, or **ih tsung boo-sah** 一尊菩薩.

A Taoist god or idol, **ih tsung zung-dau°** 一尊神道.

A piece of bread, **ih kwhe° men-deu** 一塊饅頭.

A piece of meat, **ih khwe° nyok** 一塊肉.

Khoo (顆) is the classifier used with plants, trees and flowers.

A tree, **ih khoo zu°** 一顆樹.

A flowering plant, **ih khoo hwo** 一顆花.

Cotton seed, **hwo-°ts** 花子.

A Chinese mile, **ih °li** 一里, or **ih °li-loo°** 一里路.

To regret, to be placed in an embarrassing position, **nan-we-dzing** 難爲情.

Exercises

(Translate into English)

(1) Di°-kuh °liang kuh ‘auh-sang-°ts °ngoo ’veh °hyui tsheh chi° beh-siang° we°-ts la° ‘auh-daung °li siang mo° °lau.

(2) Di° kyui° seh-wo° kuh i°-s° °ngoo ’veh °toong °tshing sien-sang °ka-seh.

(3) Di°-tsak °tiau fi le kau-le-°si.

(4) Tsauh-dzak-°ts i-kuh zuh iau° yoong° ih kung zung vok-lau-°ts.

(5) Di° khoo hwo kuh ngan suh ’man tshui°.

(6) Ya°-°li kwhung° kuh z-‘eu° tung iau° tsh °iung.

(7) °Ngoo faung° la° tshaung-°kheu laung° kuh ih tsang °ts-deu peh foong tsh-theh tse.

(8) Zak-zen °tshing khak °lau m-meh °tsieu °z nan-we-dzing kuh.

(9) ’Veh iau° pho°, di°-tsak °keu ’veh °ngau kuh.

(10) °Ngoo tau° miau° °li khoen°-kyien° ih tsung veh °lau too-°hau boo-sah.

(11) °Ngoo thing-tuh °yeu nyung la° khau °koo.

(12) Di°-deu tau° °Zaung-°he °yeu °so-°ng °li-loo°.

(13) Soe-zen di° khoo zu° ’man °hau khoen°, zen-r ’veh khe hwo kuh.

(14) Zak-zen noong° iau° tau° san laung°, nyang° °ngoo kung noong° chi°.

(15) Men-deu °tshing noong° tshih-khe-le peh ih kwhe° la° °ngoo chuh.

(16) Bing° sang le ’man °dzoong, yien°-°dze i-sung m-meh maung°-deu.

(17) Tsoong°-dien-nyung nau hwo-°ts san°-khe-le.

(18) ‘Auh-sang-°ts beh-siang° ’man kau-hyung°, dok su ’veh da° kau-hyung°.

(19) Li-khe-ts °Zaung-°he nan-meh °ngoo tau° Soo-tseu chi° tse.

(20) °Ngoo po-maung° yi le, ’veh hyau°-tuh yi na°-nung wan ’veh zung le.

(一) 第個兩個學生子我勿許出去勃相爲之拉學堂裏相駡佬.
(二) 第句說話個意思我勿懂請先生解釋.
(三) 第隻鳥飛來高來死.
(四) 捉着之一個賊要用一根繩縛牢之.
(五) 第顆花個顏色蠻趣.
(六) 夜裏睏個時候燈要吹隱.
(七) 我放拉窗口上個一張紙頭撥風吹脫哉.
(八) 若然請客佬無沒酒是難爲情個.
(九) 勿要怕第隻狗勿咬個.
(十) 我到廟裏看見一尊佛佬多化菩薩.
(十一) 我聽得有人拉敲鼓.
(十二) 第頭到上海有十五里路.
(十三) 雖然第顆樹蠻好看然而勿開花個.

(十四) 若然儂要到山上讓我跟儂去.

(十五) 饅頭請儂切開來撥一塊拉我吃.

(十六) 病生來蠻重現在醫生無沒望頭.

(十七) 種田人拿花子散開來.

(十八) 學生子勃相蠻高興讀書勿大高興.

(十九) 離開之上海難末我到蘇州去哉.

(二十) 我把望伊來勿曉得伊那能還勿曾來.

(Translate into Chinese)

(1) The dog bit the sheep two or three times; it will probably die.

(2) To-day there is no wind, and so it is not cold.

(3) Men ought not to drink too much wine.

(4) I have eaten a slice of meat and drunk a cup of tea, and now am able to walk.

(5) Men can walk, only birds can fly.

(6) There are many trees and flowers on the hill.

(7) Many Chinese worship Buddhist and Taoist idols.

(8) I wanted to follow you, but the teacher would not permit me.

(9) Let me go and tell him that you have already returned.

(10) I will use my knife and cut open the pear.

(11) I heard the dogs barking in the night and so could not sleep.

(12) Children like to play at beating the drum.

(13) These flowers are of many different colours.

(14) How many miles is it to Soochow?

(15) When the pupils take an advanced lesson, the teacher should first explain it to them.

(一) 狗咬之羊兩三回恐怕要死脫.

(二) 今朝無沒風所以勿冷.

(三) 人勿應該多吃酒.

(四) 我已經吃之一塊肉咾一碗茶咾現在走得動哉.

(五) 人會走必過鳥會飛.

(六) 山上有多化樹咾花.

(七) 多化中國人拜菩薩佬神道.

(八) 我要跟儂但是先生勿許我去.

(九) 讓我去告訴伊儂已輕轉來哉.

(十) 我要用我個刀切開第隻生梨.

(十一) 夜裏我聽得狗垃拉叫所以睏勿着.

(十二) 小囝歡喜敲鼓做勃相.

(十三) 第顆花是五顏六色個.

(十四) 到蘇州有幾化里路.

(十五) 學生子要上書先生應該先對伊拉解釋.

NOTES.

(1) In the Buddhist religion in China a Buddha or one of his manifestations is known as a *'veh*, the bodhisattvas are known as *Boo-sah.*

(2) A Chinese mile is about one-third of an English mile.

(3) In the sixteenth sentence of the First Exercise notice the expression *'man °dzoong*, "very heavy." This is the way the Chinese speak of a serious illness. They also speak of a disease being light, *chung*, just as we do.

(4) In the eighteenth sentence of the First Exercise *'veh da°* means "not very," This is a very frequent expression.

(5) In the seventh sentence of the First Exercise, *tshaung-°kheu laung°* means "on the window sill."

Lesson XIX

Asking Questions, Expecting Negative and Affirmative Answers

In addition to the interrogative forms already given there are ways of asking questions when a negative, or when an affirmative answer is expected.

Thus when the negative answer is expected, the clause begins with ***°chi*** (豈) and ends with ***nyi*** (呢). Thus ***°Chi °yeu sa° yoong°-deu nyi*** (豈有啥用頭呢). "Is it of any use?" It implies that it is not of any use and expects the negative answer. ***°Chi*** (豈) corresponds to the Latin ***num***, and implies No, or a negative of the proposition conveyed.

When the affirmative answer is expected the clause begins with ***°chi 'veh*** (豈吙) and ends with the usual interrogative ***va°*** (否).

Thus ***°Chi 'veh iung-ke tsoo° va°*** (豈吙應該做否), "Ought you not to do it?" Implies that you ought to do it and expects the affirmative answer.

It will be seen that in this case also the ***°chi*** (豈) expects the negative of the proposition conveyed, that is, the negative of a negative proposition which is an affirmative. In other words the answer is, "That you ought not not to do it," or "You ought to do it."

Vocabulary

Every place or everywhere, **kauh tshu°** 各處, or **kauh-tau°-lauh-tshu°** 各到落處.

Of course, **z°-zen** 自然.

Afterwards, hereafter, **°'eu-°seu** 後首, **°'eu-le** 後來, or **°i-°'eu** 以後.

Until, **dzuk-tau°** 直到; wait until, °tung-tau° 等到.

Daily, **nyih nyih** 日日, or **nyih-dzok** 日逐.

About, **iak-kwe** 約規, or **iak-tsak** 約酌.

About the same (not much difference), **tsho-'veh-too** 差吥多.

Secretly, **'en°-'en°-°li** 暗暗裏.

True, **tsung** 眞.

False, **°ka** 假.

Secure, **°'wung-taung°** 穩當.

A long time, **dzang-°yoen** 長遠, **dzang-°yoen-tse** 長遠哉, or **ta-z-tse** 多時哉.

Phih (疋) is the classifier denoting whole pieces of dry goods.

A piece of cloth, **ih phih poo°** 一疋布.

A piece of shirting, **ih phih yang poo°** 一疋洋布.

A piece of silk, **ih phih dzeu** 一疋綢.

A piece of satin, **ih phih doen°-°ts** 一疋緞子.

Grass, **°tshau** 草.

Vegetation in general, **hwo-°tshau-zu°-mok** 花草樹木.

Coal, **me** 煤.

To add, **ka** 加.

To add a little, **ka-°thien** 加點.

Honest, lau-zeh 老實.

A piece of land, **ih kwhe° di°-bi** 一塊地皮.

A piece of stone, **ih kwhe° zak-deu** 一塊石頭.

To pawn, **taung°** 當, or **taung°-theh** 當脫.

To mortgage, **ah** 押, or **ah-theh** 押脫.

To change a dollar into cash, **de°** 兌.

A ten cent piece, **ih kauh** 一角.

One cent, **ih fung** 一分.

Twenty cents, **°liang kauh** 兩角, **si° khe** 四開.

A half a dollar, **pen° kwhe° yang-dien** 半塊洋錢.

Small money, **°siau kauh-°ts** 小角子, or **°siau yang-dien** 小洋錢.

Change, **°tsau-deu** 找頭.

Ricksha coolie, **tsho-foo** 車夫.

A great many, **kyau-kwan** 交關.

Exercises

(Translate into English)

(1) We°-ts °lang °lau °hoo-loo °li iau° ka-°thien me.

(2) °Ma °hau-ts, °tsau-deu iau° peh °ngoo.

(3) 'Veh zung °zoo toong-yang-tsho iung-ke tah tsho-foo sien °kaung ding° peh yi °kyi kauh.

(4) I-kuh nyung °i-kyung taung°-theh-ts i-kuh i-zaung.

(5) °Ngoo iau° °ma i-kwhe° di°-bi dan°-°z °ngoo thing-tuk °i-kyung ah-theh tse.

(6) °Mo 'man hwen-°hyi chuh °tshau.

(7) °Ngoo pih-koo° °yeu pen° kwhe° yang-dien °soo-°i °ma-'veh-°chi.

(8) Yi 'veh °khung lau-zeh wo° °soo-°i °ngoo 'veh °hau siang-sing°.

(9) Noong° °chi 'veh iung-ke tsoo° dzuk-tau° tsoo° °hau va°?

(10) °Ngoo soe-zen kauh-tau° lauh-tshu° zing °'a zing-'veh-dzak.

(11) Noong° wo° lau-zeh wo°, nyung z°-zen siang-sing° kuh.

(12) Nyih nyih dok su z°-zen °khau-°i 'auh kuh.

(13) °Tung tau° noong° dok-wen °ts di°-°pung su nan-meh noong° we° wo° tsoong-kok wo°.

(14) Di°-kuh °liang phih poo° kuh ngan-suh tsho-'veh-too ih yang° kuh.

(15) 'En°-'en°-°li tsoo° z°-°thi °chi °yeu sa° yoong°-deu nyi?

(16) Di°-deu tau° Soo-tseu °yeu °kyi-hau° °li soo? Iak-kwhe °yeu san pak °li-loo°.

(17) Di°-kwhe° zak-deu iau° °pa le °'wung-taung° °tien.

(18) Yi chi°-ts dzang-°yoen-tse wan 'veh zung °tsen le.

(19) °Ngoo sien iau° 'auh dok su °'eu-le 'auh °sia z°.

(20) Hwo-°tshau-zu°-mok nyung nyung hwen-°hyi khoen°.

(21) Doo° yang-dien de°-°ts °siau yang-dien iau° taung sing iung-we° °yeu too-hau° °siau kauh-°ts °z °ka kuh.

(22) Tsung °lau °ka van-nan khoen°-tuh-tsheh.

(23) Di°-°pung su °yeu kyau-kwan z° °ngoo suh-'veh-tsheh kuh.

(一) 爲之冷佬火爐裏要加點煤.

(二) 買好之找頭要撥我.

(三) 勿曾坐東洋車應該搭車夫先講定撥伊幾角.

(四) 伊個人已經當脫之伊個衣裳.

(五) 我要買伊塊地皮但是我聽得已經押脫哉.

(六) 馬蠻歡喜吃草.

(七) 我必過有半塊洋錢所以買勿起.

(八) 伊勿肯老實話所以我勿好相信.

(九) 儂豈勿應該做直到做好否?

(十) 我雖然各到落處尋也尋勿着.

(十一) 儂話老實話人自然相信個.

(十二) 日日讀書自然可以學個.

(十三) 等到儂讀完之第本書難末儂會話中國話.

(十四) 第個兩疋布個顏色差勿多一樣個.

(十五) 暗暗裏做事體豈有啥用頭呢?

(十六) 第頭到蘇州有幾化里數?約規有三百里路.

(十七) 第塊石頭要擺來穩當點.

(十八) 伊去之長遠哉還勿曾轉來.

(十九) 我先要學讀書後來學寫字.

(二十) 花草樹木人人歡喜看.

(廿一) 大洋鈿兌之小洋錢要當心因爲有多化小角子是假個.

(廿二) 眞佬假煩難看得出.

(廿三) 第本書有交關字我識勿出個.

(Translate into Chinese)

(1) I do not know where the child has gone to; I have looked for him everywhere and do not know where to find him.

(2) Call the servant to come and add some coal.

(3) I told the pupil to sit here until the teacher returned.

(4) I was almost beaten to death by him.

(5) Take the dollar and change it into cash.

(6) An honest man speaks true words.

(7) I thought he was coming, but afterwards he wrote a letter to me and told me he could not come.

(8) The children have played for a long time and now they should go to sleep.

(9) Can you say that you did not know this?

(10) Is it not good to do things so as to please others?

(11) I had to walk here because I had no small money, and so could not call a ricksha.

(12) If he said he would do it, of course he will do it.

(13) How many cash can you get for a dollar?

(14) That man is not at all honest, and he has already pawned a lot of clothes which were not his own.

(15) This man wears silk and satin; he must have a lot of money.

(一) 小囝到那裏去我勿曉得,我各到落處去尋伊尋勿着.

(二) 叫傭人來加點煤.

(三) 我叫學生子坐拉第頭等到先生轉來.

(四) 我差勿多撥伊打殺哉.

(五) 拿第塊洋錢兌銅錢.

(六) 老實個人話眞個說話.

(七) 我想伊要來但是後來伊寫一封信來話伊勿好來.

(八) 小囝勃相之長遠哉現在應該去睏.

(九) 儂豈可以話第個是儂勿曉得否?

(十) 做事體撥別人快活豈吓是好否?

(十一) 因爲我無沒小洋錢勿能彀叫東洋車所以我只好走.

(十二) 若然伊話要做個難末自然要做個.

(十三) 一塊洋錢可以兌幾化銅錢?

(十四) 伊個人一顏勿老實已經當脫之多化勿是伊自家個衣裳.

(十五) 第個人着之綢佬緞子個衣裳伊一定有多化洋錢.

NOTES.

(1) In the third sentence of the First Exercise the expression °*kaung ding*° (講定) means "to settle the price." Literally it signifies declaiming to a fixed point.

(2) In the sixteenth sentence of the First Exercise °*Soo* (數) is added after °*li* (里) for the sake of euphony.

(3) In the twenty-third sentence of the First Exercise *suh* (識) is used. This is always used of knowing characters in the Chinese language. Sometimes it is used in the expression *Suh hoo° kuh* (識貨個), meaning "to understand affairs." A man who does not *suh hoo°* is a stupid fellow.

Lesson XX

More Verbal Idioms

Tuk dzu° (得住) and ***'veh dzu°*** (勿住) are often used after the verb ***Lih*** (立) to stand, and give the sense of "able to stand," or "unable to stand." Thus ***Lih-tuh-dzu°*** (立得住) means "able to stand," and ***Lih-'veh-dzu°*** (立勿住) unable to stand. The same words are used after other verbs also. Thus we have ***Khau°-tuh-dzu°*** (靠得住), meaning "Worthy to be trusted" and ***Khau°-'veh-dzu°*** (靠勿住), meaning "Unworthy to be trusted."

Tuh-koo° (得過) is also used after verbs, and ***'Veh-koo°*** (勿過). Thus we have ***°Tang-tuh-koo°*** (打得過), meaning "Able to beat him." Literally "Beat, obtain surpass." ***°Tang-'veh-koo°*** (打勿過) means "Unable to beat him." Literally "Beat, not surpass."

The expressions ***I°-tuh-koo°*** (意得過) and ***I°-'veh-koo°*** (意勿過) are also idiomatic. The former means, "Within the range of pity;" the latter "Beyond the range of pity," or "greatly to be commiserated."

Vocabulary

Year, **nyien** 年, or soe° 歲.

To steal, **theu** 偷.

To beg, **°thau** 討.

A beggar, **°thau-van°-kuh** 討飯個. Lit. "To beg rice," or **kau°-hwo°-°ts** 告化子.

To marry a wife, **°thau-nyang-°ts** 討娘子. Lit. "To beg for a wife." See note.

To tie (as a small parcel), **tsah** 紮.

To bind with a cord, **°paung** 綁

To command, **fung-foo°** 分付.

Price, **ka°-dien** (價錢) or **'aung-dzing** 行情. Most frequently used is the market.

How much is it, or what is the price? **Sa° ka°-dien**? 啥價錢 or **sa° 'aung-dzing**?

A soldier, **ih kuh ping-ting** 一個兵丁.

A thief, **ih kuh zuh** 一個賊.

A robber, **ih kuh °jang-°dau** 一個強盜.

A magistrate or mandarin, **ih kuh kwen-°foo**, or **ih kuh kwen** 一個官府. **ih we°** (一位) is often used as the classifier.

Mandarin dialect, **kwen wo°** 官話 or **kok-nyui°** 國語.

Shanghai dialect, **°Zaung-°he °thoo-bak** 上海土白.

A Buddhist priest, **ih kuh oo-zaung°** 一個和尙.

A Taoist priest, **ih kuh dau°-z** 一個道士.

A nun, **ih kuh nyi-koo** 一個尼姑.

Number, **soo°-mak** 數目.

Tsang (張) is the classifier used for sheets of things.

A newspaper, **ih tsang sing-vung-°ts** 一張新聞紙.

A proclamation, **ih tsang kau°-z°** 一張告示.

A sheet of paper, **ih tsang °ts-deu** 一張紙頭.

Pau (包) is the classifier used for bales of things.

A bale of merchandize, **ih pau hoo°-suh** 一包貨色.

Te (堆) is the classifier used for piles of things.

A pile of timber, **ih te mok-deu** 一堆木頭.

A pile of bricks, **ih te lok-tsen** 一堆磟磚.

°Kwen (管) is the classifier for tubular things.

A flute, **ih °kwen dih** 一管笛.

A pen, **ih °kwen pih** 一管筆.

A pencil, **ih °kwen khan-pih** 一管鉛筆.

Green, **lok** 綠.

Red, **'oong** 紅.

Blue, **lan** 藍.

Yellow, **waung** 黃.

Black, **huh** 黑.

Few, **°sau** 少.

Truly, **zeh-°dze** 實在.

More than, **’veh °ba** 勿罷. More than a hundred men is **’veh °ba ih pak nyung** 勿罷一百人.

Less than, **’veh siau** 勿消, or **’veh °men** 勿滿.

A small quantity of, **°tien** (used after the verb) 點.

People, **pak-sing°** 百姓.

Tea, **dzo** 茶.

Tea leaf, **dzo-yih** 茶葉.

The whole of a thing, **ih tshih** 一切.

A man or two, **koen-°po-nyung** 干把人.

About (used with a number), **°po** 把.

About a hundred, **pak °po** 百把.

Nearly, **mau** 毛.

Nearly three miles, **mau san °li-loo°** 毛三里路.

A queue, **ih diau °bien-°ts** 一條辮子.

Hair on the head, **deu-fah** 頭髮.

News, **sing°-sih** 信息.

To take things by force, **°tsiang** 搶, or **°tsiang doeh** 搶奪.

To tie up, **°paung** 綁, or **vok** 縛.

To put forth a proclamation, **tsheh kau°-z°** 出告示.

Exercises

(Translate into English)

(1) I-kuh zuh dzang-tsaung le theu meh-z°, tsauh dzak-ts meh iau° °paung yi °chi-le.

(2) °Ngoo khoen°-kyien° sing-vung-°ts laung° wo° kwen-°foo °i-kyung tsheh kau°-z° tsha ping-ting chi° tsauh °jang-dau°.

(3) Noong° na°-nung °lau peh yi °tang, iung-we° °ngoo °tang-’veh-koo° yi °lau.

(4) °Ngoo la° miau° °li khoen°-kyien° too-hau° ‘oo-zaung° la° pa° boo-sah.

(5) Noong° iau° ‘auh kwen-wo° nyi ‘auh °Zaung-°he °thoo-bak.

(6) ‘Oo-zaung° tah-ts dau°-z° °z °liang yang° kuh, ‘oo-zaung° m-meh deu-fah, dau° z° °yeu °bien-°ts kuh.

(7) °Ngoo dzang-°yoen ’veh khoen° sing-vung-°ts tse, kyung-tsau °yeu sa° sing°-sih va°?

(8) Di°-kuh ih pau hoo°-suh sa°-ka° dien?

(9) I-kuh °siau-noen °kyi soe° tse? Lok soe°.

(10) Nyi-°s-ziang° °i-kyung °ma-ts ih te lok-tsen yui°-be° °zau vaung-°ts.

(11) Ya°-°li °yeu nyoeh-liang°, nyung hwen-°hyi tsh dih.

(12) Di°-kuh ih pau °li-hyang° °yeu °kyi °kwen pih? °Yeu ih pak °kwen.

(13) Yi we°-sa°-°lau ’veh °thau-nyang-°ts? Iung-we° yien°-°dze °thau-’veh-°chi °lau.

(14) San laung° °Ngoo khoen° too-hau° hwo, °yeu ‘oong °lau waung °lau bak, zeh-°dze °khau-°i wo° °ng-ngan-loh-suh kuh.

(15) Nga°-kok nyung hwen-°hyi yoong° khan-pih °sia z°.

(16) Tau° °Zaung-°he ’veh °men nyan° °li-loo°, °lau ’veh °ba zeh-nyi° °li-loo°.

(17) Iung-we° °ngoo khoen°-kyien° i-kuh °thau van°-kuh dzang-°yoen ’veh chuh sa°, keh-°lau kyau° yoong°-nyung peh °tien meh-z° yi chuh.

(18) Di° kuh pau iau° tsah °hau tan tau° tien° °li chi°.

(19) °Lau-zeh kau°-soo° °ngoo °z zeh-ke° ka°-dien ’va°?

(20) S° °lau tshih °lau pah °z sa° kuh soo°-mak? °Z zeh °kyieu.

(21) Nyi-koo °z, ’veh tsheh ka° kuh °siau-°tsia.

(一) 伊個賊常莊來偷物事捉着之末要綁伊起來.

(二) 我看見新聞紙上話官府已經出告示差兵丁去捉強盜.

(三) 儂那能佬撥伊打?因爲我打勿過伊佬.

(四) 我拉廟裏看見多化和尚拉拜菩薩.

(五) 儂要學官話呢學上海土白.

(六) 和尚搭之道士是兩様個和尚無沒頭髮道士有辮子個.

(七) 我常遠勿看新聞紙哉今朝有啥信息否?

(八) 第個一包貨色啥價錢?

(九) 伊個小囝幾歲哉?六歲.

(十) 泥水匠已經買之一堆碌磚預備造房子.

(十一) 夜裏有月亮,人歡喜吹笛.

(十二) 第個一包裏向有幾管筆?有一百管.

(十三) 伊爲啥佬勿討娘子?因爲現在討勿起佬.

(十四) 山上我看多化花有紅佬黃佬白實在可以話五顏六色個.

(十五) 外國人歡喜用鉛筆寫字.

(十六) 到上海勿滿念里路佬勿罷十二里路.

(十七) 因爲我看見伊個討飯個長遠勿吃啥蓋佬叫傭人撥點物事伊吃.

(十八) 第個包要紮好拿到店裏去.

(十九) 老實告訴我是實蓋價錢否.

(二十) 四佬七佬八是啥個數目?是十九.

(廿一) 尼姑是勿出嫁個小姐.

(Translate into Chinese)

(1) If you do not read the newspaper, you will not know the news, and then when you converse with others, you will have nothing to say.

(2) When a man dies the Chinese invite Buddhist and Taoist priests to the house to perform funeral ceremonies.

(3) I put my pen and pencil on my writing table, but now I cannot find them; has any one been in and taken them?

(4) Which do you think is the pleasanter to listen to, mandarin or the Shanghai dialect?

(5) When I was young I very much liked to play the flute.

(6) A thief enters secretly and steals things, a robber kills men and enters and takes things by force.

(7) Chinese are called yellow men, foreigners white men.

(8) When you go to the shop, ask the price of the boots, and come and tell me.

(9) I caught the thief and bound him to the tree.

(10) If you use a foreign pen to write Chinese characters, they do not look well; you must learn to use a Chinese pen.

(11) The Chinese beggars in the city are numberless.

(12) When the Mandarin has important things to announce to the people, he puts forth a proclamation.

(13) I saw more than a thousand soldiers.

(14) The merchant bought more than five hundred chests of tea.

(15) Are three hundred dollars sufficient to buy the house? Less than three hundred will do.

(一) 苦然儂勿看新聞紙信息儂勿會曉得難沒儂搭別人白話儂無啥好話.

(二) 人死之末中國人請和尚佬道士到屋裏來念經.

(三) 我個筆佬鉛筆擺拉寫字檯上但是現在尋勿着, 有啥人進來拿脫否?

(四) 儂想官話佬上海土白那裏一樣好聽點?

(五) 年紀輕個時候我蠻歡喜吹笛.

(六) 賊末偷伴之進來偷物事強盜末打殺之人佬進來搶物事.

(七) 中國人是叫黃人外國人是叫白人.

(八) 儂到店裏去問鞋子個價錢來告訴我.

(九) 我捉之伊個賊佬綁伊拉樹上.

(十) 若然用外國筆佬寫中國字是勿好看個儂終要學用中國筆.

(十一) 城裏個告化子無數目拉.

(十二) 官府有要緊個事體對百姓話末伊要出告示.

(十三) 我看見勿罷一千兵丁.

(十四) 生意人買之勿罷五百箱個茶葉.

(十五) 買房子三百塊洋錢有末?勿消三百塊個.

Notes.

(1) To marry a wife is expressed by °*Thau nyang-°ts*. When we speak of a woman being married we use the expression *Tsheh ka°* (出嫁), literally to go forth from the house or family. The woman leaves her own family entirely and joins the family of the husband whom she marries.

(2) The words *'Veh-°ba* (勿罷), more than, and *'Veh siau* (勿消), less than, are used in answer to questions. The words *'Veh-°men* (勿滿) are often used for less than, meaning literally "Not full."

(3) In the second sentence of the Second Exercise "to perform funeral ceremonies" should be translated *Tsoo° koong-tuh* (做功德), or *Nyan°-kyung* (念經). It means to say masses for the soul

of the departed.

(4) In the thirteenth sentence of the Second Exercise, "More than a thousand soldiers" can be expressed *Ih tshien too* (一千多) and in the fourteenth sentence "More than five hundred chests of tea" *°Ng pak too* (五百多).

(5) In the fifteenth sentence of the Second Exercise the answer would be *'Veh siau san pak kwhe°* (勿消三百塊).

(6) In the fifth sentence of the Second Exercise "When I was young" is translated *Nyien kyi° chung° kuh z-'eu°* (年紀輕個時候), literally "The time when my years were light".

(7) In the eleventh sentence of the Second Exercise "Numberless" is translated *m-soo°-mak* (無數目), literally "Without number."

Lesson XXI

Verbal Idioms, Ordinals, and Remarks on the Expression of Time

To express the idea of "about to do a thing" in Chinese you can use the words ***tsiang-iau°*** (將要). ***Tsiang-iau°-chi°*** (將要去) means "about to go." ***Tsiang-iau° °si*** (將要死) means "about to die." Another way of expressing the same idea is by adding ***kwha° tse*** after the verb. ***Kwha°*** means "fast." ***Chi° kwha° tse*** (去快哉) means "I will go fast," that is, in a moment. ***Le kwha° tse*** (來快哉) means "will come fast," that is, in a few minutes. ***Thih-°tsung*** is often used, meaning "just on the point of doing a thing." Thus ***°Ngoo thih-°tsung iau° chi°*** (我貼準要去) means "I was just going."

The expression "According to," or "as it seems to me," is expressed in Chinese by the words ***tsau° °ngoo khoen°*** (照我看). ***Tsau° °ngoo*** (照我) used alone would mean "Follow me," "Follow my example."

The Ordinals are formed from the Numerals in a very simple way. The word ***deu*** (頭) is prefixed before the first numeral and ***di°*** (第) before all the others. Thus "the first" is ***deu ih*** (頭一), the second is ***di° nyi°*** (第二), the third is ***di° san*** (第三), and so on. When first is used with the verb in the sense of the action being prior to some other action the word ***sien*** (先) is used. Thus we have ***Noong° veh zung tsheh chi° kuh zien-deu °ngoo sien iau° kau°-soo° noong° ih tsaung z°-°thi*** (儂勿曾出去個前頭我先要告訴儂一莊事體), meaning, "Before you go I first want to tell you something." Again ***Sien tsoo° di°-yang° nan-meh tsoo° i-yang°*** (先做第樣難末做伊樣) means "First do this and then do that." Again we have for the same expression ***Sien tsoo° di° kuh, man° tsoo° i-kuh*** (先做第個慢做 伊個), "First do this, slowly do that."

Remarks on Time

About midnight, **pen°-ya°-°po** 半夜把.

Just before daylight, **thien-liang°-kwha°** 天亮快.

In the evening, **waung-hwung-deu** 黃昏頭, or **waung-hwung-°doong** 黃昏動.

Last month, **zien-nyoeh** 前月, or **zien kuh nyoeh** 前個月.

Next month, **°'au-nyoeh** 下月, or **°'au kuh nyoeh** 下個月.

First part of the month, **nyoeh deu** 月頭, or **nyoeh-deu-laung°** 月頭上.

The end of the month, **nyoeh °ti** 月底.

The middle of the month, **nyoeh-pen°** 月半.

Every month, **nyoeh-nyoeh** 月月, **nyoeh-too** 月多, or **°'me-nyoeh** 每月.

First day of the month, **tshoo-ih** 初一; second day of the month, **tshoo nyi°** 初二, and so on up to the tenth day of the month, which is **tshoo zeh**. After that **di°** 第 is used instead of **tshoo**. Thus the thirteenth of the month would be **di° zeh-san** 第十三.

A year, **ih-nyien** 一年.

Half a year, **pen°-nyien** 半年.

This year, **kyung-nyien** 今年.

Last year, **jeu°-nyien** 舊年.

Next year, **khe-nyien** 開年, **le-nyien** 來年, **ming-nyien** 明年.

Every year, nyien-nyien 年年, each year, **°'me-nyien** 每年. (See note).

The new year, **sing-nyien** 新年.

New year's day, **nyien-tshoo-ih** 年初一.

The end of the year, **nyien ya°** 年夜, literally "the night of the year." Also we have **nyien-°ti** 年底.

At the beginning of the year, **nyien-deu-laung°** 年頭上.

To pass from the old year to the new, **koo° nyien** 過年.

°Zaung-pen° and **°'au-pen°** are used with year, month, and night, just as they are used with day to denote the first half and the second half. Thus we have **°zaung-pen°-nyien** 上半年 for the first half of the year, and **°'au-pen°-nyien** 下半年 for the second half.

Rice (bought in the shop), **°mi** 米.

Work, **sang-wei** 生活.

Answer, **we-sing°** 回信.

Beginning, **°chi-deu** 起頭.

Again, **tse°** 再.

Exercises

(Translate into English)

(1) Leh-la° nyoeh-pen°, nyoeh-liang° °ting °hau khoen°.

(2) °Hoo-loo iau° °iung kwha° tse °soo-°i iau° ka-°thien me.

(3) Tsau° °ngoo khoen°, di° kuh nyung °z khau°-'veh-dzu° kuh.

(4) °Tsau-zung-deu nyih-deu tsheh le, ya°-kwha° lauh-san.

(5) Di°-kuh °z °ngoo di° nyi° kuh nyi-°ts, deu ih kuh °i-kyung tsheh mung tse.

(6) Nyien tshoo ih too-hau° nyung chi° pa° nyien.

(7) Jeu° nyien °mi kyui°-le-°si, kyung nyien jang tse.

(8) Noong° °'a-°li-deu koo° nyien? °Ngoo °siang la° ok-°li koo° nyien.

(9) Noong° su dok°-ts °kyi-z tse? Pih-koo° pen° nyien.

(10) Nyien ya° nyung nyung °yeu z°-°thi, sing-nyien °li °loong-°tsoong nyung beh-siang°.

(11) Yi tsiang-iau° chi° kuh z-'eu° °yeu nyung le kyau° yi 'veh iau° chi°.

(12) °Tshing zoo° ih hyih, sien-sang iau° le kwha° tse.

(13) Thien-liang°-kwha° °z °ting °lang kuh z-'eu°.

(14) °'Au kuh nyoeh °ngoo iau° tsheh mung, tau° Soo-tseu chi°.

(15) Jeu°-nyien sang-i° ih ngan 'veh °hau kyung-nyien po-maung° yi °hau-°tien.

(16) °Zaung-pen°-nyien di° kuh 'auh-sang-°ts su dok le man °hau, °'au-pen°-nyien ih ngan 'veh °hau.

(17) I-zak vaung-°ts °kyi-z °khau-°i °zau °hau? °Ngoo °siang khe-nyien °khau-°i °zau °hau.

(18) Lok nyoeh tshoo-san °ngoo °sia ih foong sing° peh la° yi, yien°-°dze °z tshih nyoeh tshoo-ih dan°-°z wan 'veh zung °yeu we-sing° le.

(19) Noong° 'veh zung tsheh chi°, sang-weh iau° sien tsoo° °hau.

(20) Nyoeh-deu laung° peh doong-dien, yien°-°dze 'veh °hau peh kuh.

(一) 垃拉月半月亮頂好看.

(二) 火爐要隱快哉所以要加添煤.

(三) 照我看第個人是靠勿住個.

(四) 早晨頭日頭出來夜快落山

(五) 第個是我第二個兒子頭一個已經出門哉.

(六) 年初一多化人去拜年.

(七) 舊年米貴來死今年強哉.

(八) 儂那裏頭過年?我想拉屋裏過年.

(九) 儂書讀之幾時哉?必過半年.

(十) 年夜人人有事體新年裏攏總人孛相.

(十一) 伊將要去個時候有人來叫伊勿要去.

(十二) 請坐一歇先生要來快哉.

(十三) 天亮快是頂冷個時候.

(十四) 下個月我要出門到蘇州去.

(十五) 舊年生意一顏勿好今年把望伊好點.

(十六) 上半年第個學生子書讀來蠻好下半年一顏勿好.

(十七) 伊宅房子幾時可以造好?我想開年可以造好.

(十八) 六月初三我寫一封信撥拉伊現在是七月初一但是還勿曾有回信來.

(十九) 儂勿曾出去生活要先做好.

(二十) 月頭上撥銅錢現在勿好撥個.

(Translate into Chinese)

(1) We will close the school on the fifth of next month.

(2) For how many weeks will you close the school? For about six weeks.

(3) Sometimes in the evening as the sun is sinking there are many beautiful colours in the sky.

(4) As it appears to me you can finish this book in six months.

(5) Just as I was about to go to sleep, I heard some one call out that the house was on fire.

(6) The thief enters about midnight.

(7) Before you go to school you should first wash your face and hands.

(8) On the first day of the year all the shops close their doors.

(9) When will you begin to study Chinese again? I think next year.

(10) A year has twelve months, a month has thirty days or twenty-nine days.

If it has thirty days, it is called a large month; if it has twenty-nine days, it is called a small month.

(11) Last month I was sick, but now I am better.

(12) Where were you yesterday afternoon? I had gone out to pay New Year's calls.

(13) At New Year's time every one wears their best clothes.

(14) Now I have no money; I will pay you at the end of the month.

(一) 下個月初五伲要放學.

(二) 放之幾個禮拜?約酌六個禮拜.

(三) 拉夜快日頭落山個時候常時拉天上有多化趣個顏色.

(四) 照我看第本書儂六個月功夫可以讀完.

(五) 我貼準要困個時候聽見人喊房子火着哉.

(六) 賊進來是半夜把個時候.

(七) 儂勿曾到學堂裏先要揩面伲淨手.

(八) 拉年初一攏總個店全關門個.

(九) 儂幾時再起頭讀中國書?我想開年起頭.

(十) 一年有十二個月一個月或者有三十日或者有念九日, 若然三十日是叫大月若然念九日是叫小月.

(十一) 前個月我生病哉但是現在我好點.

(十二) 昨日下半日儂拉那裏頭?我出去拜年哉.

(十三) 垃拉新年裏各人着頂好看個衣裳.

(十四) 現在無沒銅錢垃拉月底撥儂.

NOTES.

(1) In regard to the expressions *Nyien-nyien* and *Nyoek-nyoeh* it may be remarked that a very common way of forming the plural in Chinese is by the repetition of the noun. Thus *Nyung-nyung* means men in general.

(2) In the sixth sentence of the First Exercise the expression *Pa° nyien* means "to pay respects at New Year's time." *Pa°*, to worship, is used of worshipping deities, and also of worshipping or paying respect to men.

(3) In the fifth sentence of the Second Exercise the expression for a house to be on fire is *°Hoo-dzak tze*, (火着哉).

(4) In the eighth sentence of the Second Exercise "all the shops" is translated *°loong-°tsoong kuh tien° zen* (攏總個店全); the *zen* (全) makes the assertion more emphatic.

Lesson XXII

On Comparison

The usual way of forming the Comparative Degree of Adjectives has already been stated.

When two things are compared with one another in Chinese the words ***°pi*** (比) or ***°pi-ts*** (比之) are used between them. Thus ***°Mo °pi-ts °keu doo°*** (馬此之狗大) means, "the horse is larger than the dog." ***Yi °pi noong° °hau*** (伊此儂好), "He is better than you."

There are a good many other ways of expressing comparison. Thus ***'Veh jih*** (勿及) means, "not equal to." Also we have ***'Veh zu*** (勿如), meaning, "not equal to, or not up to."

Vocabulary

To present or send, to escort a person on the way, **soong°** 送.

To count, **°soo** 數.

To reckon, **soen°** 算.

To send (a person), **tsha** 差.

To send a letter, **kyi°** 寄.

To deport oneself, to treat others, **°de** 待.

To treat rudely, **°de man°** 怠慢.

To keep, observe, **°seu** 守.

To knock the head on the ground, to kowtow, **kheh-deu** 磕頭.

A loaf, **ih kuh men-deu** 一個饅頭.

A stone mason, **ih kuh zak-ziang°** 一個石匠.

A hammer, **ih kuh laung-deu** 一個榔頭, or **ih °po** 一把.

A wine shop, **ih ban °tsieu tien°** 一爿酒店.

Te° (一對) is the classifier denoting a pair or a brace.

A pair of fowls, **ih te° kyi** 一對雞.

A pair of candles, **ih te° lah-tsok** 一對臘燭.

A husband and wife, **ih te° foo-tshi** 一對夫妻.

°Kheu (口) is the classifier for some articles of furniture, and for a well.

A book case, **ih °kheu su-dzu** 一口書櫥.

Convenient, **bien°-taung°** 便當.

Clever, wise, **tshoong-ming** 聰明.

Propriety, custom, **kwe-°kyui** 規矩.

Coffin, **ih °kheu kwen-ze** 一口棺材.

Sometimes, **dzang-z** 常時.

As if, like, **°hau-°ziang** 好像.

To compare, **°pi** 比.

An account, **tsang°** 張.

Reason, **yoen-koo°** 緣故.

Exercises

(Translate into English)

(1) La° nyien ya° kauh nyung iau° soen° tsang°.

(2) Noong° we°-sa°-°lau iau° chi°? iung-we° yi tsha °ngoo chi° °lau.

(3) Sing° kyi°-tsheh chi° meh? ’Veh zung, zieu° iau° kyi° chi°.

(4) Zak-ziang° iau° yoong° °kyi kwhe° zak-deu? °Ngoo ’veh hyau°-tuh ’veh-zung soen° koo° hyih.

(5) Yi dzang-tsaung °de °ngoo ’man °hau, °soo-°i °ngoo iau° soong° °tien meh-z° la° yi.

(6) Su-dzu °li noong° °pa-ts °kyi °pung su? ’Veh °hyau-tuh we°-°ts ’veh zung °soo °lau.

(7) Khak nyung tsheh chi° meh iung-ke soong° yi tau° mung-°kheu.

(8) Di°-°kheu kwen-ze sa° nyung tsoo° kuh? Mok-ziang° tsoo° kuh.

(9) Noong° kuh °mo °pi °ngoo kuh kwha° too-hau°.

(10) Di°-kuh ‘auh-sang-°ts °pi-ts i-kuh tshoong-ming °tien.

(11) Di°-kuh ih te° lah-tsok °khau-°i °pi °pi khoen°, ih ngan m-meh doo° °siau.

(12) I-kuh °liang kuh nyung siang-mo° kuh yoen-koo° °z we°-°ts la° °tsieu tien° °li too-chuh-ts °tsieu °lau.

(13) Yien°-°dze foo° tsang° ’veh bien°-taung°, °tung tau° °‘au kuh nyoeh.

(14) Di°-kuh ih te° foo-tshi ’man °hau ih ngan ’veh siang-mo°.

(15) Di°-kuh nyung tsoo° z°-°thi, ’veh jih i-kuh nyung °hau.

(16) Pa° nyien kuh z-‘eu° °siau-noen iung-ke te° doo° nyung kheh-deu.

(17) °Nga-kok nyung chuh van° kuh zung-kwaung hwen-°hyi chuh men-deu.

(18) Di°-kuh nyung ih ngan ’veh °toong sa°, °z °hau-°ziang ’veh zung dok hyih su.

(19) Sien-sang dzang-tsaung kyau° ‘auh-sang-ts° °seu kwe-°kyui.

(20) ’Veh iau° °de man° bih nyung.

(一) 拉年夜各人要算帳.

(二) 儂爲啥佬要去?因爲伊差我去佬.

(三) 信寄出去末?勿曾,就要寄去.

(四) 石匠要用幾塊石頭?我勿曉得勿曾算過歇.

(五) 伊常莊待我蠻好所以我要送點物事拉伊.

(六) 書櫥裏儂擺之幾本書?我勿曉得爲之勿曾數佬.

(七) 客人出去末應該送伊到門口.

(八) 第口棺材啥人做個?木匠做個.

(九) 儂個馬比我個快多化.

(十) 第個學生子比之伊個聰明點.

(十一) 第個一對臘燭可以比比看一顏無末大小.

(十二) 伊個兩個人相罵個緣故是爲之拉酒店裏多吃之酒佬.

(十三) 現在付帳勿便當等到下個月.

(十四) 第個一對夫妻蠻好一顏勿相罵.

(十五) 第個人做事體勿及伊個人好.

(十六) 拜年個時候小囝應該對大人磕頭.

(十七) 外國人吃飯個晨光歡喜吃饅頭.

(十八) 第個人一顏勿懂啥好像勿曾讀歇書.

(十九) 先生常莊叫學生子守規矩.

(二十) 勿要待慢别人.

(Translate into Chinese)

(1) The Chinese use rice to make wine.

(2) This man treats his servants very well.

(3) According to Chinese custom before a man dies his coffin is made.

(4) If I wish you to come, I will send you a letter.

(5) To take the child along with us will not be convenient.

(6) He is older than you.

(7) The stone mason uses stones, the carpenter uses wood.

(8) I pay my bills at the end of the month.

(9) He and I have had a quarrel because he treated me rudely.

(10) I wish the carpenter to come and make a book case.

(11) Because I have forgotten so many characters, it is as if I had not read this book before.

(12) A scholar is wiser than a farmer.

(13) If a man takes too much wine he can not do his work.

(14) My friend came to visit me, and then I escorted him to his home.

(15) This book I will present to you, do not return it.

(一) 中國人用米做酒.

(二) 第個人待伊個用人蠻好.

(三) 照中國規矩一個人勿曾死先要做棺材.

(四) 若然要儂來末我寄一封信來.

(五) 帶小囝去是勿便當.

(六) 伊比之儂年紀大點.

(七) 石匠用石頭木匠用木頭.

(八) 我個帳是拉月底付個.

(九) 因爲伊待慢我所以我對伊相駡.

(十) 我要木匠來做一口書橱.

(十一) 因爲我忘記脫之多化字所以好像我勿曾讀歇第本書.

(十二) 讀書人比之種田人聰明點.

(十三) 若然一個人多吃之酒伊勿會做生活.

(十四) 我個朋友來望望我後來我送伊到伊屋裏去.

(十五) 第本書我送撥儂勿要還個.

NOTES.

(1) In the fifth sentence of the First Exercise notice the use of *Soong° °tien*. *°Tien* means "a few things."

(2) In the ninth sentence of the First Exercise *kwha° too-hau°* means "very much faster."

(3) In the sixteenth sentence of the First Exercise the expression *Kheh-deu* refers to the most formal salute of the Chinese. It is used by an inferior before a superior. The usual polite salutation is to clasp the hands together and move them from the feet to the forehead. This is called *Tshaung° zo°* (唱喏) or *Tsauh-ih* (作揖).

(4) In the nineteenth sentence of the First Exercise we have the expression *°Seu kwe-°kyui* (守規矩). This is very frequently used. It means to act according to the laws of propriety. It is a command frequently given to children.

Lesson XXIII

The Points of the Compass

The four cardinal points of the compass in Chinese are expressed: ***Toong, nen, si, pok*** (東, 南, 西, 北) East, South, West, North. Thus it will be seen that they do not follow the same order as we. North East is ***Toong-pok*** (東北), lit. East North. North West is ***Si-pok*** (西北), lit. West North. South East is ***Toong-nen*** (東南), and South West is ***Si-nen*** (西南).

The word ***pien*** (邊) is generally added when direction or place is indicated. Thus we have for the North ***Pok-pien***, for the West ***Si-pien***. ***Pien*** literally means "side," and is a shortened form of ***pien-deu*** (邊頭).

In giving directions as to locality, the Chinese make very frequent use of the points of the compass.If you wish a person to go towards the North you say ***dzau pok*** (朝北) "towards the North."

Vocabulary

To break, smash, **se°** 碎, **°tang-se°** 打碎, or **khau-se°** 敲碎.

To beget to nourish, **°yang** 養, or **sang °yang** 生養.

To lose, to forfeit, **seh** 失, or **seh-theh** 失脫.

To arrange, to attend to matters, to direct **ban°** 辦.

A Compradore, **°ma-ban°** 買辦.

To consult, **saung-liang** 商量, **tsung-tsak** 斟酌.

To point with the hand, **°tien** 點, or **°ts-°tien** 指點.

To separate, **fung** 分, or **fung-khe** 分開.

To hinder, oppose, **°tsoo** 阻, or **°tsoo-taung°** 阻檔.

To answer, **we-deu** 回頭, or **we-tah** 回答.

To exchange, to barter, **wen°** 換, or **diau°** 調.

To attend to a thing to make it right, **loong°** 弄, or **loong°-°hau** 弄好.

To distinguish, **fung-pih** 分別.

A difference, **ih kuh fung-pih** 一個分別.

Wages, **koong-dien** 工錢.

Salary, **sok-sieu** 束脩, **sing-foong°** 薪俸, or **sing-°soe** 薪水.

Misery, **°khoo-nau°** 苦腦.

Rain, **°yui** 雨,

To rain, **lauh °yui** 落雨.

Coolie, **tsheh-tien°** 出店.

A duck, **ih tsak ah** 一隻鴨.

A broom, **ih °po °sau-°tseu** 一把掃箒.

A snake, **ih diau zo** 一條蛇.

A stick of bamboo, **ih kung tsok-deu** 一根竹頭.

Glass, **poo-li** 玻璃.

A glass (for the table), **ih tsak poo-li pe-°ts** 一隻玻璃杯子.

°Doong (桶) is the classifier for casks, tubs and buckets.

A bucket of water, **ih °doong °s** 一桶水.

Bing (瓶) is the classifier for bottles.

A bottle of medicine, **ih bing yak** 一瓶藥.

Siang (箱) is the classifier for boxes of things.

A box of dollars, **ih siang yang-dien** 一箱洋錢.

A box of tea, **ih siang dzo-yih** 一箱茶葉.

Tired, **sa-doo** 弛瘏.

Square, **faung** 方.

Round, **yoen** 圓.

Little (to a small extent), **sau-we** 稍爲.

Thick, **°‘eu** 厚.

Thin, **bok** 薄.

Instead of, **°de-thi°** 代替.

Sufficient, **keu-z°** 穀事, **keu-z°-tse** 彀事哉, or **°yeu-tse** 有哉.

Together with (two persons doing a thing), **da-ka** 大家.

To get wet, **ling-sak** 淋濕.

Exercises

(Translate into English)

(1) Tsoong-kok tsok-deu doo° °yeu yoong°-deu, °khau-°i tsoo° lan °lau de-°ts °lau iui°-°ts °lau too-hau° meh-z°.

(2) °Ngoo mung°-°ts yi san we, dan°-°z yi ih kyui° 'veh we-deu.

(3) Tsoong°-dien-nyung °yang too-hau° kyi °lau ah.

(4) °Hau-la-va°? °Hau-la zia°-zia°.

(5) Kyung-tsau °hau-°tien va°? Zauh-ya°-deu chuh-ts yak °lau kyung-tsau sau-we °hau-°tien.

(6) Nyih-deu toong-pien tsheh °lau si-pien lauh.

(7) Pok-pien °lang °lau nen-pien °noen.

(8) °Ngoo-nyi iau° da-ka saung-liang na°-nung tsoo°-deu.

(9) Di°-kuh poo-li 'man bok kuh, yoong-yi° °tang-se°.

(10) Khoen°-kyien° nyung iau° tsoo° 'veh °hau kuh z°-°thi meh, iung-ke °tsoo-taung° yi.

(11) Khoen°-yang-nyung seh-theh-ts ih tsak yang °lau iau° chi° zing yi.

(12) Sien-sang iau° °kyi-hau° sok-sieu? Iau° san-seh kwhe° °yang-dien ih nyoeh.

(13) Noong°-kuh yoong°-nyung °kyi-hau° koong-dien ih nyoeh? Zeh kwhe° yang-dien ih nyoeh.

(14) Toong-pok foong iau° lauh °yui.

(15) Yien°-°dze la° lauh °yui, tsoong-iau° tan ih °ting san° °sang-°ts ling sak.

(16) Zauh-nyih °ngoo °tseu-°ts san-seh °li-loo°, °soo-°i kyung-tsau 'man sa-doo.

(17) °Ngoo °tien peh yi khoen° ih diau zo.

(18) Di°-kuh kwen-°foo 'veh we° ban° z°-°thi.

(19) Noong° °tau le-tse, °ngoo thih-tsung iau° tau° noong° han-deu chi°.

(20) Di°-kuh nyung seh-theh-°ts yi-kuh sang-i °lau sang-°ts dzang-yoen kuh bing° zeh-dze °khoo-nau° tuh-juh.

(21) Di°-tsak siang-°ts °z faung kuh, di°-tsak °doong °z yoen-kuh.

(22) Tsheh-tien° le wo° iau° doong-dien we°-ts iau° chi° °ma ih °po °sau-

°tseu °lau.

(23) Di°-kuh °ts-deu thuh bok iau° noong° chi° wen° °‘eu-°tien kuh.

(24) Noong° thuh sa-doo, °ngoo le °de noong° tsoo°.

(25) Di°-sen° °mung ’veh °hau khe, chi° kyau° mok-ziang loong °hau.

(26) Yi-kuh seh-wo° tah-ts noong°-kuh seh-wo° °yeu fung-pih.

(27) Di°-kuh °liang kuh nyung dzang-tsaung siang-mo°, fung-khe meh °hau.

(一) 中國竹頭大有用頭可以做籃佬檯子佬椅子佬多化物事.

(二) 我問之伊三回但是伊一句勿回頭.

(三) 種田人養多化雞佬鴨.

(四) 好拉否?好拉謝謝.

(五) 今朝好點否?昨夜頭吃之藥佬今朝稍爲好點.

(六) 日頭東邊出佬西邊落.

(七) 北邊冷佬南邊煖.

(八) 我伲要大家商量那能做頭.

(九) 第個玻璃蠻薄個容易打碎.

(十) 看見人要做勿好個事體末應該阻擋伊.

(十一) 看羊人失脫之一隻羊佬要去尋伊.

(十二) 先生要幾化束脩?要三十塊洋錢一月.

(十三) 儂個用人幾化工錢一月?六塊洋錢一月.

(十四) 東北風要落雨.

(十五) 現在拉落雨終要擔一頂傘省之淋濕.

(十六) 昨日我走之三十里路所以今朝我蠻弛瘏.

(十七) 我點擦伊看一條蛇.

(十八) 第個官府勿會辦事體.

(十九) 儂倒來哉我貼準要到儂𡍲頭去.

(二十) 第個人失脫之伊個生意佬生之長遠個病實在苦惱得極.

(廿一) 第隻箱子是方個第隻桶是圓個.

(廿二) 出店來話要銅錢爲之要去買一把掃帚佬.

(廿三) 第個紙頭忒薄要儂去換厚點個.

(廿四) 儂忒弛瘏我來代儂做.

(廿五) 第扇門勿好開去叫木匠弄好.

(廿六) 伊個說話搭之儂個說話有分別.

(廿七) 第個兩個人常莊相駡分開末好.

(Translate into Chinese)

(1) Is there any answer? Yes, please wait until I write it.

(2) The cold wind blows from the North; you ought to wear more clothes.

(3) The scholar was unable to answer what the teacher asked him.

(4) I want to consult with you on an important matter.

(5) When it rains the children cannot go out to play.

(6) I have a fan, you have a knife, I want a knife, you want a fan, let us exchange.

(7) I killed the snake with a stick.

(8) Tell the compradore what you want to buy and he can buy it for you.

(9) I have lost my watch and am willing to give five dollars to the man who finds it and returns it to me.

(10) My salary is not sufficient; I must ask you to increase it.

(11) This coolie wipes and sweeps very clean.

(12) I pointed out the river to him on the map.

(13) I cannot go away until I have arranged this matter.

(14) I could not study diligently to-day because I was too tired.

(15) How many bottles of medicine have you taken? I have already finished three.

(一) 有啥回信否?有個,請等一歇等我寫好之.

(二) 冷風從北邊吹來儂應該多着點衣裳.

(三) 先生問個,學生子回頭勿出.

(四) 我要搭儂商量要緊個事體.

(五) 落之雨小囝勿好出去勃相.

(六) 我有一把扇子儂有一把刀我要一把刀儂要一把扇子讓我伲調一調.

(七) 我用之一根棒打殺之一條蛇.

(八) 儂對買辦話儂要買啥伊可以對儂買個.

(九) 我失脫之我個表情願撥拾着之佬還撥我個人五塊洋錢.

(十) 我個薪水勿彀事我終要請儂加點.

(十一) 第個出店揩佬掃蠻割瀝.

(十二) 地圖上我點撥伊看一條河.

(十三) 我勿曾辦好第莊事體我勿能殼出去.

(十四) 今朝我勿能殼用心讀書因爲我忒弛痻.

(十五) 儂吃之幾瓶藥?我已經吃完之三瓶.

Notes.

(1) Those learning to speak Chinese must be careful never to refer to the remuneration given to their teachers as *koong-dien* (工錢), but to use the polite form of speech, *sok-sieu* or *sing-foong* (束脩, 薪俸). *Sok-sieu* means literally "dried meat," and comes from the ancient custom of paying a teacher in kind. The teacher himself could refer to remuneration as *sing° soe* (薪水).

(2) *°Eu* (厚) and *Bok* (薄) refer to things. In speaking of a person being thin we use the word *seu°* (瘦), and of being fat, the word *tsaung°* 壯.

(3) The fourth sentence of the First Exercise is the usual salutation meaning, "How do you do?" "Does it go well with you?" The answer is also the usual one.

(4) In the ninth sentence of the Second Exercise *Zing nyoen°* (情願) means "to be willing."

(5) In the seventh sentence of the First Exercise *°Noen* means "warm" (煖).

(6) In the eleventh sentence of the First Exercise *Koen°-yang-nyung* means "shepherd." Literally "Look-sheep-man."

(7) In the twenty-fifth sentence of the First Exercise the word *Loong* has a very wide meaning. There is hardly anything in China that you cannot *Loong-°hau*, that is, "put to rights."

Lesson XXIV

Some Remarks on Gender

As already remarked, words in Chinese do not change their form to indicate gender. Sometimes, however, words indicating gender are placed before them. ***Nen*** (男), "Male" and °***Nyui*** (女), "female", are used with human beings in this way. Thus we have ***Nen nyung*** (男人) for "man", and °***Nyui nyung*** (女人) for "woman". ***Nen noen*** (男囝) means "a male child," and °***Nyui noen*** (女囝) "a female child."

When speaking of the male and female of animals ***Yoong*** (雄) and ***Tsh*** (雌) are used. Thus we have ***Yoong kyi*** (雄鷄) for "cock," and ***Tsh kyi*** (雌鷄) for "hen," ***Yoong s-°ts*** (雄獅子) for "lion," and ***Tsh s-°ts*** (雌獅子) for "lioness."

Vocabulary

To crow, **di** 啼.

To offend, **tuh-°dzoe** 得罪.

To hide oneself, **ben°-°loong** 背攏.

To hide a thing, **khaung°-°loong** 园攏, or **khaung°** 园.

To gain or make a profit, **dzan°** 賺.

Profits in business, **dzan°-deu** 賺頭.

To lose in business, **zeh** 折, **zeh-theh** 折脫, **zeh-°pung** 折本.

To congratulate a person, **koong-°hyi** 恭喜.

To become rich, **fah-dze** 發財.

To lock, **°soo** 鎖.

To bar or bolt the door, **sen** 閂.

The bar, or bolt of the door, **sak** 柵.

To plant, **tsoong°** 種.

To examine carefully, **dzo** 查, or **dzo-°khau** 查考.

To examine a class, **°khau-su** 考書.

To fall, **tih** 跌.

To save, **kyeu°** 救.

To stop, **ding** 停.

Stop a minute, **ding-ih-ding** 停一停.

Garden, **hwo-yoen** 花園.

College, **su-yoen°** 書院.

University, **da°-'auh** 大學.

A lock, **ih °po °soo** 一把鎖.

A key, **ih °po yak-dz** 一把鑰匙.

A creek or canal, **ih diau pang** 一條浜.

A two story house, **ih zoo° leu** 一座樓, or **leu-vaung** 樓房.

Dzung (層) is the classifier for a story of a house or for anything like a ladder.

A three-storied house, **san dzung leu** 三層樓.

A ladder, **ih dzung voo-thi** 一層扶梯.

Dzaung° (幢) is the classifier denoting things piled one on top of the other.

A pile of clothes, **ih dzaung° i-zaung** 一幢衣裳.

Da° (埭) is the classifier for rows of things.

A row of trees, **ih da° zu** 一埭樹.

Spring (the first of the seasons), **tshung** 春.

Summer, **'au°** 夏.

Autumn, **tshieu** 秋.

Winter, **toong** 冬.

A season, **kyi°** 季.

The four seasons, **s°-kyi°** 四季.

Politeness, **khak-chi°** 客氣.

Happiness, **fok-chi°** 福氣.

Slippery, **wah** 滑.

Hard, **ngang°** 硬.

Soft, °**nyoen** 軟.

Smooth, **kwaung** 光.

Rough, **mau** 毛.

Good (moral), °**zen** 善.

Wicked, **auh** 惡.

Fierce, **hyoong** 凶.

Precious, °**pau-pe°** 寶貝.

Clear, **tshing** 清.

Muddy, **wung** 渾.

Level, **bing** 平.

Light (opposite of dark), **liang°** 亮.

Dark, **en°** 暗.

At last (in the end), **tau°-°ti** 到底.

Exercises

(Translate into English)

(1) Di°-laung° wah lau, taung-sing °tien °tseu.

(2) S°-kyi° kyau° tshung 'au° tshieu toong.

(3) °Ngoo bang°-dzak-ts ih kuh nyung °lau iau° yi nyang° loo°, °soo-°i te° yi wo° tuh-°dzoe, tuh °dzoe. Yi wo° 'veh iau° khak-chi°.

(4) Noong° tsoo° °di-kuh sang-i, ih nyien iau° dzan° °kyi-hau°? m-sa° dzan°-deu °tau zeh-°pung.

(5) Nyien tshoo ih, bang°-dzak-ts nyung tsau° kwe-°kyui iung-ke te° yi wo° koong-°hyi, fah-dze.

(6) Nyung tsoo° auh kuh z°-°thi, °z la° en°-°li tsoo° kuh.

(7) We°-ts pho° bih nyung iau° dzo-dzak °lau, i-kuh nyung chi° ben°-°loong.

(8) Ya°-°li tsoong-iau° °soo mung°, °khoong-pho° zuh tsing° le theu meh-z°.

(9) Tsoong-kok mung° yoong° sak le sen kuh, nga°-kok mung° yoong° yak-dz le °soo kuh.

(10) °Siau-noen la° beh-siang° kuh z-'eu° tih la° pang °li, kwha°-°tien chi° kyeu° yi.

(11) Yoong tiau we° kyau°, tsh tiau 'veh we° kyau°.

(12) Tsh s-°ts °pi-ts yoong s-°ts kung°-ka hyoong.

(13) Di°-kuh nyung °yeu san kuh nen-noen, °lau ih kuh °nyui-noen, zeh-dze °yeu fok-chi°.

(14) Di°-kuh meh-z° °z °pau-pe° kuh, iau° khaung° °hau.

(15) °'Au-°li-pa°, su-yoen° °li iau° °khau-su.

(16) Di°-kuh ih da° vaung-°ts kau-le-°si, °loong-°tsoong °z s° dzung leu.

(17) Di°-diau loo° 'veh bing, van-nan °tseu kuh.

(18) Tshing °s °hau chuh kuh, wung °s 'veh °hau chuh.

(19) Zak-deu °z ngang° kuh, men-deu °z °nyoen kuh.

(20) Tau°-°ti meh °zen nyung ih ding° iau° tuh-dzak fok-chi°.

(一) 地上滑佬當心點走.

(二) 四季叫春夏秋冬.

(三) 我碰着之一個人佬要伊讓路, 所以對伊話得罪得罪, 伊話勿要客氣.

(四) 儂做第個生意一年要賺幾化?無啥賺頭倒折本.

(五) 年初一碰着之人照規矩應該對伊話恭喜發財.

(六) 人做惡個事體是拉暗裏做個.

(七) 爲之怕別人要查着佬,伊個人去背攏.

(八) 夜裏終要鎖門,恐怕賊進來偷物事.

(九) 中國門用栅來閂個,外國門用鑰匙來鎖個.

(十) 小囝拉勃相個時候跌拉浜裏,快點去救伊.

(十一) 雄鴬會叫,雌鴬勿會叫.

(十二) 雌獅子比之雄獅子更加凶.

(十三) 第個人有三個男囝佬一個女囝,實在有福氣.

(十四) 第個物事是寶貝個,要囥好.

(十五) 下禮拜,書院裏要考書.

(十六) 第個一埭房子高來死,攏總是四層樓.

(十七) 第條路勿平,煩難走個.

(十八) 淸水好吃個,渾水勿好吃.

(十九) 石頭是硬個,饅頭是軟個.

(二十) 到底末善人一定要得着福氣.

(Translate into Chinese)

(1) In the garden the gardeners have planted three rows of apple trees.

(2) After the cock crows in the morning I am unable to sleep any more.

(3) This man is very polite, and so every one likes him.

(4) In the winter we close all the doors and windows and light a fire, in the summer we open all the doors and windows.

(5) The water in the creek is muddy and not fit to drink.

(6) Some men become rich in business, and some lose money.

(7) Lock the door and do not let the cat come in.

(8) The child fell off the chair and therefore cries.

(9) Yesterday I went to see a seven storied pagoda.

(10) This account is not right; it is not reckoned clearly.

(11) I cannot find out that this man has done anything wicked.

(12) When I met the robber I cried out to others to come and save my life.

(13) This man is very fierce; he is always fighting.

(14) At the end of the year, all the scholars in the college must be examined.

(15) I have lost my key and cannot open my box.

(16) I think you have not lost it, but you have hidden it away somewhere, and have forgotten where you put it; let me go and look for it.

(一) 拉花園裏種花園個種三埭蘋菓樹.

(二) 早晨頭雞啼個以後我勿能再睏.

(三) 第個人是蠻客氣所以攏總人歡喜伊.

(四) 冬天個時候我伲關攏總個門佬窗佬生火夏天個時候我伲開攏總個門佬窗.

(五) 浜裏水是渾佬勿好吃個.

(六) 有人做生意是發財有人末折本.

(七) 鎖門佬勿要讓貓進來.

(八) 小囝從椅子上跌下來所以拉哭.

(九) 昨日我去看七層樓個塔.

(十) 第個帳勿對個算來勿淸爽.

(十一) 我查勿出第個人做啥惡事.

(十二) 我碰着之強盜我喊人來救命.

(十三) 第個人凶來死所以常莊相打.

(十四) 拉年底書院裏攏總個學生子要考書.

(十五) 我失脫之我個鑰匙佬勿好開我個箱子.

(十六) 我想儂勿曾失脫恐怕儂已經囥好佬忘記擺拉啥地方, 讓我去尋尋看.

Notes.

(1) *Tuh-°dzoe*, *tuh-°dzoe* (得罪) is the usual expression for making an apology in Chinese, It literally meant, "I have sinned against you."

(2) A two storied house is generally called *leu vaung* (樓房).

(3) In the fifth sentence of the First Exercise we have the formal salutation used on New Year's Day *Koong-°hyi, fah-dze* (恭喜發財) meaning, "may you be happy and grow rich."

(4) In the twelfth sentence of the Second Exercise the expression to save life should be *Kyeu° ming°* (救命).

(5) In the tenth sentence of the Second Exercise "this account is not reckoned right" should be translated *di°-kuh tsang° 'veh te° kuh* (第個帳勿對個); *te°* means "not in agreement."

Lesson XXV

Weights and Measures

The following three Tables are very commonly used in China, and the speaker of the language should be familiar with them.

Measure of Weight

One ounce, ***ih °liang*** 一两.

One catty (16 ounces), ***ih kyung*** 一斤.

One picul (100 catties), ***ih tan°*** 一担.

Measure of Distance

1/10th of an inch, ***ih fung*** 一分.

One inch, ***ih tshung°*** 一寸.

One foot (ten inches in Chinese measure), ***ih tshak*** 一尺.

Tea feet, ***ih °dzang*** 一丈.

Measure of Area

One square foot, ***ih faung tshak*** 一方尺.

One hundred square feet, ***ih faung*** 一方.

A mow, ***ih °m*** 一畝 (one sixth of an acre).

Currency

Until recently, aside from copper cash, the Chinese had no regular system of currency. An ounce of silver was taken as a standard. The following Table is based upon that:—

An ounce of silver, ***ih °liang nyung-°ts*** 一兩銀子.

(1/10th of an ounce, ***ih dzien*** 一錢.

(1/10th of a dzien, ***ih fung*** 一分.

(1/10th of a fung, ***ih li*** 一釐.

(1/10th of a li, ***ih 'au*** 一毫.

Vocabulary

To expound, explain, **°kaung** 講.

To preach, **°kaung-su** 講書.

To exhort, **choen°** 勸, **choen°-mien** 勸勉, **choen°-'oo** 勸和.

To gather, as fruit or flowers, **°tshe** 採.

To boil **zah** 煠, (used in regard to water), or **°kwung** 滾.

To weigh, **tshung** 稱.

To measure, **liang** 量, or **°ien** 演.

To carry in arms like a child, **°bau** 抱.

To carry a load (one man, with load suspended on two ends of a bamboo), **thiau** 挑.

To carry a load (load suspended on a bamboo pole between two men), **kaung** 扛.

To carry a load on the back, **pe°** 背.

To carry a load on the shoulder, **jien** 掮.

To carry a load in one hand, **ling** 拎.

A tiger, **ih tsak °lau-°hoo** 一隻老虎.

A dish, **ih tsak dzang bung-°ts** 一隻長盆子.

A saucer, **ih tsak dzo bung-°ts** 一隻茶盆子.

A wine glass, **ih tsak °tsieu pe** 一隻酒杯.

A cooking stove, **ih tsak thih-tsau°** (foreign), 一隻鐵灶, tsau°-deu (Chinese), 灶頭.

Gold, **kyung-°ts** 金子.

Silver, **nyung-°ts** 銀子.

Iron, **thih** 鐵.

Tin, **sih** 錫.

Brass, **doong** 銅.

Lead, **khan** 鉛.

A railroad carriage, **ih boo °hoo-tsho** 一部火車.

A steam boat, **ih tsak °hoo-lung-zen** 一隻火輪船.

A pair of spectacles, **ih foo° °ngan-kyung°** 一副眼鏡.

A set of tools or instruments, **ih foo° ka-sang** 一副傢生.

A cannon, **ih tsung phau°** 一尊炮.

Cotton, **hwo** 花.

Cotton stalks, **hwo-ji** 花萁.

Cotton (already ginned), **mien-hwo** 棉花.

A plant of wheat, **ih khoo mak** 一棵麥.

A plant of rice, **ih khoo dau°** 一棵稻.

Vegetables, **tshe°** 菜.

Dishes of vegetables and meat placed on the table for meals, **°siau-tshe°** 小菜.

A shoulder, **ih tsak kyien ka** 一隻肩胛.

A bag, **ih tsak de** 一隻袋.

Back, **pe°** 背.

A field, **ih khwe° dien** 一塊田.

Soil, mud, **lan°-nyi** 爛泥.

Poor man, **joong-nyung** 窮人.

Rich man, **dze-°tsu-nyung** 財主人.

°Kwhung (梱) is the classifier denoting bundles of things.

A bundle of fuel, **ih °kwhung za** 一梱柴, **ih °kwung dau-za** 一梱稻柴.

Still, yet, **dzung-jeu°** 仍舊.

Among, **taung-tsoong** 當中.

All (collective), **zen** 全.

Exercises

(Translate into English)

(1) Noong° choen°-choen° yi 'veh iau° °doong-chi°.

(2) Khoen°-kyien° °liang kuh nyung siang-°tang meh iung-ke choen°-'oo yi-la.

(3) Di°-tsak siang-°ts °ngoo °i-kyung liang-koo°-hyih-tse °z san tshak dzang °lau nyi° tshak s° tshung kwheh.

(4) La° hwo-yoen °li °tshe hwo °z 'man °hau beh-siang°.

(5) Di°-kuh °liang tsak siang-°ts ih kuh nyung thiau-'veh-°chi °z iung-ke kaung kuh.

(6) Kyung, nyung, doong, thih, sih, Tsoong-kok nyung kyau° °ng kyung.

(7) Tsoong°-dien-nyung la° toong °li tsoong° mak, la° tshung laung° tsoong° hwo.

(8) La° °ng kyung taung-tsoong thih °z °ting °yeu yoong°-deu, doo° °lau °siau kuh meh-z° zen °khau-°i tsoo° kuh.

(9) °Ngoo-kuh bang-yeu °z °jung-z°-°ngan °soo-°i iau° ta° °ngan-kyung°.

(10) °S faung° la° thih-tsau° laung°, °kwung-ih-°kwung.

(11) Dze-°tsu-nyung tsak dzeu°-doen° °lau joong-nyung tsak poo°.

(12) Di°-kuh nyung °kaung-su °kaung le 'man °hau thing.

(13) Dih la kuh °mi tshung-tshung khoen° kyung-°liang te° va°.

(14) Di° kwhe° di°-be °yeu °kyi °m? iak-tsak °yeu lok °m.

(15) La° °ya-seu° taung-tsoong Tsoong-kok nyung °ting pho° kuh °z °lau-°hoo.

(16) We°-ts °siau-noen la° khok °lau, °nyui-nyung °bau la° seu °li.

(17) Nyok °lau tshe° ih-dau° kyau° °siau-tshe°.

(18) Lok-tsen °z lan°-nyi tsoo° la° kuh, °zau vaung-°ts °ting °yeu yoong°-deu.

(19) Di°-kuh yang-dien 'veh °hau, 'veh °z nyung-ts, °z khan kuh.

(20) °Ngoo wan iau° °ma dzang-bung-°ts, dzo-bung-°ts, °lau °tsieu-pe.

(21) Tung-loong °khau-°i ling la° °seu °li, ih kung mok-deu °khau-°i jien la° kyien-ka laung°, de meh pe° la pe° laung°.

(22) °Ng-seh nyien zien-deu, Tsoong-kok m-meh °hoo-tsho °lau °hoo-lung-zen, yien°-°dze zen °yeu-kuh.

(23) Tsau-zung-deu °ngoo thing-tuh ping-ting faung° phau°.

(24) Yien°-°dze m-meh za, 'veh °hau sang °hoo, iau° noong° chi° °ma °liang

san °kwhung.

(25) Nyeu °lau °mo la° dien °li chuh °tshau.

(一) 儂勸勸伊勿要動氣.

(二) 看見兩個人相打末應該勸和伊拉.

(三) 第隻箱子我已經量過歇哉,是三尺長佬二尺四寸闊.

(四) 拉花園裏採花是蠻好勃相.

(五) 第個兩隻箱子一個人挑勿起是應該扛個.

(六) 金銀銅鐵錫中國人叫五金.

(七) 種田人拉冬裏種麥拉春上種花.

(八) 拉五金當中鐵是頂有用頭,大佬小個物事全可以做個.

(九) 我個朋友是近視眼所以要戴眼鏡.

(十) 水放拉鐵灶上滾一滾.

(十一) 財主人着綢緞佬窮人着布.

(十二) 第個人講書講來蠻好聽.

(十三) 糴拉個米稱稱看觔兩對否?

(十四) 第塊地皮有幾畝?約酌有六畝.

(十五) 拉野獸當中,中國人頂怕個是老虎.

(十六) 爲之小囝拉哭佬,女人抱拉手裏.

(十七) 肉佬菜一淘叫小菜.

(十八) 碌磚是爛泥做拉個,造房子頂有用頭.

(十九) 第個洋錢勿好,勿是銀子是鉛個.

(二十) 我還要買長盆子茶盆子佬酒杯.

(廿一) 燈籠可以拎拉手裏,一根木頭可以掮拉肩胛上,袋末背拉背上.

(廿二) 五十年前頭中國無沒火車佬火輪船,現在全有個.

(廿三) 早晨頭我聽得兵丁放炮.

(廿四) 現在無沒柴勿好生火,要儂去買兩三捆.

(廿五) 牛佬馬拉田裏吃草.

(Translate into Chinese)

(1) The Chinese make most of their clothing out of cotton.

(2) Among the pupils this one is the brightest.

(3) I will tell you a wonderful thing: two men were fighting, and a woman came and exhorted them to peace.

(4) Among the metals, gold is the most precious.

(5) The dollars used in China are made of silver.

(6) How many men will it take to carry the stove?

(7) I think four men can carry it.

(8) How much ought I to give the ricksha coolie?

(9) I think thirty cents is sufficient.

(10) There are still many men in Shanghai who have never been in a railway carriage.

(11) Most of the Chinese scholars wear spectacles.

(12) I have been gathering apples and peaches in the garden.

(13) The carpenter has not brought his tools, and so can do no work.

(14) A Chinese foot has ten inches, a foreign foot has twelve.

(15) In China, wood and rice and cotton stalks are used as fuel.

(一) 中國人做衣裳用棉花布個是頂多.

(二) 拉學生子當中第個是頂聰明個.

(三) 我要告訴儂一椿希奇個事體, 兩個人拉相打, 一個女人來勸和.

(四) 拉五金當中金子是頂寶貝個.

(五) 中國個洋錢是銀子做拉個.

(六) 第隻火爐幾個人好扛.

(七) 我想四個人好扛個.

(八) 拖東洋車個人我應該撥伊幾錢?

(九) 我想三角有哉.

(十) 拉上海還有多化人勿曾坐過歇火車個.

(十一) 中國讀書人大一半末是戴眼鏡.

(十二) 我拉花園裏拉採蘋果佬桃子.

(十三) 木匠勿曾帶傢生來听以勿好做生活.

(十四) 中國尺是十寸外國尺有十二寸.

(十五) 中國人用木頭佬稻佬花萁做柴.

NOTES.

(1) In the fifth sentence of the First Exercise *Thiau 'veh-°chi* (挑勿起) means "unable to carry."

(2) In the sixth sentence of the First Exercise *°Ng-kyung* (五金) is generally pronounced as *°oo kyung*, as it is a *vung-li* expression.

(3) In the ninth sentence of the First Exercise *°Jung-z°-°ngan* (近視眼) means "near-sighted."

(4) In the thirteenth sentence of the First Exercise notice that "to buy rice" is *dih °mi* not *°ma °mi.*

(5) In the ninth sentence of the Second Exercise "sufficient" may be translated *°yeu-tse* (有哉).

Lesson XXVI

Family Relations

The relations in Chinese are exceedingly complex. Here only the simplest will be given. To be able to understand the complicated ramifications will take a long time, and can only be learnt by long experience.

It must be noted that different words are used when one speaks of his own relations from what are used when another person is referring to them. In the latter case more polite language is employed.

Thus the following words for "father" are used: If you yourself are speaking of your father, you might call him ***Ya*** (爺), or °***Lau-nyang-ka*** (老娘家), or ***Kya-°voo*** (家父), or °***Voo-tshing*** (父親), or ***Kya-nyien*** (家嚴). Other people would refer to your father if they were polite as ***Tsung-da°-zung*** (尊大人) Lit. "The honorable great man." ***Kya*** (家) or ***Ling°-tsung*** (令尊). Children often call their father ***Tia-tia*** (爹爹), or ***Ya-ya*** (爺爺), or ***Pak-pak*** (伯伯).

So in regard to mother. If you speak of her you say ***Nyang*** (娘), or ***Kya-°moo*** (家母), or °***Moo-tshing*** (母親), or ***Kya-dz*** (家慈). If you speak of the mother of another person you may say ***Ling°-daung*** (令堂).

Brother is different as to whether you refer to an older or a younger one. An older brother is ***Ak-koo*** (阿哥). A younger brother is ***Hyoong-°di*** (兄弟). Brothers (plural) is ***Di°-hyoong*** or ***hyoong-°di*** (弟兄). A familiar term for a younger brother is °***Di-°di*** (弟弟). An older sister is ***Ah-°tsi*** (阿姊). A younger sister is ***Me°-me°*** (妹妹). °***Tsi-me°*** (姊妹) means sister or sisters.

In referring to a son a father would call him ***Nyi-°ts*** (兒子) or °***Siau-noen*** (小囝); others would refer to your son by saying ***Ling°-laung*** (令郎) or (公郎) ***Koong-laung***. In speaking of one's own daughter you would say °***Siau-°nyui*** (小女); others would refer to her as ***Tshien-kyung*** (千金) Lit. "A thousand catties of gold," or ***Ling°- e°*** (令嫒).

Vocabulary

To love, **e°** 愛.

To love reciprocally, **siang-e°** 相愛.

To injure, **'e°** 害.

To be injured, **°zeu-'e°** 受害.

To begin, **°chi** 起.

A beginning, **°chi-deu** 起頭, or **khe-dzang** 開場.

To repair, **sieu** 修, or **seu-tsauh** 收作.

Repairs, **sieu-°li** 修理.

To take hold of, to grasp, **nyah** 捏.

To receive or accept, **°zeu** 受.

To suffer, **°zeu-°khoo** 受苦, or **°zeu-nan°** 受難.

To hand, to deliver in person, **dzeu°** 授.

To save, be economical, **°sang** 省, or **tsoo° nyung-ka** 做人家.

To save time, **°sang koong-foo** 省功夫.

To waste, to be extravagant, **saung** 傷.

To seal officially, or to seal an envelope; to deify; to exalt to a high station, **foong** 封.

To rely upon, to entrust, **khau°** 靠, **khau°-thauh** 靠托, or **thauh** 托.

A battery or a fort, **ih kuh phau°-de** 一個礮台.

A deer, **ih tsak lok** 一隻鹿.

To hunt, **°tang-lih** 打獵.

A hare, **ih tsak thoo°-°ts** 一隻兔子.

A fox, **ih tsak 'oo-li** 一隻狐狸.

A wolf, **ih tsak za-laung** 一隻豺狼.

A squirrel, **ih tsak soong-°su** 一隻松鼠.

A weasel, **ih tsak waung-laung** 一隻黃狼.

A pheasant, **ih tsak °ya-kyi** 一隻野鷄.

A goose, **ih tsak ngoo** 一隻鵝.

A set of dice, **ih foo° deu°-°ts** 一副骰子.

To gamble with cash, **°too doong-dien** 賭銅錢.

To gamble with dice, **zak deu°-°ts** 擲骰子.

A set of dominoes, **ih foo° ba** 一副牌.

To gamble with dominoes, **teu° ba** 鬪牌.

Again, **tse°** 再.

Medicine, **yak** 藥.

Tobacco, **ien** 烟.

A gun, **ih °kwen yang-tshiang** 一桿洋槍.

Powder, **°hoo-yak** 火藥. Lit Fiery medicine.

Tide flowing out, **lauh-°s** 落水.

Tide coming in, **tsang°-°s** 漲水.

Firmly, **lau** 牢.

As, **ziang** 像.

All (collective), **thok** 禿.

Exercises

(Translate into English)

(1) Zauh-nyih °ngoo tan-°ts yang-tshiang tau° san laung° chi° °tang-lih, °tang-dzak-ts san tsak lok lau s° tsak thoo°-°ts °lau ih tsak soong-°su.

(2) °Ngoo °bang-dzak-°ts ih kuh nyung la° °tang °tiau, yi °i-kyung °tang-dzak-°ts s° tsak °ya-kyi °lau ih tsak °ya-ngoo.

(3) Teu° ba °lau zak deu-°ts thok °z 'veh °hau.

(4) Di°-kuh phau°-de °yeu °ng tsung phau° °lau too-°hau °hoo-yak.

(5) Zauh-ya°-deu °yeu waung-laung theu kyi, 'veh hyau°-tuh °z waung-laung nyi wan-°z 'oo-li, kyung-ya°-deu °ting °hau °tung yi le °lau yoong° yang-tshiang °tang-sah yi.

(6) °Ngoo la° yi han-deu °zeu-°ts too-hau° meh-z°, iau° soong°-°tien sa° la° yi.

(7) Di°-foong sing° iau° foong-°hau dzeu° peh la° i-sung.

(8) Seu-tsauh vaung-°ts zieu° iau° °chi-deu, iung-we° °yeu too-hau° di°-faung iau° sieu-°li, zak-zen °tse an° meh °khoong-pho° le-'veh ji°.

(9) Too chuh °tsieu °lau too chuh ien° °z saung sung-°thi.

(10) Di°-kuh bing° °dzoong-tuh-juh, chuh yak °'a m-yoong°-deu.

(11) Tsoo° nyung-ka meh, °khau-°i nyih-nyih °sang doong-dien.

(12) Di°-kuh si-°tse hwen-°hyi °too doong-dien °lau chuh °tsieu, zeh-dze

khau°-'veh-dzu° kuh.

(13) °Ngoo thauh noong° tsoo° ih tsaung z°-thi, noong° we°-sa° 'veh zung tsoo°?

(14) Zeh-°ke tsoo°-deu saung koong-foo, iau° tsau° °ngoo wo° meh °hau.

(15) Di°-hyoong iung-ke da-ka siang-e°, 'veh iau° siang-mo° °lau siang-°tang.

(16) Tsung-da°-zung °hau-la°-va? Zia°-zia°, °lau-nyang-ka °hau-la°.

(17) Ya-nyang °i-kyung tsheh mung, pih-koo° ak-koo la° ok-°li.

(18)°Ngoo °yeu ih kuh ah-°tsi °lau °liang-kuk me°-me°.

(19) °Kyi-z iau° khe zen? Lauh-°s zieu° khe.

(20) Za-laung °z 'man hyoong-kuh °ya-seu°, hwen-°hyi chuh yang.

(21) Di°-kuh ih pe yak iau° peh la° bing° nyung chuh.

(22) Noong° °yeu °kyi-we° °ling-laung? °Yeu °liang-kuh °siau-noen.

(一) 昨日我担之洋槍到山上去打獵, 打着之三隻鹿佬四隻兔子佬一雙松鼠.

(二) 我撞着之一個人拉打鳶, 伊已經打着之四隻野雞佬一隻野鵝.

(三) 鬥牌佬擲骰子禿是勿好.

(四) 第個砲台有五尊炮佬多化火藥.

(五) 昨夜頭有黃狼偷雞, 勿曉得是黃狼呢還是狐狸, 今夜頭頂好等伊來佬用洋槍打殺伊.

(六) 我拉伊墻頭受之多化物事, 要送點啥拉伊.

(七) 第封信要封好授撥拉醫生.

(八) 收作房子就要起頭, 因爲有多化地方要修理, 若然再晚末恐怕來勿及.

(九) 多吃酒佬多吃烟是傷身體.

(十) 第個病重得極吃藥也無用頭.

(十一) 做人家末可以日日省銅錢.

(十二) 第個西崽歡喜賭銅錢佬吃酒實在靠勿住個.

(十三) 我托儂做一樁事體爲啥勿曾做.

(十四) 實蓋做頭傷工夫要照我話末好.

(十五) 弟兄應該大家相愛勿要相罵佬相打.

(十六) 尊大人好拉否? 謝謝, 老娘家好拉.

(十七) 爺娘已經出門必過阿哥拉屋裏.

(十八) 我有一個阿姊佬兩個妹妹.

(十九) 幾時要開船?落水就開.

(二十) 豺狼是蠻凶個野獸歡喜吃羊.

(廿一) 第個一杯藥要撥拉病人吃.

(廿二) 儂有幾位令郎?有兩個小囝.

(Translate into Chinese)

(1) You should do to others as you would they should do to you.

(2) If we do not call the carpenter and mason to repair this house, we shall not be able to live in it.

(3) When I began I considered the study of Chinese very difficult; now I consider it easier.

(4) The younger brother should listen to the older brother's words.

(5) You should love others as yourself.

(6) On the other side of the river there are many forts.

(7) This man wastes his money in drinking wine.

(8) Where did you get the money to buy these clothes? I saved it from my wages.

(9) The deer can run faster than the dog, but gets tired sooner.

(10) The father is head of the house.

(11) Hand this bowl of tea to the guest.

(12) I trust to you to help me do the work.

(13) The fox comes at night to steal chickens.

(14) Pheasants are fine birds to look at and are very good to eat.

(15), Geese and ducks like to remain in the water.

(16) The older sister takes care of her little sister.

(17) Take hold of it firmly in your hand and do not let it fall on the ground.

(18) According to what Chinese say, to become a good man you must repair your heart.

(一) 儂要人那能待儂儂也應該那能待別人.

(二) 若然伲勿叫木匠佬泥水匠來修房子,我伲勿好住拉化.

(三) 我起頭讀個晨光我算中國書是煩難讀個, 現在算是容易點.

(四) 弟兄應該聽阿哥個說話.
(五) 儂應該愛別人像愛自家.
(六) 垃拉河過邊有多化砲台.
(七) 第個人吃酒佬傷脫伊個銅錢.
(八) 買第個衣裳儂那裏頭來個銅錢?我工錢上省下來個.
(九) 鹿比之狗可以跑來快點,但是鹿先要弛瘏.
(十) 爺末是一家個主.
(十一) 第個一碗茶授撥拉客人.
(十二) 我托儂相幫我做第樁事體.
(十三) 狐狸是夜頭來偷雞.
(十四) 野雞是蠻好看個寫也是蠻好吃個.
(十五) 鵝佬鴨歡喜垃拉水裏向.
(十六) 阿姊是當心伊個小妹.
(十七) 捏牢拉手裏勿要放伊落拉地上.
(十八) 照中國人話成功好個人終要修儂個心.

NOTES.

(1) In the sixth sentence of the First Exercise notice the expression *Soong°-°tien-sa°* 送點啥, meaning "to make a small present."

(2) In the eighth sentence of the First Exercise notice the expression *°Tse an°* (再晚). Lit. "again late;" the idea is "if we wait any longer."

(3) In the fourteenth sentence of the First Exercise notice the expression *Tsau° °ngoo wo° meh °hau* (照我話末好), Lit. "Follow my saying then good."

(4) In the first sentence of the Second exercise the sentence would be turned round in Chinese, and we would say, *Noong° iau° nyung na°-nung °de noong°, noong° °a iung-ke na°-nung °de bih nyung* (儂要人那能待儂,儂也應該那能待別人).

Lesson XXVII

Compound Verbs

By compound verbs we mean those made up of more than one verb. As we have already seen, Chinese words having a distinct meaning when used by themselves also form part of larger compound words. This is true especially of verbs. A good example is the verb °*Tang* (打) to strike. It enters into combination with many other words to form compound verbs.

Thus:

To fight a battle, *°tang-tsang°* 打仗.

To attack an enemy, *koong-°tang* 攻打.

To gain a victory, *°tang-yung* 打贏, or *°tang-sung°-tsang°* 打勝仗.

To suffer a defeat, *°tang-su* 打輸, *tang°-ba°* 打敗, or *°tang-ba°-tsang°* 打敗仗.

To wound, *°tang-saung* 打傷.

To make inquiries, *°tang-thing* 打聽.

To fool with one another, *°tang-bang°* 打棚.

To injure by striking, *°tang-wa°* 打壞.

To consider, *°tang-soen°* 打算.

To dress in a showy manner, *°tang-pan°* 打扮.

Vocabulary

To collect, to receive payment, **seu** 收.

To collect accounts, **seu-tsang°** 收帳.

To receive payment for a lease, **seu-tsoo** 收租.

To be imprisoned, **seu-kan** 收監.

To build a wall, **tshi°** (砌), or **tshi° ziang** 砌牆.

To build a partition, **tshi° pih** 砌壁.

To mend a path, **tshi° ka** 砌街.

To be wounded, **°zeu-saung** 受傷.

To prosecute at law, **°tang-kwen-s** 打官司.

To cut with a sharp knife, **koeh** 割.

To cut in two, **koeh-°doen** 割斷.

To cut with sword, or heavy knife or axe, **tsan** 斬.

To split, **phih** 劈.

To saw, **zih** 截 or **ka°** 解.

To boil, **zah** 煤.

To grill, to broil, **tsien** 煎.

To smoke (meat), **hyuin** 燻.

To bake, **hoong** 烘.

To sew, to stitch, **ling** 紉.

To take a stitch, **ling-ih tsung** 紉一針, (**tsung** means needle).

To iron, to burn, to scald, **thaung°** 燙.

To brush, **seh** 刷.

To rise (as the tide), **tsang°** 漲.

To fall, **lauh** 落.

Duty, **ming-vung°** 名分.

Rumours, **yau-yien** 謠言.

Receipt, **seu-phiau°** 收票, or **seu-diau** 收條.

A bell, **tsoong** 鐘.

Piles (such as are driven into the ground), **tsaung** 樁.

Tide, **dzau** 潮, or **dzau-°s** 潮水.

A cake, **ih kuh kyi dan°-kau** 一個個雞蛋糕.

Japanese. **Toong-yang-nyung** 東洋人, or **Zeh-°pung-nyung** 日本人.

Pain, **thoong°** 痛.

Wheat, **mak** 麥.

Dirty, **auh-tshauh** 齷齪.

Miserable, **khoo-°nau** 苦腦.

Russians, **Ngoo-kok nyung** 俄國人.

A biscuit, **ih kuh thah-°ping** 一個餲餅.

A grate, **ih kuh °hoo-khaung** 一個火匟.

A sparrow, **ih tsak mo-tshiak** 一隻麻雀, or **mo-tsiang** 麻䳰.

A swallow, **ih tsak ien°-°ts** 一隻燕子.

A pigeon, **ih tsak keh-°ts** 一隻鴿子.

An ax, **ih °po °foo-deu** 一把斧頭.

A saw, **ih °po ke°-°ts** 一把鋸子.

A file, **ih °po tshoo°-tau** 一把銼刀.

A plane, **ih tsak bau°** 一隻刨.

A quilt or blanket, **ih diau °bi-deu** 一條被頭.

A sheet, **ih diau tan-°bi** 一條單被.

Unripe or raw, **sang** 生.

Ripe, **zok** 熟. Also used in the sense of being thoroughly cooked.

Shameful, **than-tshoong°** 坍銃.

Face (cheek), **°nyi-kwaung** 耳光.

Spread out, **than** 攤, **than-khe** 攤開.

Exercises

(Translate into English)

(1) Kyau° tsoong°-hwo-yoen-kuh la° hwo-yoen °li tsan-theh i-kuh °liang khoo zu°.

(2) Di°-diau ka ih ngan 'veh bing, iau° tse° tshi°.

(3) Sing-vung-°ts laung° °ngoo khoen° °tang-tsang° kuh zung-kwaung, Toong-yang-nyung dzang-tsaung °tang sung°-tsang°, °lau Ngoo-kok-nyung dzang-tsaung °tang-ba°.

(4) Di°-°po tau kwha°-°le-°si, °khoong-pho° °siau-noen iau° koeh thoong° °seu.

(5) °Nyui-nyung kuh ming-vung° la° ok-°li sau van°, tsoo° i-zaung, taung-sing °siau-noen; nen-nyung kuh ming-vung° la° nga°-deu tsoo° sang-i°.

(6) I-zaung koen-°ts meh nan-meh iau° thaung°-ih-thaung°.

(7) La° ka laung° yi-la tsauh-°ts ih kuh zuk, yien°-°dze soong° tau° kwen

han-deu seu-kan.

(8) Di°-saung ‘a-°ts noong° seh le ’veh °hau, ih ngan ’veh liang°.

(9) Khau-°ts tsoong °loong-°tsoong kuh ‘auh-sang-°ts zieu° iau° tsing° chi° dok su, ‘auh-daung-°li iau° °zoo-ding°, °tung sien-sang le, ’veh iau° da-ka °tang-bang°.

(10) Iau° tshi° ziang meh sien iau° °tang tsaung.

(11) Dzau tsang° meh zieu° iau° khe zen ‘ang tau° bing °s °lau ding.

(12) Di°-kuh mok-za iau° yoong° °foo-deu le phih-khe-le.

(13) Noong° foo°-°ts yang-dien meh, °ngoo peh seu-diau noong°.

(14) Di°-kuh dan° zah le thuh sang, iau° zok-°tien.

(15) Kyung-tsau °yeu khak-nyung le, iau° noong° tsoo° kyi-dan°-kau °lau thah-°ping.

(16) Peh bih nyung °tang °nyi-kwaung meh soen° °ting than-tshoong° kuh z°-°thi.

(17) Dien-°li kuh mak seu °hau meh? Wan ’veh zung we°-ts dzang-tsaung lauh °yui °lau.

(18) Iau° noong° chi° °tang-thing °tang-thing sa° nyung °zau di°-kuh yau-yien.

(19) Di°-kuh men-deu tan tau° °hoo-khaung° pien-deu chi° hoong-hoong.

(20) Kyau° mok-ziang° le yoong° ke°-°ts °ka-khe di°-kuh mok-deu.

(21) Tau° mok-ziang° han-deu chi° tsia° ih °po tshoo°-tau °lau ih tsak bau°.

(22) Mo-tshiak °lau ien°-°ts °z °siau kuh °tiau, ’veh °hau chuh, keh-°ts meh °hau chuh kuh.

(23) Tan-°bi °lau °bi-deu than °hau la° zaung laung°.

(24) Ng hyuin °hau meh tan le peh °ngoo chuh chuh khoen.

(25) I-kuh nyung koong-°tang le, °ngoo dih-’veh-dzu° yi, peh yi °tang-saung.

(26). Tsheh-chi° pa° khak kuh z-‘eu° sien iau° °tang-pan°.

(一) 叫種花園個人拉花園裏斬脫伊個兩棵樹.

(二) 第條街一顔勿平要再砌.

(三) 新聞紙上我看打仗個辰光東洋人常莊打勝仗佬俄國人常莊打敗.

(四) 第把刀快來死恐怕小囝要割痛手.

(五) 女人個名分拉屋裏燒飯做衣裳當心小囝, 男人個名分拉外頭做生意.

(六) 衣裳乾之末難末要燙一燙.

(七) 拉街上伊拉捉之一個賊,現在送到官壋頭收監.

(八) 第雙鞋子儂刷來勿好一顏勿亮.

(九) 敲之鐘攏總學生子就要進去讀書學堂裏要坐定等先生來勿要大家打棚.

(十) 要砌牆末先要打樁.

(十一) 潮漲末就要開船行到平水佬停.

(十二) 第個木柴要用斧頭來劈開來.

(十三) 儂付之洋錢末我撥收條儂.

(十四) 第個蛋煠來忒生要熟點.

(十五) 今朝有客人來要儂做鷄蛋糕佬餲餅.

(十六) 撥別人打耳光末算頂坍銃個事體.

(十七) 田裏個麥收好末?還勿曾爲之常莊落雨佬.

(十八) 要儂去打聽打聽啥人造第個謠言.

(十九) 第個饅頭担到火匠邊頭去烘烘.

(二十) 叫木匠來用鋸子解開第個木頭.

(廿一) 到木匠壋頭去借一把銼刀佬一隻刨.

(廿二) 麻雀佬燕子是小個篤勿好吃,鴿子末好吃個.

(廿三) 單被佬被頭攤好拉床上.

(廿四) 魚燻好末担來撥我吃吃看.

(廿五) 伊個人攻打來,我敵勿住伊,撥伊打傷.

(廿六) 出去拜客個時候先要打扮.

(Translate into Chinese)

(1) In cold countries the swallows fly away in the winter and return in the spring.

(2) To have a lawsuit is a miserable affair, for you must use as much money.

(3) My clothes were very dirty, so I told my servant to brush them well.

(4) In the summer when it is warm you do not need a quilt, but in the winter you do.

(5) The mandarin gave orders to cut off the robber's head.

(6) Some wicked people do not fear shame.

(7) Has the school bell rung? If so I am late.

(8) What is the matter with your foot? It was scalded by hot water.

(9) When the tide rises the boat can travel very fast.

(10) In front of my house I want to erect a fence.

(11) Put some coal in the grate; probably to-night I will want to light a fire.

(12) When you have split the fuel, tie it up in a bundle.

(13) At the beginning the boys were only fooling, but afterwards they began to fight, and one of them was hurt.

(14) A hammer, a saw, a plane, and a file are useful implements.

(15) These pears and apples are unripe; if you eat them you will become ill.

(16) At the end of the month the man goes out to collect his accounts.

(17) Every one should do his duty.

(一) 拉冷個地方到之冬天燕子飛出去到之春上末轉來.

(二) 打官司是苦腦個事體因爲儂總要用多化銅錢.

(三) 我個衣裳齷齪來死所以我叫我個用人刷刷好.

(四) 夏天熱個辰光儂勿要用被頭到之冬天末要個.

(五) 官府分付殺脫第個強盜個頭.

(六) 有個惡人勿怕坍銃.

(七) 鐘敲好末?若然已經敲好之末我晚哉.

(八) 儂個脚那能?是撥滾水燙之佬.

(九) 潮漲末船可以行來快來死.

(十) 拉我個房子個門前我要打笆.

(十一) 火匠裏要擺煤,今夜頭恐怕我要生火.

(十二) 柴劈好之末要紮之一梱一梱.

(十三) 起頭個辰光小囝必過拉打棚但是後來末就相打一個末受傷.

(十四) 一個榔頭一把鋸子一隻刨一把銼刀是有用頭個傢生.

(十五) 第個生梨佬蘋果是生個,吃之要生病.

(十六) 拉月底一個人要去收帳.

(十七) 各人應該盡伊個名分.

NOTES.

(1) In the ninth sentence of the First Exercise, notice the expression °*zoo-ding*° (坐定), "to sit quiet."

(2) In the eleventh sentence of the First Exercise *Khe zen* (開船) means "to start the boat." Literally it is "to open the boat." In the same sentence *bing °s* (平水) means "slack water."

(3). In the eighteenth sentence of the First Exercise *zau-yau-yien* (造謠言) means "to start a rumor."

(4) In the twenty-fifth sentence of the First Exercise *dih-'veh-dzu°* (敵勿住) means "unable to oppose."

(5) In the fifth sentence of the Second Exercise, "to cut off the robber's head," is *sah-theh °di-kuh °jang-dau° kuh deu* (殺脫第個強盜個頭).

(6) In the ninth sentence of the Second Exercise "to travel" is *'ang* (行).

(7) In the tenth sentence of the Second Exercise "to erect a fence," is *°tang-po* (打笆).

Lesson XXVIII

Abstract Nouns formed from two Adjectives of opposite meaning

Very often two adjectives of opposite meaning are joined together to form an abstract noun of quality. Naturally the Chinese language is defective in abstract nouns, and their lack is partially supplied is this way. Thus ***Too-°sau*** (多少), "Much-little," means "quantity."

Dzang-°toen (長短), "Long-short," means "length." ***°Yoen-°jung*** (遠近), "Far-near," means "distance." ***Kau-ti°*** (高低), "High-low," means "height." ***°'Eu-bok*** (厚薄), "Thick-thin," means "thickness." ***Kwheh-'ah*** (闊狹), "Broad-narrow," means "breadth." ***°Lang-nyih*** (冷熱), "Cold-hot," means "temperature." ***Sung-°tshien*** (深淺), "Deep-shallow," means "depth." ***Chung-°dzoong*** (輕重), "Light-heavy," means "weight." ***Tshoo-si°*** (粗細), "Coarse-fine," means "texture" (of cloth).

Verbs are also used in much the same way. Thus we have ***Le-°waung*** (來往). "Come-go," meaning "intercourse," or ***Le-chi°*** (來去), "Come-go," meaning, "going back and forth." It generally occurs as ***Le-le-chi°-chi°***. ***°Ma-ma°*** (買賣), "Buy-sell," means "business."

Vocabulary

To kneel, **°jui** 跪.

To forgive, **nyau-°so** 饒赦, **kwhen-°an** 寬限, **nyoen-liang°** 原諒, or **kwhen-yoong** 寬容.

To comfort, **oen-we°** 安慰.

To sharpen, **moo** 磨.

To drive away, **°koen** 趕, **°koen-theh** 趕脫.

To criticize, phi-bing 批評, or phi-thah 批撻.

To roll, °**kwung** 滾, or °**kwung 'au° chi°** 滾下去.

To plaster, °**fung** 粉. To plaster a partition, °**fung pih** 粉壁.

To string, (as cash), **tshen** 串.

To thread a needle, **tshen °yung-sien°** 穿引線.

To slander, **wo°-°liau** 話料, **hwe°-°paung** 毀謗, or **wo°-wa°** 話壞.

To accompany, or stay with a person, **be** 陪.

To nurse, **su-°tsang** 輸帳.

To crawl, **ban** 蹩.

To climb, **bo** 爬.

To jump, to leap, **thiau°** 跳.

To reject, **the** 推, or **the-theh** 推脫.

To feel, to touch, **mok** 摸.

To hoist (as a sail or flag), **tsha** 扯.

To run, as water, **lieu** 流.

To turn over, **fan** 翻, or **fan-°tsen-le** 翻轉來.

To upset (as water), °**tang-fan** 打翻.

To turn round, **zien** 旋, or **zien-°tsen-le** 旋轉來.

To manage, **kyung-°seu** 經手.

To pray, **jeu** 求.

To offer prayer, °**tau-kau°** 禱告.

To repent, **hwe°-°ke** 悔改.

To regret, **au-lau°** 懊憹.

A crow, **ih tsak °lau-au** 一隻老鴉.

A hawk, **ih tsak iung** 一隻鷹, or °**lau-iung** 老鷹.

A butterfly, **ih tsak 'oo-dih** 一隻蝴蝶.

A pair of scissors, **ih °po °tsien-tau** 一把剪刀.

So that, **i-ts** 以致.

A screen, **ih sen° bing-foong** 一扇屏風.

A sail, **ih sen° boong** 一扇篷.

Scales, **thien-bing** 天秤.

A gong, **ih mien° kyung-loo** 一面金鑼.

Flour, **koen-mien°** 乾麵.

Butter, **°na-yeu** 乳油.

Milk, **nyeu-°na** 牛乳.

Sugar, **daung** 糖.

Exercises

(Translate into English)

(1) Di°-sen° bing-foong °kyi-hau° kwheh-‘ah?

(2) Di°-tsak siang-°ts iau° liang-liang-khoen° dzang-°toen, kau-ti °lau kwheh-‘ah.

(3) Iau° noong° chi° °ma ih tsang °ts-deu theh di° tsang ih yang° °‘eu-bok.

(4) Thien-bing °z iau°-°kyung kuh ka-sang, °khau-i tshung meh-z° kuh chung-°dzoong.

(5) °Ngoo °jui la° yi mien°-zien jeu yi nyau-°so.

(6) °Siau-noen sang bing° meh, nyang ’veh li-khe yi, °zoo la° zaung pien-deu su-°tsang yi.

(7) ’Veh phi-bing bih nyung, keh-meh ’veh °zeu bih nyung kuh phi-bing.

(8) We°-ts °khoong-pho° loo° ’veh zok, °soo-i °tshing bih nyung be °ngoo chi°.

(9) Di°-°po °tsien-tau ih ngan ’veh kwha°, iau° chi° moo-moo.

(10) Kyau° sau-van°-kuh nau °tien koen-mien°, dan°, nyeu-°na, °lau daung, tsoo° kyi-dan°-kau.

(11) Thah °tien °na-yeu la° men-deu laung°, keh-meh °hau chuh °tien.

(12) ‘Auh-sang-°ts la° khok we°-°ts bih nyung wo°-°liau yi, sien-sang kyau° yi ’veh iau° khok, °lau oen-we° yi.

(13) °Ngoo kyau°-°ts yi meh, yi zieu° zien-°tsen-deu le khoen°.

(14) Di°-kuh ih tsaung z°-°thi sa° nyung kyung-°seu kuh.

(15) Bo zu° meh ’veh da° °wung-taung°, °khoong-pho° iau° tih thoong° °lau tih saung.

(16) Iung-ke °koen-theh i-tsak °keu, °khoong-pho° iau° °ngau °siau-noen.

(17) Tsha boong meh, zen ‘ang le kwha°.

(18) Tsoong° dien-nyung ’veh hwen-°hyi °lau-au, we°-°ts yi-la° chuh-theh yi-la° san° la°-kuh °ts.

(19) Dzang-z °lau-iung dzoong thien laung° fi-'au°-le chuh-theh-°ts °siau kyi.

(20) Tshen-°hau di°-kuh doong-dien, °lau soen°-soen° khoen° °yeu °kyi-hau°.

(21) Ping-ting tsheh-chi° °tang-tsang°, khau koo °lau kyung-loo.

(22) Di°-kuh zak-deu dzoong san °ting laung° °kwung 'au°-le.

(一) 第扇屏風幾化闊狹.

(二) 第隻箱子要量量看長短高低佬闊狹.

(三) 要儂去買一張紙頭對第張一樣厚薄.

(四) 天秤是要緊個傢生可以稱物事個輕重.

(五) 我跽拉伊面前求伊饒赦.

(六) 小囝生病末娘勿離開伊坐拉床邊頭輸帳伊.

(七) 勿批評别人蓋末勿受别人個批評.

(八) 爲之恐怕路勿熟所以請别人陪我去.

(九) 第把剪刀一顏勿快要去磨磨.

(十) 叫燒飯個拿點乾麵蛋牛乳佬糖做鷄蛋糕.

(十一) 搨點乳油拉饅頭上蓋末好吃點.

(十二) 學生子拉哭爲之别人話料伊先生叫伊勿要哭佬安慰伊.

(十三) 我叫之伊末伊就旋轉頭來看.

(十四) 第個一樁事體啥人經手個.

(十五) 爬樹末勿大穩當恐怕要跌痛佬跌傷.

(十六) 應該趕脱伊隻狗恐怕要咬小囝.

(十七) 扯篷末船行來快.

(十八) 種田人勿歡喜老鴉爲之伊拉吃脱伊拉散拉個子.

(十九) 常時老鷹從天上飛下來吃脱之小雞.

(二十) 串好第個銅錢佬算算看有幾化.

(廿一) 兵丁出去打仗敲鼓佬金鑼.

(廿二) 第個石頭從山頂上滾下來.

(Translate into Chinese)

(1) These two men constantly have intercourse with one another.

(2) The servant did not take care, and so upset a bucket of water.

(3) Butterflies are very pretty, and children like to catch them.

(4) Children before they learn to walk can first crawl on the ground.

(5) If a man wants to be forgiven he should first repent.

(6) What is the depth of this creek?

(7) If you wish to know the texture of the cloth, you must feel it with your hand.

(8) If you do not wear spectacles when you are old, you will be unable to thread your needle.

(9) I drove away that beggar, because he followed after me calling out.

(10) What is the distance between the sun and the earth? About ninety-two millions of miles.

(11) The cat climbed up the tree and the dog could not catch it.

(12) The little girl has no time to study, because her mother is sick, and she must stay at home and nurse her.

(13) The water flows down from the top of the hill.

(14) I regret that I told him, because he went and told everyone, and now every one knows it.

(15) When you pray you should kneel down.

(一) 第個兩個人常庄大家來往.

(二) 用人勿當心所以打翻之桶水.

(三) 蝴蝶是蠻好看所以小囝歡喜捉個.

(四) 小囝勿曾學會走先會得�拉地上.

(五) 一個人要得着饒赦先應該悔改.

(六) 第條浜有幾化深淺?

(七) 若然儂要曉得第塊布個粗細儂終要用手摸模看.

(八) 年紀老之佬勿戴眼鏡恐怕勿能彀穿引線眼.

(九) 我趕脫之伊個告化子因爲伊跟拉後頭佬喊.

(十) 地球離開日頭有幾化遠近?約酌有九千二百萬英里.

(十一) 貓爬到樹上所以狗捉伊勿着.

(十二) 小囝無沒工夫讀書因爲伊個娘生病伊終要登拉屋裏輸帳伊.

(十三) 水從山頂上流下來.

(十四) 我懊憦我告訴伊因爲伊去對攏總人話以致攏總人全曉得個.

(十五) 儂禱告個時候應該跽下來.

NOTES.

(1) In the seventh Sentence of the First Exercise notice how *phi-bing* is used both as a noun and as a verb.

(2) In the eighth sentence of the First Exercise *Zok* (熟), which means "ripe" of fruit, also means "well-known." It also has the meaning of "thorough" as in the expression *dok-zok* (讀熟) meaning "to read thoroughly."

(3) In the thirteenth sentence of the First Exercise notice the position of the *deu* (頭), "head" between the °*Tsen* (轉) and the *le* (來). This is usual in Chinese. Verbs are often broken up in this way.

(4) In the fifteenth sentence of the First Exercise °*wung-taung*° (穩當) means "safe."

Lesson XXIX

Some Useful Phrases

As will be seen from the lessons already gone over Chinese is very largely composed of idiomatic phrases. The only way to become acquainted with these phrases is by the constant hearing of the spoken language. We shall introduce in this lesson a few useful phrases and show how they occur in sentences.

"All one's life," ***ih sang-ih-s°*** (一生一世). Lit. "One life, one world." "To run about," ***Bau-le-bau-chi°*** (跑來跑去). Lit. "Run come, run go." "To decide," ***Lih-ding-°tsu-i°*** (立定主意). Lit. "To stand still the will."

Good-bye (French, *au-revoir*), ***An°-hyih-we°*** (宴歇會). Lit. "We will meet later," or ***Tse°-we°*** (再會). Lit. "I will see you again."

The ordinary way of saying "good-bye" when you have been to call on a person is to say ***Chi°-tse*** (去哉). Lit. "I am going." Your host will say ***Man°-chi°*** (慢去), meaning "Go slowly."

The expression. ***Kan-nyih-we°*** (間日會) would mean: "I will see you in a day or two."

"Universal" ***°Phoo-thien-'au°*** (普天下), or ***'Eh-thien-°ti-°'au*** (合天底下). Lit. "Beneath the whole of heaven."

"Useless, in vain," ***Bak-bak-°li*** (白白裏). "Indispensable" is ***°Ba-'veh-tuk*** (罷勿得).

Vocabulary

If it be so, **kyi°-zen zeh-ke** 既然實蓋.

By chance, **°ngeu-zen** 偶然.

Purposely, **°yeu-i°** 有意, or **koo°-i°** 故意.

At the point of, °**kyi-oo** 幾乎.

For the most part, generally, **da°-liak** 大略.

Suddenly, **hweh-zen** 忽然.

Instantaneous, **lih-khuh** 立刻.

Advantage, profit, **iuh-tshu°** 益處, or °**hau-tshu°** 好處.

Lord, °**Tsu** 主.

Master, °**tsu-nyung** 主人, or **toong-ka** 東家.

Heavenly Lord (a term used for God), **Thien-°tsu** 天主.

God, **Zung** 神 °Zang-ti° 上帝.

Omnipotent, **voo-°soo-peh-nung** 無所不能.

Omnipresent, **voo-°soo-peh-°dze** 無所不在.

Omniscient, **voo-°soo-peh-ts** 無所不知.

Life, **sing°-ming°** 性命.

A dragon, **ih diau loong** 一條龍.

An account book, **ih °pung tsang°-°boo** 一本帳簿.

A small blank book, **ih °pung °boo-ts** 一本簿子.

Carefully, °**ts-si°** 仔細.

To waste, **fi°-theh** 廢脫.

A carpet, **ih diau mau-°than** 一條毛毯.

°*Boo* (部) is the classifier for sets of books.

A set of books, **ih °boo su** 一部書.

A flag, **ih mien° ji** 一面旗.

Angry, **doong-chi°** 動氣.

Still, **dzung-jeu°** 仍舊.

Originally, °**pung-le** 本來.

Drowned, **dzung-sah** 沉殺.

Sign, symbol, **'au°** 號.

A mirror, **ih mien° kyung°-°ts** 一面鏡子.

Exercises

(Translate into English)

(1) Noong° zeh-ke° tsoo° meh, °khoong-pho° ih-sang-ih-s° iau° au-lau° tse.

(2) °Ngoo bak-bak-°li te° yi wo°, yi dzung-jeu° ’veh thing.

(3) Sien-sang tsiang iau° chi° yi te° °ngoo wo°, chi°-tse°, °lau °ngoo te° yi wo°, man°-chi°.

(4) Noong° iung-ke lih-ding-°tsu-i° ’veh tsoo° zeh-ke° than-tshoong° kuh z°-°thi.

(5) Thien-°tsu °z voo-°soo-peh nung, voo-°soo-peh-°dze, °lau voo-°soo-peh-ts°.

(6) Nyung iau° khoen° z°-ka mien°-khoong meh, ih mien° kyung°-°ts °z °ba-’veh-tuk-kuh.

(7) Tuh-dzak° °phoo-thien-‘au° °lau se-theh-°ts z°-ka-kuh sing°-ming° meh °yeu sa° iuh-tshu° nyi?

(8) Di°-tsak °mo la° dien °li bau-le-bau-chi°, van-nan tsauh-dzak kuh.

(9) Di° °boo su °yeu °kyi °pung? °Yeu nyan° °pung.

(10) Kyi° zen zeh-ke°-nung, nan-meh °ngoo ’veh °hau wo° sa°.

(11) ‘Auh-sang-°ts °tang-se° poo-li °z °yeu-i° nyi wan-z °ngeu-zen kuh z°-°thi?

(12) I-kuh nyung tih la° pang °li, °kyi-‘oo dzung-sah, dan°-°z °yeu ih kuh nyung le thoo yi chi°-le.

(13) °‘Au-pen°-nyih hweh-zen fah-°chi doo° foong le.

(14) ‘Auh-daung-°li °loong-°tsoong °yeu °kyi-kuh ‘auh-sang-°ts? Da°-iak °yeu san pak kuh.

(15) °Ngoo kyau° yi lih-khuh °doong-sung.

(16) Tsoong-kok ji-‘au° °z ’man °hau khoen°.

(17) Di°-kuh nyung °pung-le °z auh nyung, yien°-°dze hwe°-°ke-tse.

(18) °Ngoo au-lau° °ma-°ts di°-diau mau-°than, we°-ts °than la° khak-daung °li thuh °siau.

(19) Noong° seu-tsing°-le °lau foo-°tsheh-chi°-kuh °loong-°tsoong iau° kyi° la° tsang°-°boo laung°.

(20) Di°-kuh ‘auh-sang-°ts iau° the°-theh, iung-we° su dok-’veh °zaung.

(一) 儂實蓋做末恐怕一生一世要懊憦哉.

(二) 我白白裏對伊話伊仍舊勿聽.

(三) 先生將要去伊對我話去哉我對伊話慢去.

(四) 儂應該立定主意勿做實蓋坍銃個事體.

(五) 天主是無所不能無所不在佬無所不知.

(六) 人要看自家面孔末一面鏡子是罷勿得個.

(七) 得着普天下佬失脫之自家個性命末有啥益處呢.

(八) 第隻馬拉田裏跑來跑去煩難捉着個.

(九) 第部書有幾本?有念本.

(十) 既然實蓋能難末我勿好話啥.

(十一) 學生子打碎玻璃是有意呢還是偶然個事體.

(十二) 伊個人跌拉浜裏幾乎沉殺但是有一個人來拖伊起來.

(十三) 下半日忽然發起大風來.

(十四) 學堂裏攏總有幾個學生子?大約有三百個.

(十五) 我叫伊立刻動身.

(十六) 中國旗號是蠻好看.

(十七) 第個人本來是惡人現在悔改哉.

(十八) 我懊憹買之第條毛毯爲之攤拉客堂裏忒小.

(十九) 儂收進來佬付出去個攏總要記拉帳簿上.

(二十) 第個學生子要退脫因爲書讀勿上.

(Translate into Chinese)

(1) The man is very sick, even at the point of death.

(2) One should not only think how to get profit for oneself, but how to give advantage to others.

(3) In the evening the master gave the servants their wages.

(4) I think that he offended me purposely, and therefore I am angry.

(5) A student should not only learn while in school, but should be learning all his life.

(6) I saw a dragon come up suddenly out of the water.

(7) Truly all men under heaven are brethren, and ought to love one another.

(8) A business man can see from his account book how much he has gained in his business or how much he has lost.

(9) If you really ran very fast, how is it that you did not arrive sooner?

(10) I have looked over this book in a general way, but I have not read it carefully.

(11) If you wish to repent and become a good man, the first thing is to make up your own mind.

(12) I knew the boat was a Chinese one, because they hoisted the Chinese flag.

(13) A man's life is most precious, so he ought to take care of his body.

(14) When I had finished the work I found he had already done the same thing, and so I had wasted my time to no purpose.

(15) The children like to run about and play in the garden.

(一) 第個人毛病蠻重幾乎要死.

(二) 人勿但要想到自家個益處也要想到別人個益處.

(三) 拉夜快主人發工錢拉伊個用人.

(四) 我想伊有意得罪我所以我動氣.

(五) 學生子勿但拉學堂裏要學,一生一世應該學個.

(六) 我看見一條龍從水裏忽然上來.

(七) 普天下人實在是弟兄應該大家相愛.

(八) 生意人從帳簿上可以看伊賺之幾化或者失脫之幾化.

(九) 既然儂跑來快爲啥佬勿早點到?

(十) 我大略看過第本書但是勿曾仔細看.

(十一) 若然儂要悔改成功好個人,頭一要自家立定主意.

(十二) 我曉得第隻船是中國船因爲伊扯拉個是中國旗.

(十三) 人個性命是頂寶貝個所以應該當心自家個身體.

(十四) 我做好之第個生活我看別人搭我一樣個所以我白白裏廢脫第個工夫.

(十五) 小囝拉花園裏歡喜跑來跑去孛相.

NOTES.

(1) *Thien-°tsu* is the term used for God by the Romanists and by some Protestants. The other terms used for God are *Zung* (神), Lit. "a Spirit" and *°Zang-ti°* (上帝), Lit. "The Celestial Ruler."

(2) In the fourteenth sentence of the Second Exercise for "to no purpose," one can say *Bak-bak-li-fi°-theh*, or the *bak* (白) can be used with the verb. Thus we can say *Bak fi°-theh* (白廢脫). *Bak* is often need in this way with verbs. Thus *Bak-tsoo°* (白做), "to do in vain." *Bak °siang* (白想), "to think in vain, to no purpose," etc.

(3) In the eleventh sentence of the First Exercise *Wan°-z* may be translated "or."

Lesson XXX

More Useful Words and Phrases

In the preceding lessons emphasis has been laid upon idiom and construction. Here a few useful words and phrases are given for the purpose of increasing the vocabulary of the student.

Vocabulary

Sound of a character, **z°-iung** 字音.

To aspirate, **tsheh-foong** 出風.

Baggage, **'ang-°li** 行李.

Bank, **nyung-'aung** 銀行.

Bedding, **phoo°-ke°** 鋪蓋.

Button, **°nyeu-°ts** 鈕子.

Charcoal, **than°** 炭.

Chimney, **ien-tshoong** 烟囱.

Post Office (Foreign) **su-sing°-°kwen** 書信館, or **sing°-jok** 信局, or **yeu-tsung°-jok** 郵政局.

Church, **°li-pa°-daung** 禮拜堂.

Cook, (head) **da°-°s-voo°** 大司務.

Cook, (ordinary) **sau-van°-kuh** 燒飯個.

Dust, **boong-dzung** 埲塵.

Coal, (hard) **bak-me** 白煤.

Coal, (soft) **ien-me** 烟煤.

Enough, **°yeu-tse** 有哉, or **keu°-°z** 彀是.

Farmer, **tsoong°-dien nyung** 種田人.

Fresh, (of meat or fish) **sing-sien** 新鮮.

Hospital, **i-yoen°** 醫院.

Jetty, **°mo-deu** 碼頭.

Kerosene, **°hoo-yeu** 火油.

Kettle, (copper) **doong-‘oo** 銅壺.

Market, **°z-mien°** 市面.

Marks or signs, **kyi°-‘au°** 記號.

Mistake, not correct, **veh-te°** 勿對, or **tsho** 差.

Relative, (family) **tshing-kyoen°** 親眷.

Salt, (noun) **yien** 鹽.

Salt, (adj.) **‘an** 鹹.

Soup, **thaung** 湯.

Trousers, **khoo°-°ts** 褲子.

Washerman, **da° i-zaung-kuh** 汏衣裳個, or **zing° i-zaung-kuh** 淨衣裳個.

Postage stamp, **nyung-deu** 人頭, or **yeu-phiau** 郵票.

I supposed, **°ngoo dau-nyung-ts** 我道認之.

Exercises

(Translate into English)

(1) Di°-kuh z°-iung iau° tsheh foong nyi ’veh iau tsheh-foong.

(2) °Ngoo-kuh ‘ang-°li iau° tsaung la° tsho-ts° laung°.

(3) Di°-kuh san pak kwhe° yang-dien iau° dzung la° nyung-‘aung °li.

(4) Da°-°s-voo° di°-kuh nyoeh °li sau-ts pen° tung° ien me.

(5) Kyung-ya°-deu kuh thaung thuh ‘an, ming-tsau sau faung°-°tien yien.

(6) °Zaung-°he °li-pa°-daung °lau i-yoen° ’veh °sau.

(7) Tsoong°-dien-nyung thiau too-hau° siau-tshe tau° °z-mien laung° chi° ma°-kuh.

(8) Di°-foong sing° iau° nau tau° yeu-tsung°-jok °li, iau° °ma nyung-deu thih la laung°.

(9) Di°-diau khoo°-°ts peh la da°-i-zaung kuh zing°.

(10) Too-hau° nyung tau° °mo-deu laung° soong° bang-°yeu tau° nga°-kok chi°.

(11) Di°-kuh tsang° 'veh-te °tse iau° khe ih tsang° tshing-°saung-°tien kuh.

(12) De-°ts laung° kuh boong-dzung iau° kha theh.

(13) °Hoo-yeu keu° meh? Keu°-tse.

(14) Di°-kuh ien-tshoong 'veh thoong.

(15) °Ngoo hyau-tuh di°-tsak doong-'oo °z °ngoo-kuh iung-we° °ngoo tsoo° kyi°-au° la° laung°.

(一) 第個字音要出風呢勿要出風?

(二) 我個行李要裝拉車子上.

(三) 第個三百塊洋錢要存拉銀行裏.

(四) 大司務第個月裏燒之半噸烟煤.

(五) 今夜頭個湯忒鹹明朝少放點鹽.

(六) 上海禮拜堂佬醫院勿少.

(七) 種由人挑多化小菜到市面上去賣個.

(八) 第封信要拿到郵政局裏要買人頭貼拉上.

(九) 第條褲子撥拉汰衣裳個淨.

(十) 多化人到碼頭上送朋友到外國去.

(十一) 第個賬勿對再要一張清爽點個.

(十二) 檯子上墣塵要揩脫.

(十三) 火油穀末?穀哉.

(十四) 第個烟囱勿通.

(十五) 我曉得第隻銅壺是我個因爲我做記號拉上.

(Translate into Chinese)

(1) My relative is sick in the hospital.

(2) Salt is good, but if it has lost its savour, wherewithal shall it be salted?

(3) I told the cook to buy some stamps at the Post Office.

(4) How much money have you in the bank?

(5) When you are going on a journey, you should take your bedding along with you.

(6) To-day is Sunday, and I went to church in the morning.

(7) I told him to buy some charcoal, some hard coal and some soft coal.

(8) There is much dust in the market place.

(9) In the summer time it is important to eat only these things which are fresh.

(10) If there is no oil in the lamp, how can you light it?

(11) Your pronunciation of this word is not correct. It is aspirated.

(12) I met a friend on the jetty, who had just come from America.

(13) Put the kettle on the stove.

(14) The farmers are busy in the spring of the year.

(15) If the wind blows down the chimney, the room will be full of smoke.

(一) 我個親眷生病拉醫院裏.

(二) 鹽是好個失脫之鹽個味道那能鹹呢?

(三) 我對大司務話書信館買點人頭.

(四) 銀行裏有幾化洋錢?

(五) 出門末終要帶鋪蓋.

(六) 今朝是禮拜日早晨已經到禮拜堂去過.

(七) 我對伊話叫伊買白煤烟煤佬炭.

(八) 市面上蓬塵多來.

(九) 夏天末必定要吃新鮮個物事.

(十) 燈裏嘸沒油末那能可以點呢.

(十一) 儂個聲音勿對第個字音要出風.

(十二) 我拉碼頭上掽着一個朋友美國纔纔來.

(十三) 銅壺放拉火爐上.

(十四) 種田人春上訂忙.

(十五) 風吹到之烟囪末房間裏禿是烟哉.

NOTES.

(1) In the third sentence of the First Exercise the verb *dzung* (存) means deposit.

(2) In the fourth Sentence of the First Exercise *tung*° (噸) means ton.

(3) In the tenth sentence of the First Exercise *Soong° bung-°yeu* (送朋友) means to send on his way, or as we put it "to see off."

Lesson XXXI

Polite Language

In the Chinese language there are a great many polite phrases used in conversation. The ability to use these is a sign of education. Every student of the language should become acquainted with the most common ones, for he will have occasion to use them constantly. Some of these phrases have been introduced and explained in these lessons already, but here an attempt will be made to gather together all those that would be ordinarily used is conversation.

When you meet any one for the first time, according to Chinese etiquette you are at liberty to ask him what his honorable name may be. The expression for this is ***Tsung sing°*** (尊姓), or ***Kwe°-sing°*** (貴姓). In answer he will tell you his surname, but in doing so he will refer to it as his humble name. Thus he will say ***Bi°-sing° Tsang*** (敝姓張) (if his surname is Tsang).

Next you might proceed to inquire what his other name was, that is, his private name in distinction from his surname. This you would ask by saying ***°Tshing kyau° da° 'au°*** (請叫大號), "Please teach me your great appellation" or ***The °foo*** (台甫). In answer he might say ***°Tshau-z° Kya-foo*** (草字嘉甫), meaning "the grass characters are ***Kya-foo***," or he might say ***°Siau-ming*** (小名). (***Kya-foo*** is taken as an example of a name).

Then you might proceed to ask his age. This you would do by saying ***Too-sau kwe°-kang*** (多少貴庚). The answer would be ***°Ngoo hyui doo° san seh soe°*** (我虛度三十歲). Lit. "I have vainly passed thirty years." If you ask an old gentleman his age, you would say ***°Kyi-hau° kau-zeu°*** (幾化高壽). Lit. "What is your high longevity?"

If you ask a person how he is, as has been already intimated, you would say ***°Hau-la°-va°*** (好拉否). The answer might be ***Khau° fok*** (靠福), meaning "I depend upon you for my happiness."

If a person asked you how many years you had been in China, he would say

Tau°-ts bi°-kok °kyi z-tse (到之敝國幾時哉). You would answer ***°Ngoo tau°-ts kwe°-kok nyan nyien*** (我到之貴國念年). "I arrived in your honorable country twenty years ago" (or any length of time you had been in the country).

When you are asking a guest to take a seat, if he is at all an honorable guest, you must request him to take an honorable seat. This you do by saying ***°Tshing °zaung-deu °zoo*** (請上頭坐), meaning "Please sit up higher."

In asking how many children you have your guest would say ***°Kyi-we °sau-kyuin*** (幾位少君), "How many little princes have you." Your answer is ***San kuh °siau-koen*** (三個小干), or ***°san kuh °siau-noen*** (三個小囝), or ***san kuh °siau-°choen*** (三個小犬).

At table, if you finish before others, you raise your chop-sticks and say to the others ***Man°-yoong°*** (慢用), "use slowly." Then place the chop-sticks on top of the bowl. Your host could answer ***Yoong°-°pau*** (用飽), meaning, "Take plenty."

When a guest is leaving, in addition to saying ***Chi°-tse***, he may say ***Kyung-tshau*** 驚吵), meaning, "I have troubled you." Your answer may be ***De-man de-man*** (待慢), meaning, "I have treated you without proper respect." Or he may say, as he is walking away ***°Tshing lieu kyung-boo°*** (請留經步), meaning, "Please restrain your orderly footsteps"; or simply ***Lieu-boo°***, meaning "Don't trouble to come out." If you have to excuse yourself after a short stay, you should say ***Sau-be*** (少陪).

Vocabulary

England, **Iung-kok** 英國.

America, **°Me-kok** 美國, or **Hwo-ji-kok** 花旗國. Lit., Kingdom of the Flowery Flag.

France, **Fah-kok** 法國.

Germany, **Tuh-kok** 德國.

Russia, **Ngoo-kok** 俄國.

Antiquity, anciently, **°koo-z-kan** 古時間.

Neighbor, **ling-°so** 鄰舍.

A godown, **°dzan-vaung** 棧房.

Inconceivable, **°siang-'veh-tau** 想勿到.

Lazy, **°lan-phok** 懶朴, or **°lan-doo°** 懶惰.

Tricky, **diau°-bi** 掉皮.

Communication, intercourse, **le-°waung** 來往.

Matches, **z°-le-°hoo** 自來火.

Next (juxtaposition), **kah-pih** 隔壁.

Promise, **iung°-°hyui** 應許.

Recently, **°jung-le** 近來.

To meet with misfortune, **chuh °khoo** 吃苦. Literally, "Eat bitterness."

Comfortable, **suh-i°** 適意.

The earlier the better, **yoeh-°tsau yoeh-°hau** 越早越好.

To relax the mind, **san° sing** 散心.

Soap, **bi-zau°** 肥皂.

To strike a match, **wak** 劃.

Exercises

(Translate into English)

(1) Di°-foong sing° iau° noong° tan tau° yeu-tsung°-jok °li chi°.

(2) °Koo-z-kan Tsoong-kok tah-ts bih-kuh kok-doo° ih ngan 'veh le-°waung.

(3) °Jung-le Ngoo-kok tah-ts Toong-yang da°-ka °tang-tsang°.

(4) Dzu° la kah-pih kuh nyung °z kyau° ling-°so.

(5) Di°-kuh nyung 'veh ba° °z °lan-phok, 'a-z diau°-bi.

(6) Sang-i°-nyung la° °dzan-vaung °li tsaung-ts too-hau° hoo°-suh.

(7) °Tshing °zoo la° bih-kuh iui°-°ts laung°, °i-tsak 'veh da° suh-i°.

(8) °Ngoo iung°-°hyui °ngoo kuh si-tse, zak-zen tsoo° le °hau meh iau° ka yi-kuh koong-dien.

(9) I-kuh nyung we°-ts chuh °tsieu, °too doong-dien, °lau 'veh °lau-zeh °i-kyung chuh-ts too-hau° khoo.

(10) Tsoong-kok tah °Me-kok tsho-'veh-too ih yang° doo°-°siau.

(11) °Pung-le °Me-kok nyung °z dzoong Iung-kok le kuh.

(12) Di°-foong sing° °kyi-z iau° °ngoo °sia kuh? Yoeh-°tsau yoeh-°hau.

(13) I-kuh nyung zeh-ke° diau°-bi zeh-°dze °siang-'veh-tau°-kuh.

(14) °Seu °lau mien°-khoong iau° kha le koen-zing meh °tsoong iau° yoong° bi-zau°.

(15) Iau° wak z°-le-°hoo tsoong iau° wak la° 'ah-°ts laung°, 'veh zen meh 'veh we° yaung.

(一) 第封信要儂担到郵政局裏去.
(二) 古時間中國搭之別個國度一顏勿來往.
(三) 近來俄國搭之東洋大家打仗.
(四) 住拉隔壁個人是叫鄰舍.
(五) 第個人勿罷是懶朴也是掉皮.
(六) 生意人拉棧房裏裝之多化貨色.
(七) 請坐拉別個椅子上伊隻勿大適意.
(八) 我應許我個西崽若然做來好末要加伊個工錢.
(九) 伊個人爲之吃酒賭銅錢佬勿老實已經吃之多化苦.
(十) 中國搭美國差勿多一樣大小.
(十一) 本來美國人是從英國來個.
(十二) 第封信幾時要我寫個?越早越好.
(十三) 伊個人實蓋掉皮實在想勿到個.
(十四) 手佬面孔要揩來乾淨末終要用肥皂.
(十五) 要劃自來火終要劃拉匣子上勿然末勿會旺.

(Translate into Chinese)

(1) You should love your neighbor as yourself.

(2) All over China now there are post offices, and you can send a letter to any part of China for three cents.

(3) America is called the Kingdom of the Flowery Flag, because its flag is very beautiful.

(4) A lazy man likes to get up late in the day, and during the day he likes to go to sleep.

(5) Germany and France are next to one another on the map.

(6) The fox is one of the most tricky of all the animals.

(7) How long have you been in my humble country? I arrived in your honorable country only about one year ago.

(8) Since I have promised it, I will certainly do as I said.

(9) In ancient times most men were unable to read and write; now a large portion of the people can do so.

(10) Children should not play with matches because they might set the house on fire.

(11) Men can not always be using their minds; they must at times relax their

minds.

(12) Yesterday I felt very wretched, and was in bed all day; to-day I am more comfortable.

(一) 儂應該愛鄰舍像愛自家.

(二) 垃拉中國各處地方有郵政局三分洋錢可以送一封信到隨便那裏頭.

(三) 美國是叫花旗國因爲伊個旗是蠻好看.

(四) 懶朴個人是歡喜晚碌起來日裏也要睏.

(五) 德國搭之法國垃拉地理圖上是隔壁.

(六) 拉中牲當中狐狸蠻掉皮個.

(七) 到之敝國幾時哉?到之貴國不過年把.

(八) 我旣然應許個一定要照我話個佬做.

(九) 拉古時間攏總人勿會讀書佬寫字現在大一半人可以個.

(十) 小囝勿應該拿自來火來弄勃相恐怕要弄開火來.

(十一) 人勿可以常莊用心有常時末終要散心.

(十二) 昨日我一顏勿好一日睏拉床上今朝稍爲適意點.

NOTES.

(1) In the third sentence of the First Exercise *da-ka* (大家) means "together."

(2) In the fifteenth sentence notice the *'Veh zen meh* (勿然末), meaning, "If not so."

(3) In the tenth sentence of the Second Exercise "to set the house on fire," may be translated *Loong khe °hoo le* 弄開火來.

(4) In the eleventh sentence of the Second Exercise *Yoong°-sing* (用心) and *San°-sing* (散心) are just the opposite of one another.

Lesson XXXII

Proverbs

As is well known, the Chinese are very fond of proverbs. Their language is exceedingly rich with sententious sayings. They also make use of many felicitous expressions on New Year's Day, at marriages, etc. Here is a short list of those in common use. Most of them are in literary style, but are used in ordinary speech.

一念之差終身之悔.
ih nyan° ts tsho tsoong sung ts hwe°.
The evil done in a moment's thought may entail the repentance of a life time.

一言已出駟馬難追.
Ih yien i tsheh, s° °mo nan tsoe.
When a word has gone forth, four horses cannot overtake it.

一心舉念.
Ih sing °kyui nyan°.
A heart holding one thought; a mind set on one purpose.

一榻糊塗.
Ih thah oo-doo.
Everything in confusion.

吃人碗半,由人使換喚.
Chuh zung °wen pen°, yeu *zung s° hwen°.
If you eat half a bowl of rice of another man, you thereby are placed under obligations.

*Note that the character for man is pronounced Nyung in the vernacular and Zung in the literary language.

皇天不負苦人心.
Waung Thien peh veu° °khoo zung sing.
Great Heaven never forgets the desire of a person in misery.

敗子回頭金不換.
Ba°-°ts we deu kyung peh wen°.
The repentance of a prodigal is more precious than gold.

推車撞之壁.
The tsho dzaung ts pih.
To wheel the cart against the wall,—equivalent to knock your head against a stone wall.

捨近而求遠.
So° °jung r jeu °yoen.
To forfeit what is near and seek what is far. It implies the folly of giving up the bird in the hand for the bird in the bush.

忘恩負義.
Vaung° ung veu° nyi°.
To forget benefits received.

順風扯旗.
Zung° foong °tsha ji.
To float the flag in the wind. This implies "to follow the crowd," and applies to a person of weak character.

人心皆同.
Zung sing kya doong.
Human nature is one.

惡有惡報,善有善報,若使勿報,時刻未到.
Auh °yeu auh pau°, °zen yeu °zen pau°, zak-s 'veh pau°, z khuk vi tau°.
Evil has an evil recompense—virtue has a good recompense. If the recompense does not appear, it is because the time has not yet arrived.

冤有頭,債有生.
Ioen °yeu deu, tsa° °yeu tsu.
Enmity has a source, just as debt has a creditor.

欺人自欺自.
Chi zung z° chi z°.
To cheat others is to cheat oneself.

樹高千丈,葉落歸根.
Zu° kau tshien °dzang, yih lauh kwe kung.
*Although the tree may be ten thousand feet high, its leaves fall down to the roots.

*This means that all, sooner or later, return to their original homes.

人面獸心.
Zung mien° sen° sing.
He has the face of a man and the heart of an animal.

看死捻鼻頭.
Khoen° °si nyah pih-deu.
To catch hold of the note of a man who is dying. Equivalent to the expression "To hit a man when he is down."

落水搇.
Lauh °s chung.
To press a drowning man down in the water. This has much the same meaning as the preceding.

近朱者赤,近墨者黑.
°Jung tsu tse tshuh, °jung muh tse huh.
Contact with red ink makes you red. Contact with black ink makes you black.

損人利己眞小人.
Sung zung li° kyi tsung °siau zung.
To injure another to benefit yourself, is the part of a mean fellow.

欺衆不欺一.
Chi °tsoong peh chi ih.
In dealing harshly with all, you do not deal harshly with any one in particular.

狗看滿天星.
°Keu khoen° °men thien sing.
The dog looks at the sky full of stars. This describes a stupid person who does not understand what he sees.

始終如一.
°S tsoong xu ih.
To continue the same from the beginning to the end.

半途而廢.
Pen° doo r fi.
To give up half-way.

謀事在人,成事在天.
Meu z° dze zung, dzung z° dze thien.
Man contrives, God accomplishes. Equivalent to "Man proposeth, God disposeth."

步步升高.
Boo°-boo° sang kau.
May you rise step by step.

壽比南山,福如東海.
Zeu° °pi nen san, fok zu toong °he.
May your longevity be like the Southern Mountain, and your happiness like the Eastern Sea.

琴瑟調和.
Jung seh diau 'oo.
May the harp and guitar harmonize. Note. This is a wedding wish, the harp and guitar signifying the bride and groom.

百年偕老.
Pak nyien kya °lau.
May you have happiness for a hundred year. A wedding wish.

成雙到老.
Dzung saung tau° °lau.
May the couple remain united until old age. A wedding wish.

稱心如意.
Tshung sing zu-i°.
May everything be according to your own wishes.

壽年千歲.
Zeu° nyien tshien soe°.
May you have a long life of a thousand years.

一路順風.
Ih loo° zung° foong.
May you have favorable winds journey.

恭喜發財.
Koong-°hyi fah ze.
*May wealth and happiness both be yours.

*This wish is often used at New Year's time.

四季平安.
S° kyi° bing-oen.
May you have peace through the four seasons.

Chinese-English Vocabulary

A

Ah, 押, to mortgage.

Ah, 鴨, a duck.

Ah-koo, 阿哥, an older brother.

Ah-theh, 押脫, to mortgage.

Ah-°tsi, 阿姐, an older sister.

An°, 晏, late.

‘Ang-°li, 行李, baggage.

An°-hyih-we°, 晏歇會, good-by.

Au°-°lau, 懊佬, to regret.

Auh, 惡, wicked.

Auh-tshauh, 齷齪, dirty.

‘A-°ts, 鞋子, shoes.

°‘A, 亦 or 也, also.

°‘A-°li, 那裏, which.

°‘A-°z, 亦是, also.

‘Ah, 狹, narrow.

‘Ah-°ts, 盒子, a small box.

‘An, 鹹, salt (adj.).

‘Au, 毫, 1/10 of a li (in currency).

‘Au-sau°, 豪燥, quickly.

°‘Au, 下, down.

°‘Au-deu, 下頭, below.

°‘**Au-kuh-nyoeh**, 下個月, next month.

°‘**Au-le**, 下來, to come down.

°‘**Au-nyoeh**, 下月, next month.

°‘**Au-pen°-nyien**, 下半年, last half of year.

°‘**Au-pen°-nyih**, 下半日, afternoon.

°‘**Au-pen°-nyoeh**, 下半月, last half month.

°‘**An-pen°-ya°**, 下半夜, last half night.

°**Au-°ti**, 下底, below.

°**Au-°ti-deu**, 下底頭, below.

°‘**Au-zen**, 下船, to go on board a ship.

‘**Au°**, 夏, summer.

‘**Auh**, 學, to learn.

‘**Auh-daung**, 下堂, school.

‘**Auh-sang-°ts**, 學生子, a scholar, a pupil.

‘**Aung-dzing**, 行情, price.

B

Ba, 排, to arrange in order.

°**Ba-tse**, 罷哉, (after verb), gives force of completed action.

°**Ba-’veh-tuh**, 罷弗得, indispensable.

Bak, 白, white.

Bak-bak-°li, 白白裏, useless, in vain.

Bak-me, 白煤, hard coal.

Bak-wo°, 白話, to converse.

Ban, 爿, a classifier for shops.

Ban°, 跘, to crawl.

Ban°, 辦, to direct, to attend to a matter.

Bang-°yeu, 朋友, a friend.

Bang°, 碰, to strike against.

Bang°-dzak, 捧着, to meet.

Bau, 跑, to run.

Bau-le-bau-chi°, 跑來跑去, to run about.

°**Bau**, 抱, to carry in the arms.

Bau°, 刨, a plane.

Baung-pien, 旁邊, by the side of.

°**Baung**, 棒, a cane, a stick.

Be, 陪, to accompany, to stay with a person.

Beh-siang°, 孛相, to play, to take recreation.

Ben°, 伴, to hide.

Ben°-°loong, 伴攏, to hide oneself.

Bi-zau°, 皮皂, soap.

°**Bi-deu**, 被頭, a quilt, a blanket.

°**Bien-°ts**, 辮子, a queue.

Bien°-taung°, 便當, convenient.

Bih, 別, other.

Bih-deu, 鼻頭, the nose.

Bing, 瓶, a bottle.

Bing, 平, level.

Bing-foong, 屏風, a screen.

Bing-°koo, 蘋果, an apple.

Bo, 爬, climb.

Bok, 薄, thin.

Boo°, 步, classifier of carriages.

Boo°, 部, classifier for sets of books.

Boo-sah, 菩薩, a Buddhist idol.

°**Boo-°ts**, 簿子, a small blank book.

Boong, 篷, a sail.

Boong-dzung, 塳塵, dust.

Bung-°ts, 盆子, a plate.

C

Cheu, 怵, bad.

°**Chi**, 起, to begin.

°**Chi**, 豈, an interrogative particle.

°**Chi-deu**, 起頭, the beginning.

°**Chi-le**, 起來, to arise; expresses action going on.

°**Chi-lih**, 起立, to stand up, standing.

Chi°, 去, to go.

Chi°-lih, 氣力, strength.

Chi°-tse, 去哉, good-by, gone.

Choen°, 勸, to exhort.

Choen°-°mien, 勸勉, to exhort.

Choen°-‘oo, 勸和, to exhort.

Chung, 輕, light (in weight).

Chung-chung-nung, 輕輕能, gently.

Chung-°dzoong, 輕重, weight.

Chuh, 吃, to eat.

Chuh-°khoo, 吃苦, to meet with misfortune.

Chuh-van°, 吃飯, eat a meal.

Chuh-van°-de-°ts, 吃飯檯子, a dining table.

Chuh-van°-kan, 吃飯間, a dining room.

D

Da°, 埭, classifier of rows of things.

Da°-i-zaung-kuh, 汏衣裳個, a washerman.

Da°-ka, 大家, together.

Da°-ke°, 大概, all in general, most.

Da°-liak, 大略, for the most part, generally.

Da°-°s-voo°, 大司務, the chief cook.

Da°-tshing-kok, 大清國, (Former name of) China.

Dan°, 蛋, an egg.

Dan°-°z, 但是, but.

Dau-nyung-ts, 道認之, to suppose; to think.

Dau-°ts, 桃子, a peach.

°**Dau-za**, 稻柴, a bundle of fuel.

°**Dau**, 稻, a plant of rice.

Dau°-°z, 道士, Taoist priest.

Daung, 糖, sugar.

De-°ts, 檯子, a table.

De°, 兌, to exchange a dollar into cash.

°De, 待, to deport oneself, to treat others.

°De-man°, 待慢, to treat rudely.

De°-thi°, 代替, instead of.

Deu, 頭, head, the chief, the first.

Deu-fah, 頭髮, hair on the head.

Deu-°ts, 骰子, dice.

Di, 啼, to crow.

°Di, 第, this, the, a series.

°Di-deu, 第頭, here.

°Di-°di, 弟弟, young brethern.

°Di-hyoong, 弟兄, brothers.

°Di-ih, 第一, the first.

°Di-kuh, 第個, this, these.

°Di-mien, 第面, the side, here.

°Di-yang, 第樣, this sort.

Di°, 地, the earth.

Di°-faung, 地方, place.

Di°-jeu, 地球, the earth.

Di°-°li-doo, 地理圖, a map, a chart.

Diau, 條, classifier for long, winding, or limber objects.

Diau°, 調, to exchange, to barter.

Diau°-bi, 調皮, tricky.

Dien, 甜, sweet.

Dih, 笛, a flute.

Dih-'veh-dzu°, 敵勿住, to unable to oppose.

Ding, 停, to stop.

Ding-ih-ding, 停一停, stop a minute.

Doen°-°ts, 緞子, a piece of satin.

Dok, 讀, to read.

Dok-su, 讀書, to study.

Dok-su-nyung, 讀書人, a scholar.

Dok-°z, 獨是, but, only.

Doo, 圖, a map, a chart.

Doo°, 大, large.

Doo°-°siau, 大小, size.

°Doong, 桶, classifier for tubes and buckets, a bucket.

Doong-‘oo, 銅壺, a copper kettle.

Doong, 銅, brass.

Doong, 同, with.

Doong-dien, 銅錢, a cash.

°Doong, 動, lift, to move, to excite.

°Doong, 動, to move a thing.

°Doong-°‘a-’veh-°doong, 動也勿動, immovable.

°Doong-°lau-°doong, 動佬動, loose, unstable.

°Doong-°seu, 動手, to commence work.

°Doong-sung, 動身, to start (on a journey).

Dung°, 鈍, dull.

Dzan-vaung, 棧房, a godown.

Dzan°, 賺, to gain or make a profit.

Dzan°-deu, 賺頭, profit in business.

Dzang, 長, long.

Dzang-bung-°ts, 長盆子, a dish.

Dzang-dzang, 常常, always.

Dzang-°toen, 長短, length.

Dzang-tsaung, 常莊, always.

Dzang-°yoen, 長遠, a long time.

Dzang-°yoen-tse, 長遠哉, a long time.

Dzang-°z, 常是, sometimes.

°Dzang, 丈, ten feet.

Dzau, 潮, tide.

Dzau-°s, 潮水, tide.

Dzaung°, 幢, classifier denoting things piled one on top of the other.

Dze-nga°, 在外, besides, in addition.

Dzeu, 綢, silk.

Dzeu°, 授, to hand, to deliver in person.

Dzien, 錢, 1/10 Of an ounce of silver.

Dzo, 茶, tea.

Dzo, 查, examine carefully.

Dzo-bung-°ts, 茶盆子, saucer.

Dzo-°khau, 查考, to examine carefully.

Dzo-kwen°, 茶館, a tea shop.

Dzo-‘oo, 茶壺, a teapot.

Dzo-yih, 茶葉, tea leaves.

Dzoe-bien°, 隨便, whichever.

Dzoe-bien°-°kyi-z, 隨便幾時, whatever time you please.

Dzoe-bien°-sa°, 隨便啥, whatever, no matter what.

Dzoong, 從, from.

°Dzoong, 重, heavy.

Dzu, 除, to take off (a hat).

Dzu-vaung, 厨房, a kitchen.

Dzu°, 住, to live.

Dzu°-la°, 住拉, to live.

Dzuh-tau°, 直到, until.

Dzung, 層, classifier for stories of a house or ladder.

Dzung, 城, a city.

Dzung-jeu°, 仍舊, still, yet.

Dzung-koong, 成功, to complete.

E

E°, 愛, to love.

En°, 暗, dark.

En°-en°-°li, 暗暗裏, secretly.

'E°, 害, to injure.

'Eh-thien-'au°, 合天下, universal.

'Eu-°ts, 兒子, a son.

'Eu°, 候, after.

°'Eu, 厚, thick.

°'Eu-bok, 厚薄, thickness.

°'Eu-deu, 後頭, behind.

°'Eu-le, 後來, afterwards.

°'Eu-nyih, 後日, day after to-morrow.

°'Eu-°seu, 後首, afterwards.

°'En-°ti, 後底, behind.

°'Eu-°ti-deu, 後底頭, behind.

F

Fah-dze, 發財, to become rich.

Fah-kok, 法國, France.

Fan, 翻, to turn over.

Fan-°tsen-le, 翻轉來, to turn over.

Faung, 方, square.

Faung, 方, one hundred square feet.

Faung-tshak, 方尺, a square foot.

Faung°, 放, to place, let go.

Faung°-'auh, 放學, to dismiss school.

Fi, 飛, to fly.

Fi-theh, 廢脫, to waste.

Fok, 幅, classifier for paintings or engravings.

Fok-chi°, 福氣, happiness.

Foo-tshi, 夫妻, husband and wife.

°Foo-deu, 斧頭, an ax.

Foo°, 付, to pay.

Foong, 封, classifier of letters and sealed parcels.

Foong, 風, wind.

Foong, 封, to seal officially, to seal, to exalt to a high position.

Fung, 分, a cent.

Fung, 分, to separate.

Fung, 分, 1/10 of an inch, 1/10 of a dzien.

Fung-khe, 分開, to separate.

Fung-bih, 分別, a difference; to distinguish.

°**Fung**, 粉, to plaster.

°**Fung-pih**, 粉壁, to plaster a wall.

H

Han-deu, 壖頭, place.

Han°, 喊, to call.

°**Hau**, 好, good, very, superlative.

°**Hau-siau°**, 好笑, laughable.

°**Hau-tse**, 好哉, completed action.

°**Hau-tshu°**, 好處, advantage, profit.

°**Hau-°ziang**, 好像, as if, like.

°**Hoo**, 火, fire.

°**Hoo-dzak-tse**, 火着哉, on fire.

°**Hoo-khaung°**, 火炕, a grate.

°**Hoo-loo**, 火爐, a stove.

°**Hoo-lung-tsho**, 火輪車, a railway engine.

°**Hoo-lung-zen**, 火輪船, a steam boat.

°**Hoo-yak**, 火藥, gunpowder.

Hoo°-suh, 貨色, merchandize.

°**Hoo-yeu**, 火油, kerosene.

Hoong, 烘, to bake.

Huh, 黑, black.

°**Hwaung-°tshia**, 況且, moreover.

Hwe°-ke, 悔改, to repent.

°**Hwe-paung°**, 毀謗, to slander.

Hweh-zen, 忽然, suddenly.

Hwen-°hyi, 歡喜, to like, to enjoy.

Hwo, 花, a flowering plant.

Hwo, 花, cotton, flower.

Hwo-ji, 花萁, cotton stalks.

Hwo-ji-kok, 花旗國, America.

Hwo-‘oong, 花紅, a crab apple.

Hwo-°ts, 花子, cotton seed.

Hwo-°tshau-zu°-mok, 花草樹木, vegetation in general.

Hwo-yoen, 花園, a garden.

°Hyau-tuh, 曉得, to know.

Hyi-ji, 希奇, to wonder, to be surprised.

Hyi°-siau°, 戲笑, to ridicule.

Hyih, 歇, to rest.

Hyih-ih-hyih, 歇一歇, to wait a little.

Hyih-khe-le, 揭開來, to open a box.

Hyoong, 凶, fierce.

Hyoong-°di, 兄弟, a young brother, brothers.

°Hyui, 許, to permit.

Hyuin, 燻, to roast (meat).

I

I-deu, 伊頭, there.

I-°hau, 醫好, to heal.

I-kuh, 伊個, that, those.

I-khwe°, 伊塊, there.

°I-kyung, 已經, already.

I-nyih-°ts, 伊日子, at that time.

I°-s°, 意思, thought, meaning.

I-sung, 醫生, a doctor.

°I-°‘eu, 以後, afterwards, hereafter.

°I-ts°, 以致, so that.

°I-tuh-koo°, 以得過, permissible and proper, leading to no embarrassment.

I°-'veh-koo°, 意勿過, unpermission, because very embarrassing.

I-yoen, 醫院, hospital.

I-zaung, 衣裳, a garment.

Iak-kwe, 約規, about.

Iak-tsak, 約着, about.

Iau°, 要, to want, to wish, will.

Iau°-°kyung-kuh, 要緊個, it is important.

Ien, 烟, tobacco.

Ien-me, 烟煤, soft coal.

Ien-tshoong, 烟囱, a chimney.

°Ien-seu, 演手, to make motions.

Ien°-°ts, 燕子, a swallow.

Ih, 一, a, one.

Ih-dau, 一淘, together, with.

Ih-ding°-iau°, 一定要, must.

Ih-fung, 一分, one cent.

Ih-kauh, 一角, ten cents.

Ih-ngan-'veh, 一顏勿, not at all.

Ih-pak, 一百, one hundred.

Ih-sang-ih-s°, 一生一世, all one's life.

Ih-thaung, 一 [illegible], one time.

Ih-we, 一回, one time.

Iuh-tshu°, 益處, advantage, profit.

Iui°-°ts, 椅子, a chair.

Iung, 鷹, a hawk.

Iung-°hyui, 應許, a promise.

Iung-ke, 應該, ought.

Inng-kok, 英國, England.

Iung-we°, 因爲, because.

J

Jang, 強, cheap.

Jang-dau°, 強盜, a robber.

Jau, 橋, a bridge.

Jau°-foo, 轎夫, a sedan chair coolie.

Jau°-don, 轎班, a sedan chair coolie.

Jau°-°ts, 轎子, a sedan chair.

Jeu, 求, to pray.

Jeu°, 舊, old.

Jeu°-nyien, 舊年, the last year.

Ji, 旗, a flag.

Jien, 掮, carry on the shoulder.

Jien°, 件, classifier of garments, baggage and affairs, an affair.

Juh, 極, forms superlative degree.

°Jui, 跽, to kneel.

°Jung, 近, near.

°Jung, 近, recently.

°Jung-z°-°ngan, 近視眼, near-sighted.

K

Ka, 街, a street.

Ka, 加, to add.

Ka-°hoo, 傢伙, furniture.

Ka-sang, 傢生, tools, implements.

Ka-°thien, 加添, to add.

°Ka, 假, false.

°Ka-seh, 解說, to explain.

Ka°, 鋸, to saw.

Ka°-dien, 價錢, price.

Kah-pih, 隔壁, next (juxtaposition).

Kan, 間, a room.

Kan-nyih-we°, 間日會, will see you in a day or two.

Kau, 高, high.

Kau-°ti, 高底, height.

Kau°, 教, to teach.

Kau°-hwo-°ts, 教花子, a beggar.

Kau°-soo°, 告訴, to tell, to narrate.

Kau°-z°, 告示, a proclamation.

Kauh, 角, a ten cent piece.

Kauh, 各, every.

Kauh-tau°-lauh-°tshu, 各到落處, everywhere.

Kauh-°tshu, 各處, everywhere.

Kaung, 扛, to carry (two men with bamboo pole).

°Kaung, 講, to expound, to explain.

°Kaung-ding°, 講定, to settle the price.

°Kaung-su, 講書, to preach.

Ke°-ts, 鋸子, a saw.

Keh-°lau, 蓋老, therefore.

Keh-ts, 鴿子, a pigeon.

°Keu, 狗, a dog.

Keu°-°z, 彀是, sufficient, enough.

Keu-°z-tse, 彀是哉, sufficient.

Kha, 揩, to wipe.

Kha-mien°-de-°ts, 揩面檯子, a washstand.

°Kha-weh, 快活, happy.

Kha-chi°, 客氣, politeness.

Khak-daung-kan, 客堂間, a guest room.

Khak-nyung, 客人, a guest, a visitor.

Khan, 鉛, lead.

Khan khan, 纔纔, just now, a little while ago.

Khan-pih, 鉛筆, a lead pencil.

Khau, 敲, to knock, strike.

°Khau-°i, 可以, can, may.

°Khau-su, 考書, to examine a class.

Khau°, 靠, to rely upon, to trust.

Khau°-thauh, 靠託, to rely upon, to trust.

Khaung°, 囥, to hide a thing.

Khaung°-°loong, 囥攏, to hide a thing.

Khe, 開, to open, open, opens.

Khe-'auh, 開學, to open school.

Khe-dzang, 開場, a beginning.

Khe-koong, 開工, to commence work.

Khe-le, 開來, to open wide.

Khe nyien, 開年, next year.

Khe-°s, 開水, boiling water.

Kheh-deu, 磕頭, to kowtow.

°Kheu, 口, classifier of furniture.

°Kheu, 口, a mouth.

Khoen°, 看, to see.

Khoen°-°hau, 看好, to heal.

Khoen°-kyien°, 看見, seen.

Khok, 哭, to cry.

Khoo, 棵, classifier of plants, trees, and flowers.

°Khoo, 苦, bitter.

°Khoo-°nau, 苦腦, misery.

Khoo°-°ts, 褲子, trousers.

Khoong-pho°, 恐怕, perhaps.

°Khung, 肯, to be willing.

Koeh, 割, to cut (with a sharp knife).

Koeh-°doen, 割斷, to cut in two.

Koen, 乾, dry.

Koen-mien°, 乾麵, flour.

Koen-po-nyung, 干巴人, a man or two.

Koen-zing°, 乾淨, clean.

°Koen, 趕, to drive away.

°Koen-theh, 趕脫, to drive away.

Koo, 鼓, a drum.

°Koo-z-kan, 古時間, antiquity, anciently.

Koo°, 過, to pass over.

Koo°-i, 故意, purposely.

Koo°-nyien, 過年, to pass from the old to the new year.

Koo°-nyih-°ts, 過日子, some past time.

Koo°-s°, 過世, to die.

Koo°-tse, 過哉, forms past tense.

Koong-dien, 工錢, wages.

Koong-foo, 功夫, time, work.

Koong-°hyi, 恭喜, to congratulate.

Koong-laung, 公郎, a son.

Koong-°tang, 攻打, to attack an enemy.

Koong-°tsoong, 共總, all.

Kuh, 个, or 個, of; sign of the genitive; a general classifier; a final particle.

Kung, 跟, to follow.

Kung, 根, a classifier denoting objects long and generally stiff.

Kung°-ka, 更加, still more.

Kwan, 關, to shut, shut.

Kwaung, 光, smooth, bright.

Kwe-°kyui, 規矩, custom, propriety.

°Kwen, 管, a classifier of tubular things.

Kwen, 官, a mandarin, a magistrate.

Kwen-°foo, 官府, a mandarin, a magistrate.

Kwen-wo°, 官話, mandarin dialect.

Kwen-ze, 棺材, a coffin.

Khwa°, 快, fast, sharp.

Khwa°-khwa°, 快快, quickly.

Khwa°-tse, 快哉, about to do a thing.

Khwan, 筷, chop-sticks.

Khwe°, 塊, a piece, a slice.

Khweh, 闊, broad.

Khweh-‘ah, 闊狹, breadth.

Khwen-°‘eu, 寬厚, to forgive.

Khwen-yoong, 寬容, to forgive.

°**Khwung**, 梱, a classifier denoting bundles of things.

Khwung°, 睏, to sleep.

°**Kwung**, 滾, to boil.

°**Kwung**, 滾, to roll.

°**Kwung-'au°-chi°**, 滾下去, to roll.

Kya-dz, 家慈, a mother.

Kya-°moo, 家母, mother.

Kya-nyien, 家嚴, father.

Kya-°voo, 家父, father.

Kyak, 脚, a foot.

Kyak-tsih-deu, 脚指頭, a toe.

Kyau-kwan, 交關, a great many.

Kyau°, 叫, to call.

°**Kyeu**, 九, nine.

°**Kyeu-seh**, 九十, ninety.

Kyeu°, 救, to save.

Kyi, 鷄, a fowl.

Kyi-dan°-kau, 鷄蛋糕, a sponge cake.

°**Kyi**, 幾, how many?

°**Kyi-hau°**, 幾化, how many

°**Kyi -'oo**, 幾乎, on the point of.

°**Kyi-z**, 幾時, when?

Kyi°, 記, remember.

Kyi°, 寄, to send a letter.

Kyi°, 季, season.

Kyi°-'au°, 記號, signs or marks.

Kyi°-tuh, 記得, to remember.

Kyi°-zen-zeh-ke, 既然實該, if that be so.

Kyoeh-°ts, 橘子 an orange.

Kyui°, 貴, dear (in price).

Kyui° seh-wo°, 句說話, a sentence.

Kyung, 斤, a catty.

Kyung-loo, 金鑼, a gong.

Kyung-nyien, 今年, this year.

Kyung-°seu, 經手, to manage.

Kyung-°ts, 金子, gold.

Kyung-tsau, 今朝, to-day.

Kyung°-°ts, 鏡子, a mirror.

L

La°, 拉, at, in, on, to, sign of past tense.

Lah-tsok, 蠟燭, a candle.

Lan, 籃, a basket.

Lan, 藍, blue.

°Lan-°doo, 懶惰, a lazy.

°Lan-phok, 懶怕, lazy.

°Lang, 冷, cold.

°Lang-nyih, 冷熱, temperature.

°Lang-siau°, 冷笑, to ridicule.

Lau, 牢, firm.

°Lau-zeh, 老實, honest.

°Lau, 佬, and.

°Lau, 老, old, venerable.

°Lau-au, 老鴉, a crow.

°Lau-dzoong, 老蟲, a rat.

°Lau-°hoo, 老虎, a tiger.

°Lau-iung, 老鷹, a hawk.

°Lau-nyung-ka, 老人家, a father.

°Lau-°ts, 老鼠, a rat.

Lauh, 落, to fall.

Lauh-°s, 落水, tide going out.

Lauh-°yui, 落雨, to rain.

Laung-deu, 榔頭, a hammer.

Laung-tsoong, 郎中, doctor.

Laung°, 上, above, upon (used after a noun).

Le, 來, to come.

Le-chi°, 來去, going back and forth.

Le-nyien, 來年, next year.

Le-°si, 來死, used in forming the superlative.

Le-tuh-ji°, 來得及, there is time.

Le-'veh-ji°, 來勿及, there is not time.

Le-°'waung, 來往, intercourse.

Leh-la°, 垃拉, there, in, on, sign of past tense.

Leh-°li, 垃裏, here, sign of present tense.

Leu, 樓, a two-storied house.

Leu-vaung, 樓房, a two-storied house.

Leu, 漏, to leak.

Li, 釐, a li (in currency).

Li-khe, 離開, to forsake, desert, depart from.

°Li, 里, a Chinese mile.

°Li, 裏, in (used after noun).

°Li-hyang°, 裏向, in (used after noun).

°Li-loo°, 里路, a Chinese mile.

°Li-pa°, 禮拜, a week.

°Li-pa°-daung, 禮拜堂, a church.

°Li-pa°-ih, 禮拜一, Monday.

°Li-pa°-lok, 禮拜六, Saturday.

°Li-pa°-°ng, 禮拜五, Friday.

°Li-pa°-nyi°, 禮拜二, Tuesday.

°Li-pa°-nyih, 禮拜日, Sunday.

°Li-pa°-s°, 禮拜四, Thursday.

°Li-pa°-san, 禮拜三, Wednesday.

Liang, 量, to measure.

°Liang, 兩, two.

°Liang, 兩, an ounce.

°**Liang-kauh**, 兩角, twenty cents.

°**Liang-thaung**, 兩遍, two times, twice.

°**Liang-we**, 兩回, two times, twice.

Liang°, 亮, light (opposite of dark).

lih, 立, to stand up.

Lih-ding°, 立定, to stand still.

Lih-ding°-°tsu-i°, 立定主意, to decide.

Lih-khuh, 立刻, instantaneous.

Ling, 拎, to carry a load in one hand.

Ling, 紉, to sew, to stitch.

Ling-ih-tsung, 紉一針, to take a stitch.

Ling-sak, 淋濕, to get wet.

Ling-°so, 鄰舍, a neighbor.

°**Ling**, 領, to lead.

Ling°-daung, 令堂, a mother.

Ling°-e°, 令嫒, a daughter.

Ling°-laung, 令郎, a son.

Ling-nga°, 另外, besides, in addition.

Ling°-tsung, 令尊, a father.

Lok, 六, six.

Lok, 趢, to get up.

Lok, 綠, green.

Lok, 鹿, a deer.

Lok-seh, 六十, sixty.

Lok-tsen, 磟磚, a brick.

Loo°, 路, a road.

Loong, 龍, a dragon.

°**Loong-°tsoong**, 攏總, all.

Loong°, 弄, to attend to a thing, to make it right.

Loong°-°hau, 弄好, to attend to a thing, to make it right.

Loong°-khe-°hoo-lo, 弄開火來, to set a house on fire.

M

M-meh, 無沒, not any.

M-sa°, 無啥, not any.

M-sa°-nyung, 無啥人, no one.

°**M**, 畝, a mow.

°**Ma**, 買, to buy.

°**Ma-ban°**, 買辦, a compradore.

°**Ma-ma°**, 買賣, business.

Ma°, 賣, to sell.

°'**Ma-theh**, 賣脫, to sell.

Mah, 襪, socks, stockings.

Mak, 麥, a plant of wheat.

Man°, 慢, slow.

Man°, 萬, ten thousand.

Man°-chi°, 慢去, good-by.

Man°-man°-nung, 慢慢能, slowly, gently.

Man°-man°-ts-°tseu, 慢慢之走, walk slowly.

'**Man**, 蠻, very.

Mau, 毛, nearly.

Mau, 毛, rough.

Mau, 貓, a cat.

Mau-bing°, 毛病, illness.

Mau-san-°li-loo°, 毛三里路, nearly three miles.

Mau-tsen, 毛氈, a carpet.

Mau°-°ts, 帽子, a hat, cap.

Maung°, 望, to desire, to expect.

Maung°, 望, to visit, to pay respects to.

Maung°-deu, 望頭, hope.

Maung°-kyi°, 忘記, to forget.

Me, 煤, coal.

°'**Me**, 每, each.

°**Me-kok**, 美國, America.

°'**Me-nyien**, 每年, every year.

°'**Me-nyoeh**, 每月, every month.

Me°-me°, 妹妹, a younger sister.

Meh, 末, at last, end, interrogative particle, a negative, a conditional particle.

Meh-z°, 物事, an affair (concrete), a thing.

Men-deu, 饅頭, bread.

°**Mi**, 米, rice (bought in shop).

Miau°, 廟, a temple.

Mien-hwo, 棉花, cotton.

Mien°, 面, classifier of flat objects.

Mien° bung, 面盆, a washbowl.

Mien°-°khoong, 面孔, a face.

Ming-bak, 明白, to understand.

Ming-nyien, 明年, next year.

Ming-tsau, 明朝, to-morrow.

Ming-vung°, 名分, duty.

Mo-tshiak, 麻雀, a sparrow.

Mo-tsiang, 麻 雀 a sparrow.

°**Mo**, 馬, a horse.

°**Mo-deu**, 碼頭, a jetty.

°**Mo-foo**, 馬夫, a coachman.

°**Mo-tsho**, 馬車, a carriage.

Mok, 摸, to feel, to touch.

Mok-deu, 木頭, wood, lumber.

Mok-ziang, 木匠, a carpenter.

Moo, 磨, to sharpen.

°**Moo-tshing**, 母親, a mother.

Muh, 墨, ink.

Muh-°s, 墨水, foreign ink.

Mung, 門, a door.

Mung-°kheu, 門口, doorway.

Mung-°kheu-deau, 門口頭, a doorway.

Mung-°ts, 蚊子, a mosquito.

Mung°, 問, to ask.

N

°Na-nung, 那能, how.

°Na-yeu, 奶油, butter.

Na°, 伲, you, ye.

Na°-kuh, 伲個, your, yours.

Nan, 難, difficult.

Nan-meh, 難末, then.

Nan-we-dzing, 難爲情, to regret, to be placed in an embarrassing position.

Nau, 拿, to take.

Nau-ehi°, 拿去, to take away.

Nau-le, 拿來, to bring here.

Nau-theh, 拿脫, to take off.

Nen, 南, south.

Nen, 男, male.

°Ng, 五, five.

°Ng-ngan-lok-suh, 五顔六色, variegated colours.

°Ng-seh, 五十, fifty.

Nga°, 外, out.

Nga°-deu, 外頭, out, outside.

Nga°-kok, 外國, foreign.

Nga°-kok-nyung, 外國人, a foreigner.

Ngan-suh, 顔色, colour.

°Ngan-kyung°, 眼鏡, spectacles.

°Ngan-tsing, 眼睛, an eye.

Ngang°, 硬, hard.

°Ngau, 咬, to bite, to bark.

Nge°-sa°-va°, 碍啥否, is it important?

Ngeh-°ts, 杌子, a stool.

°Ngeu-zen, 偶然, by chance.

Ngoo, 鵝, a goose.

Ngoo-kok, 俄國, Russia.

Ngoo-kok-nyung, 俄國人, Russians.

°Ngoo, 我, I, me.

°Ngoo-han-deu, 我壗頭, my place.

°Ngoo-kuh, 我個, mine, my.

°Ngoo-nyi°, 我伲, we, us.

°Ngoo-nyi°-kuh, 我伲個, ours, our.

°Noen, 暖, warm.

Noen°, 囡, daughter.

Noong°, 儂, thou, thee, you.

Noong°-kuh, 儂個, they, thine, yours.

Nung-keu°, 能穀, can, may.

Nung-koen°, 能幹, ability, power.

Nyah, 捻, to take bold of, to grasp.

Nyan°, 念 or 廿, twenty.

Nyan°-kyung, 念經, perform funeral ceremonies.

Nyang, 娘, mother.

Nyang°, 讓, to allow.

Nyau-so°, 饒赦, to forgive.

Nyeu, 牛, a cow.

Nyeu-°na, 牛奶, milk.

°Nyeu-°ts, 鈕子, a button.

Nyi, 呢, interrogative particle.

°Nyi-kwaung, 耳光, face (cheek).

Nyi-koo, 尼姑, nun.

Nyi-°s-ziang°, 泥水匠, a mason.

Nyi-°ts, 兒子, a son.

°Nyi-°too, 耳朵, the ear.

Nyi°, 伲, we, us.

Nyi°, 二, two.

Nyi°-kuh, 伲個, ours, our.

Nyi° seh, 二十, twenty.

Nyien, 年, a year.

Nyien-deu-laung°, 年頭上, the beginning of the year.

Nyien-nyien, 年年, every year.

Nyien-°ti, 年底, the end of the year.

Nyien-tshoo-ih, 年初一, New Year's day.

Nyien-ya°, 年夜, the end of the year.

Nyien°-de, 硯台, a Chinese ink tablet.

Nyien°-°ts, 硯子, a Chinese ink tablet.

Nyih, 日, a day, the sun.

Nyih, 熱, hot.

Nyih-dzok, 日昨, daily.

Nyih-nyih, 日日, daily.

Nyih-tsoong°, 日中, noon, in the middle of the day.

Nyoeh, 月, a month, a moon.

Nyoeh-deu, 月頭, first part of a month.

Nyoeh-deu-laung°, 月頭上, first part of a month.

Nyoeh-liang°, 月亮, the moon.

Nyoeh-nyoeh, 月月, every month.

Nyoeh-pen°, 月半, the middle of the month.

Nyoeh-°ti, 月底, the end of a month.

°Nyoen, 軟, soft.

Nyoen-liang°, 原諒, to forgive.

Nyok, 肉, meat.

°Nyui-nyung, 女人, a woman.

Nyung, 人, man.

Nyung-'aung, 銀行, a bank.

Nyung-deu, 人頭, a postage stamp.

Nyung°-tsih, 迎接, to welcome.

Nyung-°ts, 銀子, silver.

Nyung°-tuh, 認得, to know a person.

O

Oen-we°, 安慰, to comfort.

Ok-°li, 屋裏, home.

‘Ok-tse, 或着, either, or.

‘Ok-°z, 或是, either, or.

‘Oh-hwaung, 何況, how much more?

‘Oo-zaung°, 和尚, a Buddhist priest.

‘Oo, 壺, a kettle.

‘Oo, 河, river.

‘Oo-dih, 蝴蝶, a butterfly.

‘Oo-li, 狐狸, a fox.

‘Oong, 紅, red.

P

Pa, 擺, to place.

Pa°, 拜, to worship.

Pa°-khak, 拜客, to pay a ceremonial visit.

Pa°-maung°, 拜望, to visit, to pay respects to.

Pah, 八, eight.

Pah-seh, 八十, eighty.

Pak, 百, a hundred.

Pak-pak, 伯伯, father.

Pak-po, 百巴, about a hundred.

Pan, 班, a class (in school).

°Pan, 板, a board.

Pang, 浜, a canal, a creek.

Pau, 包, a bale, classifier of bales of things.

°Pau-pe°, 寶貝, precious.

°Paung, 綁, to tie up, to bind with a cord.

Pe-°ts, 杯子, a cup.

Pe°, 背, to carry on the back.

Pe°, 背, to back a book, to recite a lesson.

Peh, 撥, to give.

Peh, 撥, used to form passive.

Pen, 搬, to remove (a residence).

Pen-dzang, 搬場, to remove (a residence).

Pen°, 半, half.

Pan°-kwhe°-yang-dien, 半塊洋錢, a half of a dollar.

Pen°-nyien, 半年, half a year.

Pen°-ya°-po, 半夜巴, about midnight.

Phau°, 炮, a cannon.

Phau°-de, 炮台, a fort, a battery.

Phi-bing, 批評, to criticize, criticism.

Phi-thah, 批搨, to criticize, criticism.

Phih, 劈, to split.

Phih, 疋, a classifier of whole pieces of dry goods.

Phih, 匹, classifier of horses.

Pho°, 怕, ugly.

Phoo°-ke, 鋪蓋, bedding.

°Phoo-thien-'au°, 普天下, universal.

°Pi, 比, to compare.

°Pi-faung, 比方, for instance, an illustration.

°Pi-ts, 比之 it to compare.

°Piau, 錶, a watch.

Pien-deu, 邊頭, by the side of.

Pih, 筆, a pen.

Pih, 必, certain.

Pih-ding-iau°, 必定要, must.

Pih-koo°, 不過, only.

Ping-ting, 兵丁, a soldier.

°Ping-°tshia, 幷且, moreover.

Po-maung°, 把望, to desire, to expect, to hope.

Po, 巴, about.

°**Po**, 把, classifier of tools and articles grasped in the hand.

Pok, 北, north.

Pok-pien, 北邊, north.

Poo-li, 玻璃, glass.

Poo-li-pe-°ts, 玻璃杯子, a tumbler, a glass.

Poo°, 布, cloth.

°**Pung**, 本, classifier of books.

°**Pung-di°**, 本地, native.

°**Pung-di°-nyung**, 本地人, a native.

°**Pung-le**, 本來, originally.

R

R-°tshia, 而且, moreover.

S

°**S**, 水, water.

°**S-nyeu**, 水牛, a water buffalo.

S°, 使, to cause.

S°, 四, four.

S°-kyi°, 四季, the four seasons.

S°-seh, 四十, forty.

Sa-doo, 弛瘏, tired.

Sa, 啥, who? what? any? interrogative particle.

Sa°-'aung-dzing, 啥行情, how much is it? what is the price?

Sa°-di°-faung, 啥地方, where?

Sa°-dzang-hau°, 啥場化, where?

Sa°-ka°-dien, 啥價錢, how much is it?

Sa°-nyung, 啥人, who?

°**Sa-°'oo-daung**, 啥戶蕩, where?

Sah, 殺, to kill.

Sah-theh, 殺脫, to kill.

Sak, 閂, the bolt or bar of a door.

Sak, 濕, wet.

San, 三, three.

San, 山, a mountain, a hill.

San-dzung-leu, 三層樓, a three-storied house.

San-seh, 三十, thirty.

San-yang, 山羊, a goat.

San°, 傘, an umbrella.

San°-khe, 散開, to scatter wide cast.

San°-sing, 散心, to relax the mind.

Sang, 生, to light (a fire), to beget.

Sang, 生, unripe, raw.

Sang-bing°, 生病, to become ill.

Sang-i°, 生意, business.

Sang-li, 生梨, a pear.

Sang°-yang, 生養, to beget, to nourish.

°Sang, 省, to save, to be economical.

°Sang-koong-foo, 省工夫, to save time.

°Sang-ts, 省之, lest.

Sau, 燒, to burn, to cook.

Sau-van°-kan, 燒飯間, a kitchen.

Sau-van°-kuh, 燒飯個, a cook.

°Sau, 少, few.

°Sau-°tseu, 掃箒, a broom.

Saung, 雙, classifier for pairs of things.

Saung, 傷, to waste, to be exhausted.

Saung-liang, 商量, to consult.

Se°, 碎, to smash.

Seh, 失, to lose, to forfeit.

Seh, 刷, to brush.

Seh-theh, 失脫, to lose, to forfeit.

Seh-wo°, 說話, words.

Sen, 閂, to bar or bolt a door.

Sen°, 扇, classifier for broad objects.

Sen°-°ts, 扇子, a fan.

Seu, 收, to collect.

Seu-diau, 收條, a receipt.

Seu-kan, 收監, to be imprisoned.

Seu-phiau°, 收票, a receipt.

Seu-tsang°, 收帳, to collect accounts.

Sen-tsoo, 收租, to receive payment for a lease.

°Seu, 守, to keep, to observe.

°Seu, 手, a hand.

°Seu-kyung, 手巾, a towel.

Seu°, 瘦, thin, lean.

Si, 西, west.

Si-nen, 西南, southwest.

Si-pien, 西邊, west.

Si-pok, 西北, northwest.

°Si, 死, to die.

Si-theh, 死脫, to die.

Si°-tse°, 西崽, a table boy.

°Sia, 寫, to write.

°Sia-z°-de, 寫字檯, an office desk.

°Sia-z°-de-°ts, 寫字檯子, an office desk.

°Sia-z°-kan, 寫字間, an office.

Siang, 箱, classifier for boxes of things.

Siang-e°, 相愛, to love reciprocally.

Siang-lien, 相連, to be connected together.

Siang-mo°, 想罵, to quarrel.

Siang-paung, 相幫, to help one another.

Siang-sing°, 相信, to believe.

Siang-°tang, 相打, to fight one another.

Siang-°ts, 箱子, a trunk, a large box.

°Siang, 想, to think.

°Siang-'veh-tau°, 想勿到, inconceivable.

°Siau, 小, small.

°Siau-kauh-°ts, 小角子, small money.

°Siau-noen, 小囝, a child.

°Siau-sing, 小心, to take care.

°Siau-tsho, 小車, wheelbarrow.

°Siau-tshe°, 小菜, vegetables, dishes of food on table.

°Siau-tsia, 小姐, an unmarried woman.

°Siau-yang-dien, 小洋錢, small money.

Siau°, 笑, to laugh.

Siau°-sah-tse, 笑殺哉, very laughable.

Sien, 先, first.

Sien-sang, 先生, a teacher.

Sieu, 修, to repair.

Sieu-°li, 修理, repairs.

Sieu-tsauh, 修作, to repair.

Sih, 錫, tin.

Sing, 新, new.

Sing, 心, the heart.

Sing, 星, a star.

Sing-foong°, 薪俸, salary.

Sing-nyien, 新年, the new year.

Sing-sien, 新鮮, fresh.

Sing-°soe, 薪水, salary.

Sing-vung-°ts, 新聞紙, a newspaper.

Sing°, 信, a letter.

Sing°-°foong, 信封, an envelope.

Sing°-jok, 信局 post office (foreign).

Sing°-khauh, 信殼, an envelope.

Sing°-ming°, 性命, a life.

Sing°-sih, 信息, news.

°**So-°ng**, 十五, fifteen.

Soe-°z, 雖是, although.

Soe-zen, 雖然, although.

Soen°, 算, to reckon.

Sok-sieu, 束修, salary.

Soo-tseu, 蘇州, Soochow.

°**Soo**, 鑕, a lock.

°**Soo**, 所, relative pronoun—who, which, what.

°**Soo**, 鎖, to lock.

°**Soo**, 數, to count.

°**Soo-°i**, 所以, therefore.

Soong-°su, 松鼠, a squirrel.

Soong°, 送, to present, send, to escort a person on the way.

Su, 書, a book.

Su-dzu, 書厨, a bookcase.

Su-sing°-°kwen, 書信管, post office (foreign).

Su-°tsang, 輸張, to nurse.

Su-vaung, 書房, a study.

Su-yoen°, 書院, a college.

Suh, 識, to know a Chinese character.

Suh-i°, 適意, comfortable.

Sung, 深, deep.

Sung-°thi, 身體, the body.

Sung-°tshien, 深淺, depth.

T

Ta-z-tse, 多時哉, a long time.

Ta°, 戴, to wear (a hat).

Ta°-chi°, 帶去, to take away with you.

Ta°-le, 帶來, to bring with you.

Tah, 搭, with.

Tah-ts, 搭之, and.

Tan, 擔, to take.

Tan-°bi, 單被, a sheet.

Tan-chi°, 擔去, to take away.

Tan-le, 擔來, to bring here.

Tan-theh, 擔脫, to take away.

Tan°, 擔, a picul.

°Tang, 打, to strike.

°Tang-ba°, 打敗, to suffer a defeat.

°Tang-ba°-tsang°, 打敗仗, to suffer a defeat.

°Tang-°bang, 打棚, to fool with another.

°Tang-fan, 打翻, to upset (water).

°Tang-kwen-s, 打官司, to prosecute at law.

°Tang-lah, 打臘, to hunt.

°Tang-lih, 打獵, to hunt.

°Tang-pan°, 打扮, to dress in a showy manner.

°Tang-sah, 打殺, to kill by a blow.

°Tang-saung, 打傷, to wound.

°Tang-se°, 打碎, to smash, to break.

°Tang-soen°, 打算, to consider.

°Tang-su, 打輸, to suffer a defeat.

°Tang-sung°-tsang°, 打勝仗, to gain a victory.

°Tang-thing, 打聽, to make inquiries.

°Tang-tsang°, 打仗, to fight a battle.

°Tang-wa°, 打壞, to injure by striking.

°Tang-yung, 打贏, to gain a victory.

Tau, 刀, knife.

°Tau, 倒, on the contrary, on the other hand.

Tau°, 到, to, to arrive.

°Tau-kau°, 禱告, to offer prayer.

Taung-tsoong, 當中, among.

Taung-sing, 當心, to take care.

Taung°, 當, to pawn.

Taung°-theh, 當脫, to pawn.

Te, 堆, classifier for piles of things.

Te°, 對, classifier of a brace, a pair.

Te°, 對, to.

Teu°-ba, 鬪牌, to gamble (with dominoes).

Thah, 塔, a pagoda.

Thah-°ping, 餲餅, a biscuit.

Than-khe-le, 攤開來, to unroll.

Than-°tshoong, 坍寵, shameful.

Than°, 炭, charcoal.

°Thau, 討, to beg.

°Thau-nyang-°ts, 討娘子, to marry a wife.

°Thau-vah°-kun, 討飯個, a beggar.

Thauh, 託, to rely upon, to entrust.

Thaung, 湯, soup.

°Thaung-s°, 倘使, if.

°Thaung-zen, 倘然, if.

Thaung°, 燙, to iron, to burn, to scald.

The°, 退, to reject.

The°-theh, 退脫, to reject.

Theh, 脫, after verb a sign of completed action.

Theu, 偷, to steal.

Theu-ben°-ts, 偷伴之, secretly.

Thi°, 替, instead of.

Thiau, 挑, to carry (a load suspended from ends of a pole).

Thiau°, 跳, to jump, to leap.

Thien, 天, heaven, a day.

Thien-bing, 天平, scales.

Thien-liang°-khwa°, 天亮快, just before daybreak.

Thien-°tsu, 天主, The Heavenly Lord.

Thih, 鐵, iron.

Thih-tsau°, 鐵竈, a cooking stove (foreign).

Thih-°tsung, 貼准, on the point of (doing a thing).

Thing, 聽, to hear.

Thing-kyien°, 聽見, heard.

Thoeh, 脫, to take off.

Thoeh-theh, 脫脫, to take off.

Thok, 禿, all.

Thoo°-°ts, 兔子, a hare.

Thoong°, 痛, pain.

Thuh, 忒, for (for a person).

Thuh, 忒, too (excess).

°Ti, 底, low.

°Ti-°‘au, 底下, under, beneath.

Tia-tia, 爹爹, father.

°Tiau, 鳥, a bird.

°Tien, 點, to point with the hand.

°Tien, 點, a small quantity of (after verb).

°Tien, 點, to light (a candle).

°Tien, 點, sign of comparative degree.

°Tien-tsoong, 點鐘, an hour.

Tien°, 店, a shop.

Tih, 跌, to fall.

Ting, 叮, to sting.

°Ting, 頂, sign of superlative degree.

°Toen, 短, short

Too, 多, many, much.

Too-hau°, 多化, many, much.

Too-°sau, 多少, quantity.

Too-°taung-sing, 多當心, take much care.

°Too, 賭, to gamble.

Toong, 東, east.

Toong, 冬, winter.

Toong-ka, 東家, master.

Toong-nen, 東南, southeast.

Toong-pien, 東邊, east.

Toong-pok, 東北, northeast.

Toong-yang-nyung, 東洋人, Japanese.

Toong-yang-tsho, 東洋車, a ricksha.

°**Toong**, 懂, to understand.

Ts-loo, 猪玀, a pig, a hog.

Ts-°na, 支那, China.

°**Ts**, 紙, a sheet of paper.

°**Ts-deu**, 紙頭, a sheet of paper.

°**Ts-si**°, 仔細, carefully.

°**Ts-°tien**, 指點, to point (with the hand).

Tsah, 扎, to tie (as a small bundle).

Tsak, 着, to wear.

Tsak, 隻, classifier of animals, birds, bugs, boats, furniture on legs, etc.

Tsan, 斬, to cut (with sword, ax, or heavy knife).

Tsang, 張, classifier for sheets of things.

Tsang, 賬, an account.

Tsang°, 漲, to rise (as the tide).

Tsang°-°boo, 賬簿, an account book.

Tsang°-°s, 漲水, a rising tide.

Tsang°-°vaung-kan, 賬房間, shroff's room.

°**Tsau**, 早, early.

°**Tsau-deu**, 找頭, change.

°**Tsau-zung-deu**, 早晨頭, early in the morning.

Tsau°, 照, according to.

Tsau°-deu, 灶頭, a Chinese cooking stove.

Tsau°-kan, 灶間, a kitchen.

Tsau°-°ngoo, 照我, follow my example.

Tsau°-°ngoo-khoen°, 照我看, as it seems to me.

Tsauh, 捉, to catch, to seize; to arrest.

Tsaung, 樁, piles (as driven in ground).

Tsaung°, 壯, fat (person).

Tse, 哉, final article denoting completed action.

Tse°, 再, again.

Tse°-we°, 再會, good-by, an revoir.

°Tsen-chi°, 轉去, to return to a place.

°Tsen-le, 轉來, to return from a place.

°Tseu, 走, to walk.

Tsh, 吹 to blow.

Tsh-°iung, 吹隱, to blow out, to extinguish.

Tsh-yaung°, 吹旺, to blow into a blaze.

°Tsh-di°, 此地, here.

Tsha, 差, to send (person), to cause.

°Tsha, 扯, to hoist (as a sail).

Tshak°, 尺, a foot (10 inches).

Tshau, 匙, a spoon.

°Tshau, 草, grass.

Tshaung, 窗, a window.

°Tshe, 採, to gather (as fruit).

Tshe°, 菜, vegetable.

Tsheh-chi°, 出去, to go out.

Tsheh-ka°, 出嫁, to marry (a husband).

Tsheh-kau°-z°, 出告示, to put forth a proclamation.

Tsheh-le, 出來, to come out.

Tsheh-tien°, 出店, a coolie.

Tshen, 穿, to string (as cash).

Tshen-°yung-sien°, 穿引線, to thread a needle.

Tsheu-deu, 抽頭, a chest of drawers.

Tsheu-thi°, 抽屜, a drawer (of a table).

Tshi°, 砌, to build a wall.

Tshi°-ziang, 砌牆, to build a wall.

Tshi°-pih, 砌壁, to build a partition.

Tshi°-ka, 砌街, to mend a path.

°Tshiang, 搶, to take by force.

°Tshiang-doeh, 搶奪, to take by force.

Tshien, 千, a thousand.

Tshien-kyung, 千金, a daughter.

Tshien, 淺, shallow.

Tshieu, 秋, autumn.

Tshih, 七, seven.

Tshih-khe, 切開, to cut open.

Tshih-khe-le, 切開來, to cut open.

Tshih-seh, 七十, seventy.

Tshih-ziang°, 漆匠, a painter.

Tshing, 清, clear.

Tshing-kyoen°, 親眷, a relative (family).

Tshing-°saung, 清爽, clear, distinct.

°Tshing, 請, to invite, please.

Tsho, 叉, fork.

Tsho, 錯, mistake, not correct.

Tsho-foo, 車夫, ricksha coolie.

Tsho-°ts, 車子, a wheelbarrow.

Tsho-'veh-too, 差勿多, about same, not much difference.

Tshoo-ih, 初一, the first day of the month.

Tshoo-si°, 粗細, texture.

Tshoo°-tau, 銼刀, a file.

Tshoong-ming, 聰明, clever, wise.

Tshui°, 趣, pretty.

Tshung, 春, spring.

Tshung, 稱, to weigh.

Tshung°, 寸, an inch.

°Tsi-me, 姐妹, a younger sister.

Tsi°, 左, left.

Tsi°-°seu, 左手, left hand.

Tsia°, 借, to borrow, to lend.

Tsiang-iau°, 將要, about to do a thing.

Tsien, 煎, to grill, to broil.

°Tsien-tau, 剪刀, scissors.

°Tsieu, 酒, wine.

°Tsieu-pe, 酒杯, a wine glass.

°Tsieu-tien°, 酒店, a wine shop.

Tsih-deu, 指頭, a finger.

°Tsing, 井, a well.

Tsing°, 進, to enter, come in.

Tsoe°-°hau, 最好, form of the superlative degree.

Tsok-deu, 竹頭, a bamboo stick.

°Tsoo, 阻, to hinder, to oppose.

°Tsoo-taung°, 阻檔, to hinder, to oppose.

°Tsoo, 左, left.

Tsoo°, 做, to do, to make, to perform.

Tsoo°-koong-tuh, 做功德, to perform funeral ceremonies.

Tsoo°-nyung-ka, 做人家, to be economical.

Tsoong, 鐘, a bell.

Tsoong°-dien-nyung, 種田人, a farmer.

°Tsoong-iau°, 總要, must.

Tsoong-kok, 中國, China.

Tsoong-wo, 中華, China.

Tsoong-°z, 總是, it must be.

°Tsoong-°z-zeh-ke°, 總是實蓋, it must be so.

°Tsu, 主, a lord, master.

°Tsu-nyung, 主人, a master.

Tsuh-tuh, 只得, only.

Tsung, 尊, classifier for idols and cannons.

Tsung, 針, needle.

Tsung, 眞, true.

Tsung-da°-zung, 尊大人, a father (in addressing their father politely).

Tsung-tsak, 斟酌, to consult.

Tuh, 得, to get.

Tuh-°chi, 得起, after verb expresses ability.

Tuh-°doong, 得動, after verb expresses possibility.

Tuh-°dzoe, 得罪, to offend.

Tuh-dzu°, 得住, worthy, ability.

Tuh-ji°, 得及, time to do a thing.

Tuh-kok, 德國, Germany.

Tuk-koo°, 得過, ability.

Tuh-kuh, 得個, (after verb) it is possible.

Tuh-kyien°, 得見, possible of seeing.

Tuh-lauh, 得落, ability.

Tuh-le, 得來, able.

Tuh-tsheh, 得出, ability to hear.

Tung, 燈, a lamp.

°Tung, 等, to wait.

°Tung-ih-hyih, 等一歇, wait a little.

°Tung-ih-°tung, 等一等, wait a little.

°Tung-tau°, 等到, wait until.

V

Va°, 否, interrogative particle.

Van-°i, 凡係, whosoever.

Van-nan, 煩難, difficult.

Van°, 飯 rice (boiled).

Vaung-kan, 房間, a bedroom.

Vaung-°ts, 房子, a house.

’Veh, 勿, not, no.

Veh, 佛, a Buddhist idol.

’Veh-°ba, 勿罷, not only.

’Veh-°ba, 勿罷, more than.

’Veh-°chi, 勿起, after verb expresses inability.

’Veh-da°, 勿大, not very.

'Veh-dan°, 勿但, not only.

'Veh-dan°-°z, 勿但是, not only.

'Veh-°doong, 勿動, after verb expresses impossibility.

'Veh-hau°, 勿好, bad.

'Veh-iau°-°kyung, 勿要緊, not important.

'Veh-jih, 勿及, not equal to.

'Veh-kau-hyung°, 勿高興, not inclined to do a thing.

'Veh-koo°, 勿過, inability.

'Veh-kyien°, 勿見, (after verb) impossible.

'Veh-kyui-sa°, 勿拘啥, no matter what, whatsoever.

'Veh-lauh, 勿落, inability.

'Veh-le, 勿來, (after verb) impossible.

'Veh-lung°-sa°, 勿論啥, no matter what, whatsoever.

'Veh-lung°-sa°-nyung, 勿論啥人, no matter who.

'Veh-°men, 勿滿, less than.

'Veh-nge°-sa°, 勿碍啥, not important.

'Veh-pih, 勿必, it is not necessary.

'Veh-siau, 勿消, less than.

'Veh-te°, 勿對, mistake, not correct.

'Veh-too-°kyi-z°, 勿多幾時, just now, a little while ago.

'Veh-tsheh, 勿出, (after verb) impossible.

'Veh-tuh, 勿得, (after verb) impossible.

'Veh-zen-meh, 勿然末, if not so.

'Veh-zu, 勿如, not equal to.

'Veh-zung, 勿曾, not yet.

Vok, 縛, to tie.

Vok-lau, 縛牢, to tie firmly.

Vok-lau-dzu°, 縛牢住, to tie firmly.

Voo-°soo-peh-°dze, 無所不在, omnipresence.

Voo-°soo-peh-nung, 無所不能, omnipotent.

Voo-°soo-peh-ts°, 無所不如, omniscient.

Voo-thi, 扶梯, a ladder.

°**Voo-tshing**, 父親, father.

Vung-san, 墳山, a grave mound.

W

Wa°, 壞, to spoil.

Wa°-theh, 壞脫, to spoil.

Wah, 滑, slippery.

Wak, 劃, to strike (a match).

Wan, 還, besides, in addition.

Wan, 還, still, (addition).

Wan, 還, to return (a debt).

Wan-iau°, 還要, still.

Wan-'veh-zung, 還勿曾, still not yet.

Waung, 黃, yellow.

Waung-hwung-deu, 黃昏頭, in the evening.

Waung-hwung-doong, 黃昏同, in the evening.

Waung-laung, 黃狼, a weasel.

We-deu, 回頭, to answer.

We-tah, 回答, to answer.

We°, 會, may, can.

We°-sa°, 為啥, why?

We°-sa°-°lau, 為啥佬, why?

We°-ts, 為之, because.

Weh, 活, to live.

°'**Wen**, 碗, a Chinese eating bowl.

Wen, 完, to finish.

Wen-tse, 完哉, expresses completed action.

Wen°, 換, to exchange, to barter.

Wo°, 話, to speak.

Wo°, 畫, a painting.

Wo°-deu, 話頭, words.

Wo°-°liau, 話殰, to slander.

Wo°-wa°, 話壞, to slander.

°**Wung**, 混, muddy.

°'**Wung-taung°**, 穩當, secure, safe.

Y

Ya, 爺, father.

Ya-ya, 爺爺, father.

°**Ya-kyi**, 野雞, a pheasant.

Ya°, 夜, night.

Ya°-deu, 夜頭, at night.

Ya°-khwa°, 夜快, in the evening.

Ya°-°li, 夜裏, at night.

Yak, 藥, medicine.

Yak-dz, 鑰匙, a key.

Yang, 羊, a sheep.

Yang-dien, 洋錢, a dollar.

Yang-poo°, 洋布, shirting.

Yang-tshiang, 洋槍, a gun.

°**Yang**, 養, to beget, to nourish.

Yang°-yang°, 樣樣, things of every sort.

Yau-yien, 謠言, rumour.

Yeu-phiau, 郵票, postage stamp.

Yeu-tsung°-jok, 郵政局, post office.

°**Yeu**, 有, to have, there is.

°**Yeu-i°**, 有意, purposely.

°**Yeu-kuh**, 有個, some.

°**Yeu-nyung**, 有人, some men.

Yeu-tse, 有哉, sufficient, enough.

°**Yeu-tuh**, 有得, is there to be had?

Yeu°, 右, right (direction).

Yeu°-pan-pan, 右班班, right side.

Yeu°-pien, 右邊, right side.

Yeu°-°seu, 右手, right hand.

Yi, 伊, he, she, it.

Yien, 鹽, salt (noun).

Yi-kuh, 伊個, his, hers, its.

Yi-la°, 伊拉, they.

Yi-la°-kuh, 伊拉個, their, theirs.

Yien°-°dze, 現在, now.

Yoeh-ka, 越加, still more.

Yoeh-°tsau-yoeh-°hau, 越早越好, the earlier the better.

Yoen, 圓, round.

°Yoen-°jung, 遠近, distance.

Yoong-yi°, 容易, easy.

Yoong°, 用, to use.

Yoong°-nyung, 用人, a servant.

Yoong°-sing, 用心, to pay attention, to be diligent.

Yui°-be°, 預備, to prepare, to provide.

°Yui, 雨, rain.

Z

Z-'eu°, 時候, time.

°Z, 是, to be.

°Z-mien°, 市面, a market.

Z°, 字, a Chinese character.

Z°-iung, 字音, sound of a character.

Z°-ka, 自家, self.

Z°-le-°hoo, 自來火, a match.

Z°-ming-tsoong, 自鳴鐘, a clock.

Z°-°thi, 事體, an affair.

Z°-zen, 自然, of course.

Za, 柴, fuel.

Za-laung, 豺狼, a wolf.

Zah, 煠, boil.

Zak, 若, if.

Zak-deu, 石頭, a stone.

Zak-deu-°ts, 擲骰子, to gamble (with dice).

Zak-s°, 若是, if.

Zak-zen, 若然, if.

Zak-ziang°, 石匠, a stone mason.

°Zau, 造, to build.

Zauh-nyih, 昨日, yesterday.

Zaung, 牀, a bed.

°Zaung, 上, up.

°Zaung-chi°, 上去, to go up.

°Zaung-deu, 上頭, above.

°Zaung-°he, 上海, Shanghai.

°Zaung-°he-°thoo-bak, 上海土白, Shanghai dialect.

°Zaung-le, 上來, to come up.

°Zaung-pen°-nyien, 上半年, first half of the year.

°Zaung-pen-nyih, 上半日, before noon.

°Zaung-pen°-nyoeh, 上半月, first half of the month.

°Zaung-pen°-ya°, 上半夜, first half of night.

°Zaung-san, 上山, to go up a hill.

°Zaung-su, 上書, to take an advanced lesson.

Ze-voong, 裁縫, tailor.

Zeh, 十, ten.

Zeh, 折, to lose (in business).

Zeh-°dze, 實在, truly.

Zeh-ke°, 實蓋, thus.

Zeh-ke°-nung, 實蓋能, thus.

Zeh-pah-°sang, 十八省, China.

Zeh-°pung, 折本, to lose (in business).

Zeh-°pung-nyung, 日本人, Japanese.

Zeh-theh, 折脫, to lose (in business).

Zen, 全, all (collective).

Zen, 船, a boat.

Zen-r, 然而, moreover, yet.

°**Zen**, 善, good (moral).

°**Zeu**, 受, to receive, accept.

°**Zeu-'e°**, 受害, to be injured.

°**Zeu-°khoo**, 受苦, to suffer.

°**Zeu-nan°**, 受難, to suffer.

°**Zeu-saung**, 受傷, to be wounded.

Zia°, 謝, to thank.

Zien, 前, before.

Zien-deu, 前頭, before.

Zien-kuh-nyoeh, 前個月, last month.

Zien-nyih-°ts, 前日子, day before yesterday.

Zien-nyoeh, 前月, last month.

Zien-°tsen-le, 旋轉來, to turn around.

Zieu°, 就, immediately.

Zih, 截, to saw.

Zing, 尋, to look for.

Zing°, 浄, to wash.

Zing°-i-zaung-kuh, 浄衣裳個, a washerman.

Zing°-yok, 浄浴, to bathe.

Zo, 蛇, a snake.

Zok, 熟, ripe, thoroughly cooked, well known, thorough.

°**Zoo**, 坐, to sit.

Zoo°, 座, classifier for hills and buildings.

Zu°, 樹, a tree.

Zuh, 賊, a thief.

Zung, 神, God.

Zung, 繩, a rope.

Zung-dau°, 神道, a Taoist god or idol.

Zung-kwaung, 晨光, time.

English-Chinese Vocabuary

A

A or an *is expressed by the use of a classifier, e.g.,* ih-kuh, 一個, ih-diau, 一條.

Able, nung, 能, we°, 會, nung-keu°, 能夠.

About, iak-kwe, 約規, iak-tsak, 約酌, da-iak, 大約, *when used with a number*, 巴, —— *a hundred*, pak-°po, 百巴, —— *the same*, tsho-'veh-too, 差勿多, —— *to do a thing*, tsiang-iau°, 將要, khwa-tse, 快哉, (*used after the verb*), —— *midnight*, pen°-ya°-°po, 半夜巴.

Above, °zaung-deu, 上頭.

Accept, to, °zeu, 受, seu, 收.

Accompany, to, be, 陪, —— *a friend on leaving*, soong°, 送.

According, to, tsau, 照, tsau°-°ngoo-khoen°, 照我看.

Account, an, tsang°, 賬, *to collect* ——, seu-tsang°, 手賬, *on* —— *of*, iung-we°, 因爲.

Account book, an, ih °pung tsang°-°boo, 一本帳簿.

Add, to, ka, 加, thien, 添, ka-thien, 加添, *to* —— *a little*, ka-°tien, 加點.

Advantage, iuh-tshu°, 益處, °hau-tshu°, 好處.

Affair, an, ih °jien z°-°thi, 一件事體 *or* ih tsaung z°-°thi, 一樁事體.

After, °'eu, 後, °'eu-deu, 後頭, —— *this*, °i-°'eu, 以後, *day* —— *to-morrow*, °'eu-nyih, 後日.

Afternoon, °'au-pen°-nyih, 下半日.

Afterwards, °'eu-°seu, 後首, °'eu-le, 後來, °i-°'eu, 以後.

Again, tse°, 再, yi°, 又.

Age, kwe-kang, 貴庚, or kau-zeu, 高壽.

Ago, *a little while* ——, khan-khan, 纔纔, 'veh-too °kyi-z, 勿多幾時.

All, °loong-°tsoong, 攏總, koong°-°tsoong, 共總, ih tshi, 一切, (*collectively*), zen, 全, thok, 禿, —— *in general*, da-ke, 大概.

Allow, to, nyang°, 讓.

Already, °i-kyung, 已經.

Also, °'a-z, 也是, °'a, 也.

Although, soe-zen, 雖然, soe-°z, 雖是.

Always, dzang-tsaung, 常莊, dzang-dzang, 常常.

Am, z, 是.

America, °Me-kok, 美國, Hwo-ji-kok, 花旗國.

Among, taung-tsoong, 當中.

Anciently, °koo-z-kan, 古時間.

And, °lau, 佬, tah-ts, 搭之, *one hundred* —— *one*, ih pak ling ih, 一百零一.

Answer, to, we-deu, 回頭, we-tah, 回答.

Antiquity, °koo-z-kau, 古時間.

Anyone, dzoe-bien° sa°-nyung, 隨便啥人, *have you any?* noong° °yeu sa° va°? 儂有啥否, *not any*, m-meh, 沒末.

Anywhere, dzoe-bien° °'a-li, 隨便那裏, 'veh lung °'a-li, 勿論那裏.

Apple, an, ih tsak bing-°koo, 一只蘋菓.

Are, z, 是.

Arrange, to, ban, 辦.

Arrest, to, tsauh, 捉.

Arrive, to, tau°, 到.

As, *for example, like*, °hau-ziang, 好像, —— *it seems to me*, tsau° °ngoo khoen°, 照我看, —— *you please*, dzoe-bien° noong°, 隨便儂.

Ask, to, mung°, 問, jeu, 求, °tshing, 請.

Aspirate, to, tsheh-foong, 出風.

At, leh-la°, 垃拉, la°, 拉, —— *first*, chi deu, 起頭, —— *night*, ya° deu, 夜頭, ya°-li, 夜裏.

Attack, to, koong-°tang, 攻打.

Attend, to, *to heed*, taung-sing, 當心, yoong-sing, 用心, lieu-sing, 留心, *to* —— *to matters*, ban°, *to* —— *to a thing to make it right*, loong, 弄,

loong-°hau, 弄好.

Autumn, tshieu, 秋.

Ax, an, ih °po °foo-deu, 一把斧頭.

B

Back, the, pe°, 背, *to come* ——, °tsen le, 轉來, kyui le, 歸來, *to* —— *the book*, pe°, 背.

Bad, cheu, 怵, 'veh °hau, 勿好, —— *weather*, thien 'veh °hau, 天勿好.

Bake, to, hoong, 烘.

Baggage, 'ang-°li 行李.

Bale, *a* ——, ih pau, 一包, (*used as a classifier*), *a* —— *of merchandize*, ih pau °hoo-suh, 一包貨色.

Bamboo, *a stick of* ——, ih kung tsok-deu, 一根竹頭.

Bar, *of a door*, sak, 閂.

Bar, *to a door*, sen, 閂.

Bark, to, °ngau, 咬, kyau, 叫.

Barrow, a, ih boo° °siau tsho, 一部小車.

Barter, to, wen°, 換, diau°, 調.

Basket, a, ih tsak lan, 一隻籃.

Bathe, to, zing° yok, 淨浴.

Battery, a, ih kuh phau°-de, 一個炮台.

Battle, *to fight a* ——, °tang-tsang°, 打仗.

Be, to, °z, 是, leh la°, 垃拉.

Beat, to, °tang, 打, *to* —— *one another*, siang-°tang, 相打, *to* —— *a drum*, khau °koo, 敲鼓.

Because, iung-we°, 因爲, we°-ts, 爲之.

Bed, a, ih tsak zaung, 一隻牀 —— *room*, ih kan vaung-kan, 一間房間.

Bedding, phoo°-ke°, 鋪蓋.

Before, zien, 前, zien-deu, 前頭, *day* —— *yesterday*, koo°-nyih-°ts, 過日子, zien-nyih-°ts, 前日子, i-nyih-°ts, 伊日子.

Beg, to, °thau, 討.

Beget, to, °yang, 養, sang °yang, 生養.

Beggar, a, °thau-van°-kuh, 討飯個, kau° hwo°-°ts, 叫化子.

Begin, to, °chi, 起, *to* —— *work*, khe-koong, 開工, °doong-koong, 動工, —— *to journey*, °doong-sung, 動身.

Beginning, a, °chi-deu, 起頭, °chi-tshoo, 起初, khe-dzang, 開塲, —— *of the year*, nyien-deu, 年頭.

Behind, °'eu-ti, 後底, °'eu-ti-deu, 後底頭, °'eu-deu, 後頭.

Believe, to, sing°, 信, siang-sing°, 相信.

Bell, a, tsoong, 鐘.

Below, °'au-deu, 下頭, °'au-ti-deu, 下底頭.

Beneath, ti-°'au, 底下.

Beside, baung-pien, 旁邊, pien-deu, 邊頭.

Besides, ling°-nga°, 另外, dze-nga°, 在外, wan, 還.

Best, °ting °hau, 頂好, man °hau, 蠻好.

Better, °hau tien, 好點, *the quicker the* ——, yoeh khwa° yoeh °hau, 越快越好.

Between, taung-tsoong, 當中.

Beyond, koo, 過.

Big, doo°, 大.

Bill, ih tsang tsang°, 一張賬.

Bind, to, *with a cord*, °paung, 綁.

Bird, a, ih tsak °tiau, 一隻鳥.

Biscuit, ih kuh thah-°ping, 一個餲餅.

Bite, °ngau, 咬.

Bitter, °khoo, 苦.

Black, huh, 黑.

Blanket, a, ih diau °bi-deu, 一條被頭, *woolen*, nyoong-than, 羢毯.

Blow, to, tsh, 吹, *to* —— *out*, tsh °iung, 吹隱, *to* —— *into a flame or blaze*, tsh yaung°, 吹旺.

Blue, lan, 藍.

Board, a, ih khwe °pan, 一塊板.

Board, to, *a ship*, °zaung zen, 上船.

Boat, a, ih tsak zen, 一隻船, *steam* ——, ih tsak °hoo-lung-zen, 一隻火輪船, *to start a* ——, khe zen, 開船.

Body, a, ih kuh sung-°thi, 一個身體.

Boil, to, zah, 煠, *to* —— *water*, °kwung, 滾.

Boiling water, khe °s, 開水.

Bolt, *of a door*, sen, 閂, *of cloth*, ih phih poo°, 一疋布.

Bolt, *to* —— *a door*, sak, 閂.

Bonnet, a, ih °ting mau°-°ts, 一頂帽子, ih tsak mau°-°ts, 一隻帽子.

Book, a, ih °pung su, 一本書, *a set of* ——*s*, ih boo° su, 一部書, *an account* ——, ih °pung tsang°-°boo, 一本賬簿, *a small blank* ——, ih °pung boo°-°ts, 一本簿子.

Book-case, a, ih °kheu su-dzu, 一口書厨.

Borrow, to, tsia°, 借.

Both, liang-kuh, 兩個.

Bottle, a, (*used as a classifier*) bing, 瓶.

Bowl, *a Chinese eating* ——, ih tsak °wen, 一只碗, *a wash* ——, ih tsak mien°-bung, 一只面盆.

Box, *a large* ——, ih tsak siang-°ts, 一只箱子, *a small* ——, ih tsak ‘ah-°ts, 一只盒子, (*as a classifier*), siang, 箱.

Boy, a, ih kuh siau-noen, 一個小囝, *a table* ——, ih kuh °si-tse°, 一個細崽, *a horse* ——, ih kuh °ma-foo, 一個馬夫, *a school* ——, ih kuh °auh-sang-°ts, 一個學生子.

Brace, a (used as a classifier), ih te°, 一對.

Brass, doong, 銅.

Bread, *a loaf of* ——, ih kuh men-deu, 一個饅頭, *a piece of* ——, ih khwe° men-deu, 一塊饅頭, *a slice of* ——, ih phien° men-deu, 一片饅頭.

Breadth, khweh-‘ah, 闊狹.

Break, to, se°, 碎, °tang-se°, 打碎, khau-se°, 敲碎.

Breakfast, °tsau-van°, 早飯.

Brick, a, ih khwe° tsen-deu, 一塊磚頭, *or* lok-tsen, 碌磚, *a pile of* ——, ih te lok-tsen, 一堆碌磚.

Bridge, ih diau jau, 一條橋.

Bring, to, tan-le, 担來, nau-le, 拿來, *to* —— *with you*, ta° le, 帶來, *to* —— *out*, nau-tsheh-le, 拿出來, tan-tsheh-le, 担出來, *to* —— *back*, nau °tsen le, 拿轉來, tau-°tsen-le, 担轉來.

Broad, khweh, 闊.

Broil, to, tsien, 煎.

Broom, a, ih °po °sau-°tseu, 一把掃箒.

Brother, °di-hyoong, 弟兄, *elder* ——, ak-koo, 阿哥, *younger* ——, hyoong-°di, 兄弟, °di-°di, 弟弟.

Brush, to, seh, 刷.

Bucket, a, (*used as a classifier*), ih doong, 一桶.

Buddhist, *a* —— *idol*, ih tsung veh, 一尊佛, boo-sah, 菩薩, *a* —— *priest*, ih kuh oo-zaung°, 一個和尙.

Buffalo, *a water* ——, ih tsak °s-nyeu, 一隻水牛.

Build, to, °zau, 造, *to* —— *a partition*, tshi° pih, 砌壁, *to* —— *a wall*, tshi°, 砌, tshi° ziang, 砌牆.

Bundle, a, (*used as a classifier*), ih °khwung, 一捆.

Burn, to, sau, 燒, thaung, 烫.

Business, sang-i°, 生意, °ma-ma°, 買賣.

But, dau-°z, 但是, dok-°z, 獨是.

Butter, °na-yeu, 奶油.

Butterfly, a, ih tsak ‘oo-dih, 一隻蝴蝶.

Button, a, °nyeu-°ts, 鈕子.

Buy, to, °ma, 買.

By, (*the agent*), peh, 撥, peh-la°, 撥拉, —— *means of*, yoong, 用, —— *the side of*, pien-deu, 邊頭, —— *chance*, °ngeu-zen, 偶然, —— *what means*, na°-nung, 那能, —— *and* ——, °tung-ih-°tung, 等一等, hyih-ih-hyih, 歇一歇.

C

Cake, a, ih kuh kyi-dan°-kau, 一個鷄蛋糕.

Calculate, to, soen°, 算, °tang-soen°, 打算, *to* —— *accounts*, soen°-tsang°, 算賬.

Call, to, kyau°, 叫, han°, 喊, *to* —— *on*, maung°-maung°, 望望.

Can, *permission or ability*, °khau-°i, 可以, *physical ability*, nung-keu°, 能彀, *acquired ability*, we°, 會, —— *do it*, tsoo°-tuh-le, 做得來, —— *not do it*, tsoo°-’veh-le, 做勿來.

Canal, a, ih diau °kaung, 一條港.

Candle, a, ih kung lah-tsok, 一根蠟燭.

Candles, a, *pair of* ——*s*, ih te° lah tsok, 一對蠟燭.

Cane, a, ih kung °baung, 一根棒.

Cannon, a, ih tsung phau°, 一尊炮.

Cap, a, ih °ting, 一頂 *or* ih tsak mau°-°ts, 一只帽子.

Car, *a steam* ——, ih °boo °hoo-tsho, 一部火車.

Careful, taung-sing, 當心.

Carefully, °ts-si°, 仔細.

Carpenter, a, ih kuh mok-ziang°, 一個木匠.

Carpet, a, ih diau mau-°than, 一條毛毯.

Carriage, a, ih °boo °mo-tsho, 一部馬車, *steam* ——, ih °boo °hoo-tsho, 一部火車, *to go in a* ——, °zoo °mo-tsho, 坐馬車.

Carry, to, tan, 担, nau, 拿, *to* —— *in one hand*, ling, 拎, nau, 拿, *to* —— *in the arms like a child*, °bau, 抱, *to* —— *on the shoulder*, jien, 掮, *to* —— *on the back*, pe°, 揹, *to* —— *with bamboo pole on shoulder, one man*, thiau, 挑, *to* —— *with bamboo pole by two men*, kaung, 扛, *to* —— *a letter*, ta° ih foong sing°, 帶一封信.

Case, *a book* ——, ih °kheu su-dzu, 一口書厨, *in any* ——, dzoe-bien° na°-nung, 隨便那能.

Cash, a, ih kuh doong-dieu, 一個銅鈿.

Cask, a, (*used as a classifier*), ih doong, 一桶.

Cat, a, ih tsak mau, 一只猫.

Catch, tsauh, 捉, *to* —— *fire*, seh-°hoo, 失火, °hoo-dzak, 火着.

Catty, a, ih kyung, 一斤.

Cent, *a* ——, ih fung, 一分, *ten* ——*s*, ih kauh, 一角, *twenty* ——*s*, liang kauh, 兩角, s khe, 四開.

Chair, a, ih tsak iui°-°ts, 一只椅子, *a sedan* ——, ih °ting jau°-°ts, 一頂轎子.

Chance, *by* ——, °ngeu-zen, 偶然.

Change, °tsau-deu, 找頭.

Change, to, —— *a dollar*, de° yang-dien, 兌洋鈿, *to* —— *residence*, pen-dzang, 搬場.

Character, *a Chinese* ——, ih kuh z°, 一個字, *to know a* ——, suh, 識, *sound of a* ——, z°-iung, 字音.

Charcoal, than, 炭.

Chart, a, ih fok doo, 一幅圖, ih fok di°-°li-doo, 一幅地理圖.

Cheap, jang, 強.

Cheat, to, chi, 欺, phien°, 騙, chi-phien°, 欺騙.

Chicken, a, ih tsak kyi, 一只鷄.

Child, a, ih kuh °siau-noen, 一個小囝.

Chimney, ien-tshoong, 烟囱.

China, Tsoong-kok, 中國, Tsoong-wo, 中華, zeh-pah-°sang, 十八省, Ts-na, 支那, Tsoong-wo ming-kok 中華民國.

Chinese, Tsoong-kok, 中國, *a —— character*, ih kuh z°, 一個字, *to know a —— character*, suh, 識.

Church, a, °li-pa°-daung, 禮拜堂.

City, a, ih zoo° dzung, 一座城.

Class, a (*in school*), ih pan, 一班.

Clause, a, ih kyui°, 一句.

Clean, koen-zing, 乾淨.

Clear, tshing, 淸, tshing-°saung, 淸爽.

Clever, tshoong-ming, 聰明.

Climb, to, bo, 爬, ban °zaung-chi°, 蹩上去.

Clock, a, ih tsak z°-ming-tsoong, 一只自鳴鐘.

Cloth, *a piece of* ——, ih phih poo°, 一疋布.

Clothe, to, tsak, 着.

Clothes, i-zaung, 衣裳, *pile of* ——, ih-dzaung° i-zaung, 一幢衣裳, *to take off* ——, thoeh theh i-zaung, 脫脫衣裳.

Coachman, ih kuh °mo-foo, 一個馬夫.

Coal, me, 煤, (hard) bak-me, 白煤, (soft) ien-me, 烟煤.

Coffin, a, ih °kheu kwen-ze, 一口棺材.

Cold, °lang, 冷.

Collect, to, seu, 收, *to —— accounts*, seu-tsang°, 收賬.

College, a, su-yoen°, 書院.

Colour, ngan-suh, 顏色, *the five ——s*, °ng-suh, 五色, *variegated ——s*, °ng-ngan-lok-suh, 五顏六色.

Come, to, le, 來, —— back, °tsen-le, 轉來, —— *forth*, tsheh-le, 走來, —— *down*, °'au-le, 下來, —— *in*, tsing°-le, 進來, —— *up*, °zaung-le, 上來.

Comfort, to, oen-we°, 安慰.

Comfortable, suh-i°, 適意.

Command, to, fung-foo°, 吩咐.

Commence, to, °chi-deu, 起頭, khe-koong, 開工, *to* —— *work*, doong°-seu, 動手, khe-dzang, 開場, —— *to journey*, doong-sung, 動身.

Compare, to, °pi, 比.

Complete, to, dzung-koong, 成功.

Compradore, a, ih kuh °ma-ban°, 一個買辦.

Congratulate, to, —— *a person*, koong-°hyi, 恭喜.

Connect, *to be* ——*ed together*, siang-lien, 相聯.

Conquer, to, tuh-sung, 得勝.

Consider, to, °tang-soen°, 打算.

Consult, to, saung-liang, 商量, tsung-tsak, 斟酌.

Convenient, bien°-taung°, 便當, bien°, 便, *when* ——, bien°-z, 便時.

Converse, to, bak-wo°, 白話, dan-dan, 談談.

Cook (a chief), da°-°s-voo°, 大司務, (an ordinary) sau-van°-kuh, 燒飯個.

Cook, to, sau, 燒, sau-van, 燒飯, ——*ed roughly*, zok 熟.

Cooking, *a* —— *stove* (*Chinese*), ih tsak tsau°-deu, 一只竈頭 *a* —— *stove* (*foreign*), ih tsak thih-tsau, 一只鐵竈.

Coolie, a, tsheh-tien°, 出店, *a ricksha* ——, tsho-foo, 車夫, *a sedan* ——, ih kuh jau°-pan, 一個轎班, jau-foo, 轎夫.

Cord, *to bind with a* ——, °paung, 綁.

Cotton, hwo, 花, (*already ginned*), mien-hwo, 棉花, *a bale of* ——, ih pau mien-hwo, 一包棉花, —— *cloth*, poo°, 布, —— *seeds*, hwo-°ts, —— *stalk*, hwo-ji, 花楷.

Count, °soo, 數, soen°, 算.

Cow, ih tsak nyeu, 一只牛.

Crab apple, a, ih tsak hwo-‘oong, 一只花紅.

Crawl, to, ban, 踫.

Creek, a, ih diau pang, 一條浜, ih diau siau°-‘oo, 一條小河.

Criticise, to, phi-bing, 批評, phi-thah, 批搨.

Crow, a, ih tsak °lau-au, 一只老鴉.

Crow, to (*as a cock*), di, 啼.

Cry, to, khok, 哭.

Cup, a, ih tsak pe-°ts, 一只杯子.

Custom, kwe-°kyui, 規矩.

Cut, to, *with a sharp knife*, koeh, 割, *to* —— *with a sword, heavy knife or ax*, tsan, 斬, *to* —— *in two*, koeh-°doen, 割斷, *to* —— *open*, tshih-khe, 切開, tshih-khe-le, 切開來.

D

Daily, nyih-nyih, 日日, nyih-dzok, 日逐, me-nyih, 每日.

Dark, en°, 暗, *nearly* ——, thien en° khwa° tse, 天暗快哉.

Daughter, ih kuh noen, 一個囡, ih kuh °siau-°nyui, 一個小女, tshien-kyung, 千金, ling°-e°, 令媛.

Day, ih nyih, 一日, thien, 天, *to-day, this* ——, kyung-tsau, 今朝, *the first* —— *of month*, tshoo ih, 初一, *every* ——, nyih-nyih, 日日, nyih-dzok, 日逐, *the 15th* ——, nyoeh-pen°, 月半, —— *and night*, nyih-ya°, 日夜, *all* ——, tsoong-nyih, 終日, *half a* ——, pen°-nyih, 半日, —— *after to-morrow*, °'eu-nyih, 後日, —— *before yesterday*, koo°-nyih-°ts, 過日子, zien-nyih-°ts, 前日子, i°-nyih-°ts, 伊日子, *in the middle of the* ——, nyih-tsoong, 日中, —— *time*, nyih-li, 日裏.

Dead, °si-tse, 死哉.

Deal, a great, too-bau°, 多化.

Dear (*costly*), kyui°, 貴, —— child, °pau-pe kuh °siau-noen°, 寶貝個小囝.

Decide, to, lih-ding-°tsu-i°, 立定主意.

Deep, sung, 深.

Deer, ih tsak lok, 一隻鹿.

Defeat, to, °tang-ba°, 打敗, *to be* ——*ed*, °tang-su, 打輸, °tang-ba°, 打敗, °tang-ba°-tsang, 打敗仗.

Deify, to, foong zung, 封神.

Deliver, *to* —— *in person*, dzeu°, 授.

Depart, *to* —— *from*, li-khe, 離開.

Depend on, to, i-khau°, 依靠, khau°-thauh, 靠託.

Deport, *to* —— *oneself*, de°, 待.

Depth, sung-°tshien, 深淺.

Descend, to, °'au-chi°, 下去, *to* —— *a hill*, °'au-san, 下山.

Desert, to, li-khe, 離開.

Desire, to, maung, 望, po-maung, 巴望, iau°, 要.

Desk, *an office* ——, ih tsak °sia-z°-de-°ts, 一只寫字檯子.

Dialect, °thoo-bak, 土白, *Shanghai* ——, °Zaung-°he °thoo-bak, 上海土白, *mandarin* ——, kwen-wo, 官話.

Dice, a set of, ih foo° °deu-°ts, 一付骰子, *to gamble with* ——, zak deu°-°ts, 擲骰子.

Die, to, °si, 死, °si-theh, 死脫.

Difference, a, fung-pih, 分別, *not much* ——, tsho-'veh-too, 差勿多.

Difficult, van-nan, 煩難, nan, 難.

Diligent, *to be* ——, yoong-sing, 用心.

Dining, *a* —— *room*, ih kan chuh-van°-kan, 一間吃飯間, *a* —— *table*, ih tsak chuh-van°-de°-°ts, 一只吃飯檯子.

Direct, to, ban°, 辦.

Dirty, auh-tsauh, 齷齪.

Dish, a, ih tsak dzang bung-°ts, 一只長盆子.

Dismiss, *to* —— *school*, faung° 'auh, 放學.

Distance, °yoen-°jung, 遠近.

Distinct, tshing-°saung, 淸爽.

Distinguish, to, fung-pih, 分別.

Divide, to, fung, 分, fung-khe, 分開.

Do, to ——, tsoo°, 做, *cannot* —— *it*, tsoo°-'veh-le, 做勿來, *how* —— *you* ——? noong°-°hau-la° va? 儂好拉否, —— *for*, theh, 對.

Doctor, ih we °laung-tsoong, 一位郎中, ih we i-sung, 一位醫生.

Dog, ih tsak °keu, 一只狗.

Dollar, a, ih kuh, 一個, *or* ih khwe° yang-dien, 一塊洋錢, *half a* ——, pen° khwe° yang-dien, 半塊洋錢, *a box of* ——*s*, ih siang yang-dien, 一箱洋錢.

Dominoes, *a set of*, ih foo° ba, 一付牌, *to gamble with* ——, teu°-ba, 鬪牌.

Door, a, ih sen mung, 一扇門, *shut the* ——, kwan mung, 關門, *open the* ——, khe mung, 開門, *lock the* ——, °soo mung, 鎖門.

Doorway, a, ih kuh mung-°kheu, 一個門口, ih kuh mung-°kheu-deu, 一個門口頭.

Down, °'au, 下, *put it* ——, faung°-la°, 放拉, °pa-la°, 擺拉, *please sit* ——, tshing-°zoo, 請坐.

Dragon, a, ih diau loong, 一條龍.

Drawer, ih tsak tsheu-thi°, 一只抽屜.

Drawers, *a chest of* ——, ih tsak tsheu-teu, 一只抽斗.

Dress, to, tsak, 着, *to* —— *in a showy manner*, °tang-pan °, 打扮.

Drive, *to* —— *away*, °koen, 趕, koen-theh, 趕脫.

Drum, a, ih mien° °koo, 一面鼓.

Dry, koen, 乾.

Duck, ih tsak ah, 一只鴨.

Dull, dung°, 鈍.

Dust, boong-dzung, 塳塵.

Duty, ming-vung°, 名分.

Dwell, to, dzu, 住.

E

Each, °me, 每.

Ear, a, ih tsak °nyi-°too, 一只耳朵.

Earlier, *the* —— *the better*, yoeh °tsau yoeh °hau, 越早越好.

Early, °tsau, 早, —— *in the morning*, °tsau zung-deu, 早晨頭.

Earn, to, dzan° 賺.

Earth, the, di°, 地, di°-jeu, 地球, *the whole* ——, phoo-thien-°‘au, 普天下.

East, the, toong, 東, —— *side*, toong-pien, 東邊.

Easy, yoong-yi°, 容易, —— *to read*, °hau dok kuh, 好讀個.

Eat, to, chuh, 吃, *to* —— *rice or meal*, chuh van, 吃飯, *unable to* ——, chuh-’veh-lauh, 吃勿落, *good to* ——, °hau chuh kuh, 好吃個.

Eating, *a Chinese* —— *bowl*, ih tsak °wen, 一只碗.

Ebb-tide, the°-dzau, 退潮.

Economical, to be, °sang, 省, tsoo° nyung-ka, 做人家.

Egg, an, ih kuh dan°, 一個蛋.

Eight, pah, 八.

Eighteen, zeh-pah, 十八.

Eighty, pah-zeh, 八十.

Either, ‘ok-tse, 或者, ‘ok-°z, 或是.

Eleven, zeh-ih, 十一.

Else, ling°-nga°, 另外, wan-°yeu, 還有.

Embarrassing, *to be placed in an — position*, nan-we-dzing, 難爲情.

Emblem, an, kyi-'au°, 記號.

Enemy, *to attack an* ——, koong-°tang, 攻打.

England, Iung-kok, 英國.

Enjoy, to, hwen-°hyi, 歡喜.

Enough, °yeu-tse, 有哉, or keu°-z°, 够是.

Ensign, kyi-'au°, 記號.

Enter, to, tsing°, 進.

Entrust, to, khau°, 靠, khau°-thauh, 靠託, thauh, 託.

Envelope, an, ih kuh sing°-khauh, 一個信殼, ih kuh sing°-foong, 一個信封.

Equal, ih yang°, 一樣, *not* —— *to*, 'veh-jih, 勿及, 'veh zu, 勿如.

Erect, *to* —— *a fence*, °tang-po, 打芭.

Error, tsho, 差.

Escort, *to* —— *a person to the way*, soong°, 送.

Evening, ya°-khwa°, 夜快, waung-hwung-deu, 黃昏頭, waung hwung-°doong, 黃昏同.

Every, kauh, 各, °me, 每, —— *day*, °me-nyih, 每日, —— *place*, khauh tshu°, 各處, khauh-tau° lauh tshu°, 各到落處.

Examine, *to* —— *carefully*, dzo, 查, dzo-°khau, 查考, *to* —— *a class*, °khau-su, 考書.

Exalt, *to* —— *to a high position*, foong, 封.

Exchange, to, wen°, 換, diau, 調.

Excite, to, doong, 動.

Exhort, to, °choen, 勸, °choen-mien, 勸勉, °choen-'oo, 勸和.

Except, to, maung°, 望, po-maung°, 巴望.

Explain, to, °ka-suh, 解說, °khaung, 講.

Expound, to, °khaung, 講.

Extinguish, to, tsh-°iung, 吹隱.

Extra, ling-nya°, 另外.

Extravagant, to be, ——, saung-fi, 傷費.

Eye, an, ih tsak °ngan-tsing, 一只眼睛.

F

Face, ih kuh mien° khoong, 一個面孔, —— (*cheek*), nyi-kwaung, 耳光.

Fall, to, lauh, 落, tih, 跌, *to* —— *down*, lauh-'au°-le, 落下來, tih-'au°-le, 跌下來, *the tide is* ——*ing*, lauh-dzau, 落潮.

False, °ka, 假.

Fan, a, ih °po sen°-°ts, 一把扇子.

Farmer, tsoong°-dien-nyung, 種田人.

Fast, khwa°, 快.

Fat, (*a person being* ——), tsaung°, 壯.

Father, ya, 爺, °lau-nyung-ka, 老人家, kya-°voo, 家父, tsung-da°-nyung, 尊大人, kya, 家, ling-°tsung, 令尊, tia-tia, 爹爹, ya-ya, 爺爺, pak-pak, 爸爸.

Feel, to, mok, 摸.

Female, (*human*), °nyui, 女, (*animal*), tsh, 雌.

Fence, *to erect a* ——, °tang-po, 打芭.

Few, sau, 少.

Fierce, hyoong, 兇.

Fifteen, °so-°ng, 十五.

Fifty, °ng-seh, 五十.

Fight, *to* —— *with each other*, siang-°tang, 相打, *to* —— *a battle*, °tang-°tsang, 打仗.

File, a, ih °po tshoo-tau, 一把銼刀.

Find, to, zing, 尋, zing-dzak, 尋着, *cannot* ——, zing-'veh-dzak, 尋勿着.

Finger, a, ih tsak tshih-deu, 一只指頭.

Finish, to, wen, 完.

Fire, °hoo, 火, *to light the* ——, sang-°hoo, 生火, *on* —— (*as a house*), °hoo-dzak, 火着.

Firm, lau, 牢.

First, sien, 先, deu ih, 頭一, °di ih, 第一, *the* —— *month*, tsung nyoeh, 正月, *the* —— *day of a month*, tshoo-ih, 初一, *the* —— *part of a month*, nyoeh-deu, 月頭, nyoeh deu laung, 月頭上, *the* —— *half of a month*, *day, or year*, °zaung-pen°, 上半.

Fish, a, ih diau ng, 一條魚.

Five, °ng, 五.

Flag, ih mien° ji, 一面旗.

Flour, koen-mien°, 乾麵, mien°-°fung, 麵粉.

Flower, hwo, 花, *a* ——*ing plant*, ih khoo hwo, 一棵花.

Flute, ih °kwen-dih, 一管笛.

Fly, to, fi, 飛.

Follow, to, kung, 跟.

Food, van°, 飯, chuh-kuh meh-z°, 吃個物事.

Fool, *to* —— *with one another*, °tang-bang, 打棚.

Foot, the, ih tsak kyak, 一只脚, *a measure of 10 inches*, ih tshak, 一尺, *ten feet*, ih °dzang, 一丈, *a square* ——, ih faung tshak, 一方尺, *100 square feet*, ih faung, 一方.

For, iung-we°, 因爲, we°-ts, 爲之, —— (*instead of*), theh, 替, de°-thi°, 代替.

Force, *to take a thing by* ——, °tshiang, 搶, °tshiang-doeh, 搶奪.

Foreigner, ih kuh °nga-kok nyung, 一個 外國人.

Forfeit, to, seh, 失, seh-theh, 失脫.

Forget, to, maung-kyi, 忘記.

Forgive, to, nyau-°so, 饒赦, khwen-yoong, 寬容, nyoen-liang°, 原諒.

Fork, ih °po tsho°, 一把叉.

Forsake, to, li-khe, 離開.

Fort, a, ih kuh phau°-de, 一個炮台.

Forth, tsheh, 出, *to come* ——, tsheh-le, 出來.

Forty, s°-seh, 四十.

Four, °s, 四.

Fowl, ih tsak kyi, 一隻鷄, *a pair of* ——*s*, ih te° kyi, 一對鷄.

Fox, ih tsak ‘oo-li, 一隻孤狸.

France, Fah-kok, 法國.

Fresh (*of meat or fish*), sing-sien, 新鮮.

Friend, ih kuh bang-°yeu, 一個朋友.

Friday, °li-pa°-°ng, 禮拜五.

From, dzoong, 從.

Fuel, *a bundle of* ——, ih khwung za, 一梱柴, ih khwung dau-za, 一梱稻柴.

Furniture, *classifier for articles of* ——, °kheu, 口.

G

Gain, to, ——, dzan, 賺, *to* —— *a victory*, °tang-yung, 打贏, °tang-sung°-tsang, 打勝仗.

Gamble, to, too, 賭, *to* —— *with dice*, zak deu°-°ts, 擲骰子, *to* —— *with dominoes*, teu°-ba, 鬬牌.

Garden, hwo-yoen, 花園.

Garment, ih jien° i-zaung, 一件衣裳.

Gate, mung, 門.

Gateway, mung-kheu, 門口.

Gather, (*as fruit, flowers*), °tshe, 採.

Generally, da°-liak, 大略.

Germany, Tuh-kok, 德國.

Gentleman, sien-sang, 先生.

Gently, man°-man°-nung, 慢慢能, chung-chung-nung, 輕輕能.

Get, to, tuh, 得, tuh-dzak, 得着, *to* —— *up*, lok, 碌 lok chi° le, 碌起來.

Give, to, peh, 撥, soong°, 送.

Glad, kha°-weh, 快活, hwen-°hyi, 歡喜.

Glass, poo-li, 玻璃, *a* ——, ih tsak poo-li pe-°ts, 一只玻璃杯子, *a wine* ——, ih tsak °tsieu pe, 一只酒杯.

Go, to, chi°, 去, *to* —— *out*, tsheh chi°, 出去, *to* —— *on shore*, °zaung-ngoen°, 上岸, *to* —— *on board*, °zaung-zen, 上船.

Goat, ih tsak san-yang, —隻山羊.

God, °Zang-ti, 上帝, Thien-°tsu, 天主, Zung, 神, *a Taoist* ——, ih tsung zung-dau°, 一尊神道.

Godown, a, ih zoo °dzan-vaung, 一座棧房.

Gold, kyung-°ts, 金子.

Gong, ih mien° kyung-loo, 一面金鑼.

Good, °hau, 好, (*moral*), zen, 善.

Good-by, an°-hyih-we°, 晏歇會, tse°-we°, 再會, chi°-tse, 去哉, man°-chi°, 慢去, kan-nyih-we°, 隔日會.

Goose, a, ih tsak ngoo, 一只鵝.

Grasp, to, nyah, 揑.

Grass, a, °tshau, 草.

Grate, a, ih kuh °hoo-khaung, 一個火炕.

Grave, *a, —— mound*, ih kuh vung-san, 一個墳山.

Great, doo°, 大, *a great many*, too hau°, 多化, kyau-kwan, 交關.

Green, lok, 綠.

Guest, a, ih we° khak nyung, 一位客人, *a —— room*, ih kan khak-daung kan, 一間客堂間.

Grill, to, tsien, 煎.

Gun, a, ih kwen yang-tshiang, 一管洋槍.

H

Hair, *on the head*, deu-fah, 頭髮.

Half, a, ih pen°, 一半, *—— an hour*, pen° °tien-tsoong, 半點鐘, *—— a dollar*, pen° khwe° yang-dien, 半塊洋錢.

Hammer, a, ih kuh, 一個, *or* °po laung-deu, 把榔頭.

Hand, the, ih tsak °seu, 一只手, *the right* ——, yeu°-°seu, 右手, *the left* ——, tsi°-°seu, 左手.

Hand, to, dzeu°, 授.

Handful, a, ih °po, 一把.

Happiness, fok-chi°, 福氣.

Happy, kha°-weh, 快活.

Hard, ngang, 硬, (*difficult*), nan, 難.

Hare, a, ih tsak thoo°-°ts, 一只兔子.

Hat, ih °ting man-°ts, 一頂帽子.

Have, °yeu, 有.

Hawk, a, °ih tsak iung, 一只鷹, ih tsak °lau-iung, 一只老鷹.

He, yi, 伊.

Head, ih kuh deu, 一個頭, *to wear on the* ——, ta°, 戴, *to bow the* —— (*as to kowtow*), kheh-deu, 磕頭.

Heal, to, i-°hau, 醫好, khoen°-°hau, 看好.

Hear, thing, 聽, thing-kyien, 聽見, *cannot* ——, thing-'veh-tsheh, 聽勿出.

Heart, ih kuh sing, 一個心.

Heaven, thien, 天.

Heavy, °dzoong, 重.

Height, kau-ti, 高低.

Help, paung-dzoo°, 帮助, *to* —— *one another*, siang-paung, 相幫.

Hen, a, ih tsak ths kyi, 一只雌鷄.

Her, yi, 伊.

Here, leh-li, 垃裏, °ths-di°, 此地, di-deu, 第頭.

Hereafter, °'eu-°seu, 後首, °'eu-le, 後來, °i-°'eu, 以後.

Hers, yi-kuh, 伊個.

Hide, *to* —— *oneself*, ben°-loong, 避攏, *to* —— *a thing*, khaung°-°loong, 囥攏, khaung°, 囥.

High, kau, 高.

Hill, ih zoo° san, 一座山.

Him, yi, 伊.

Himself, yi z°-ka, 伊自家.

Hinder, to, °tsoo, 阻, °tsoo-taung, 阻擋.

His, yi-kuh, 伊個.

Hit, to, °tang, 打.

Hog, a, ih tsak ts-loo, 一只猪玀.

Hoist, to, *as a flag or a sail*, °tsha, 扯.

Hold, to, nyah, 捏, *to* —— *in the arms*, °bau, 抱.

Hole, doong, 洞.

House, ok-°li, 屋裏.

Honest, lau-zeh, 老實.

Hope, a, maung-deu, 望頭.

Hope, to, po-maung°, 巴望.

Horse, a, ih phih °mo, 一匹馬, ih tsak °mo, 一只馬, *a* —— *boy*, ih kuh °mo-foo, 一個馬夫, *to ride a* ——, ji-°mo, 騎馬.

Hospital, i-yoen°, 醫院.

Hot, nyih, 熱.

Hour, ih °tien tsoong, 一點鐘, *or* ih kuh tsoong-deu, 一個鐘頭, *half an* ——, pen° °tien tsoong, 半點鐘, *quarter of an* ——, ih khuh, 一刻.

House, ih zoo°, 一座, *or* ih zak vaung-°ts, 一宅房子, *two storied* ——, ih zoo° leu, 一座樓, ih zoo° leu-vaung, 一座樓房, *three storied* ——, san dzung leu, 三層樓.

How? °na-nung, 那能? —— *many?* °kyi-hau°, 幾化? °kyi kuh, 幾個? —— *much?* °kyi hau°, 幾化? —— *much is it* (*price*)? sa ka°-dien, 啥價錢? sa ‘aung-dzing, 啥行情? —— *much more?* ‘oo-°hwaung, 何況? nyi, 呢, (*at end of clause*) —— *are you?* noong° °hau la° °va, 儂好拉否? —— *old are you?* °kyi hau° nyien-kyi, 幾化年紀? °kyi soe°, 幾歲? °kyi-hau° kwe°-kang, 幾何貴庚? kyi-hau° kau-zeu°, 幾化高壽.

However, zen-r, 然而.

Hundred, ih pak, 一百.

Hunt, to, °tang-lih, 打獵.

Husband, *a* —— *and wife*, ih te° foo-tshi, 一對夫妻.

I

I, °ngoo, 我, —— *myself*, °ngoo z°-ka, 我 自家.

Idol, *a Buddhist* ——, ih tsung veh, 一尊佛, boo-sah, 菩薩, *a Taoist* ——, ih tsung zung-dau°, 一尊神道.

If, zak, 若, zak-s°, 若是, zak-zen, 若然, °thaung-zen, 倘然, °thaung-s°, 倘使, meh, 末 (*at end of the clause*), —— *not so*, ’veh zen meh, 勿然末, ’veh zeh-ke° meh, 勿實蓋末, —— *it be so*, kyi-zen zeh-ke°, 既然實蓋, *as* ——, °hau-°ziang, 好像.

Ill, *to become*, sang-bing, 生病.

Illness, mau-bing, 毛病.

Immediately, zieu, 就.

Immovable, °doong-°‘a-’veh-°doong, 動亦勿動.

Implement, ka-sang, 傢生.

Imprison, *to be* ——*ed*, seu-kan, 收監.

In, la°, 拉, *or* leh-la°, 垃拉, (*before noun*) °li, 裏, *or* °li-hyang, 裏向, (*after noun*), *is he* ——? yi leh-la° va°? 伊垃拉否? *come* ——, tsing°-le, 進來, *go* ——, °tsing-chi°, 進去, —— *addition*, ling°-nga, 另外, dze-nga°, 在外, wan, 環, —— *order to*, °i-°ts, 以至, —— *vain*, bak-bak-°li, 白白

裏.

Inch, an, ih tshung, 一寸.

Inconceivable, siang-’veh-tau, 想勿到.

Indispensable, °ba-’veh-tuh, 罷勿得.

Injure, ‘e°, 害, *to be* ——*ed*, zeu-°‘e, 受害, *to be* ——*ed by striking*, °tang-wa°, 打壞.

Ink, *a piece of*, ih khwe° muh, 一塊墨, *foreign* ——, muh-s, 墨水, *a Chinese* —— *tablet*, ih kuh nyien°-°ts, 一個硯池, ih kuh nyien°-de, 一個硯台.

Inquire, *to make* ——*ies*, °tang-thing, 打聽.

Inside, °li-hyang°, 裏向.

Instantaneous, lih-khuk, 立刻.

Instead of, thi°, 替, °de-thi, 代替.

Instruments, *a set of*, ih foo° ka-sang, 一副傢生.

Intercourse, le-°waung, 來往.

Invite, to, °tshing, 請.

Iron, thih, 鐵.

Iron, to, thaung, 烫.

Is, °z, 是, *there* ——, °yeu, 有, —— *there to be had?* °yeu-tuh, 有得?

It, yi, 伊, —— *is not necessary*, ’veh pih, 勿必.

Its, yi-kuh, 伊個.

J

Japanese, Toong-yang-nyung, 東洋人, zeh-°pung-nyung, 日本人.

Jetty, a, °mo-deu, 碼頭.

Journey, *to start on*, °doong-sung, 動身.

Jump, to, thiau, 跳.

Just now, khan-khan, 纔纔, ’veh too-°kyi-z, 勿多幾時, —— *on the point of doing a thing*, thih-°tsung, 貼准, —— *before daylight*, thien-liang°-khwa°, 天亮快.

K

Keep, to, seu, 守.

Kerosene, °hoo-yeu, 火油.

Kettle, s-'oo, 水壺.

Key, a, ih °po yak-dz, 一把鑰匙.

Kill, to, sah, 殺, sah-theh, 殺脫, *to —— with a blow*, °tang-sah, 打殺.

Kitchen, a, ih kan sau-van°-kan, 一間燒飯間, dzu-vaung, 厨房, tsau°-kan, 灶間.

Kneel, to, jui, 跪.

Knife, a, ih °po tau, 一把刀.

Knock, to, khau, 敲.

Know, to, °hyau-tuh, 曉得, *to —— a person*, nyung°-tuh, 認得, *to —— a Chinese character*, suh, 識.

Kowtow, to, kheh-deu, 磕頭.

L

Ladder, a, ih dzung voo-thi, 一層扶梯.

Lamp, a, ih tsan-tung, 一盞燈.

Large, doo°, 大.

Late, °an, 晏.

Laugh, to, siau°, 笑.

Laughable, °hau-siau°, 好笑, *very ——*, siau°-sah-tse, 笑殺哉.

Lazy, °lan-phok, 懶怕, °lan-doo°, 懶惰.

Lead, khan, 鉛.

Lead, to, ling, 領.

Leap, to, thiau, 跳.

Learn, to, °'auh, 學.

Left, tsoo°, 左 (*sometimes pronounced tsi°*), *—— hand*, tsi° °seu, 左手.

Lend, to, tsia, 借.

Length, dzaug-°toen, 長短.

Less than, 'veh siau, 勿消, 'veh °men, 勿滿.

Lest, °sang-ts, 省之.

Letter, a, ih foong sing°, 一封信.

Level, bing, 平.

Life, ih diau sing°-ming°, 一條性命, *all one's* ——, ih-sang ih-s°, 一生一世.

Light (*not dark*), liang, 亮.

Light (*in weight*), chung, 輕.

Light, to, (*a lamp or candle*), tien, 點, *to* —— *a fire*, sang, 生.

Like, °hau-°ziang 好像, °ziang, 像, yeu-z 猶似, tsho-'veh-too, 差不多.

Like, to, hwen-°hyi, 歡喜, siang-sing°, 相信, *as you* ——, dzoe noong, 隨儂, dzoe bien noong, 隨便儂.

Lion, a, ih tsak s-°ts, 一只獅子.

Little, °siau, 小, —— (*in quantity*), °sau, 少, —— (*to a small extent*), sau-we, 少爲, *a* ——, ih ngan, 一顏, ih ngan-ngan, 一顏顏, *differs but* ——, tsho-'veh-too, 差勿多.

Live, to, dzu°, 住, weh, 活 sung, 生.

Loaf, *a* —— *of bread*, ih kuh men-deu, 一個饅頭.

Lock, a, ih °po °soo, 一把鎖.

Lock, to, °soo, 鎖.

Long, dzang, 長, *a* —— *time*, dzang-°yoen, 長遠, dzang-°yoen-tse, 長遠哉, ta-z-tse, 多時哉.

Look, to, khoen°, 看, *to* —— *for*, zing, 尋, *take a* ——, khoen°-ih-khoen°, 看一看, *to* —— *around*, tseu-we-khoen°, 周圍看, ——*s well*, °hau khoen°, 好看, *to* —— *for* (*expect*), maung°, 望, —— *after* (*to lake care of*), tsau-koo, 照顧, taung-sing, 當心.

Loose, °doong-°lau-°doong, 動佬動.

Lord, °Tsu, 主, *the heavenly* ——, Thien-°Tsu, 天主.

Lose, to, seh, 失, seh-theh, 失脫, *to* —— *in business*, zeh, 折, zeh-theh, 折脫, zeh-pung, 折本.

Love, to, e°, 爱, *to* —— *mutually*, siang-e°, 相愛.

Low, ti, 底.

M

Magistrate, a, ih kuh, 一個, (or ih we°, 一位), kwen-°foo, 官府.

Make, to, tsoo°, 做, *to* —— *a profit*, dzan, 賺.

Male, nen, 男, *of animals*, yoong, 雄.

Man, ih kuh nyung, 一個人, *a* —— *or two*, deu-liang-kuh-nyung, 頭兩個

人.

Manage, to, kyung-°seu, 經手, ban, 辦, °kwen, 管.

Mandarin, a, ih kuh kwen, 一個官, ih kuh kwen-°foo, 一個官府, —— *dialect*, kwen-wo°, 官話.

Many, too-hau°, 多化, *how* ——, °kyi-hau°, 幾化, *a great* ——, kyau-kwan, 交關.

Map, a, ih fok doo, 一幅圖, ih fok di°-°li-doo, 一幅地理圖.

Market, °z-mien°, 市面.

Marks or signs, kyi°-'au°, 記號.

Marry, *to* —— *a wife*, °thau nyang-°ts, 討娘子, *a woman to* ——, tsheh-ka°, 出嫁.

Mason, a, ih kuh nyi-°s-ziang, 一個泥水匠.

Master, a, °tsu-nyung, 主人, toong-ka, 東家.

Matches, z°-le hoo°, 自來火, *strike a* ——, wak, 劃.

May, °khau-i°, 可以.

Me, °ngoo, 我.

Meaning, i°-s°, 意思.

Measure, to, liang, 量, °ien, 演.

Meat, *a piece* ——, ih khwe° nyok, 一塊肉.

Medicine, yak, 藥.

Meet, to, bang°-dzak, 碰着, *to go to* ——, nyung-tsih, 迎接, *to* —— *a misfortune*, chuh-°khoo, 吃苦.

Men, nyung, 人.

Mend, to, sieu, 修, °poo, 補, to —— a path, tshi° ka, 砌街.

Merchandise, hoo°-suh, 貨色.

Method, fah-tsuh, 法則.

Midday, nyih-tsoong, 日中.

Middle, kyui-tsoong, 居中, —— *of a month*, nyoeh-pen°, 月半.

Midnight, pen°-ya° °po, 半夜把.

Might, °khau-°i, 可以.

Mile, *a Chinese* ——, ih °li, 一里, ih °li-loo°, 一里路.

Milk, nyeu-°na, 牛奶.

Mind, to relax the ——, san-sing, 散心.

Mine, °ngoo-kuh, 我個.

Minute, a, ih fung, 一分.

Mirror, a, ih mien° kyung°-°ts, 一面鏡子.

Misery, °khoo-nau°, 苦惱.

Misfortune, *to meet with a* —, chuh-°khoo, 吃苦.

Mistake, 'veh-te°, 勿對, *or* tsho, 錯.

Miss, a, ih kuh °siau-°tsia, 一個小姐.

Mister, sien-sang, 先生.

Mistress, Mrs., nyang-nyang, 娘娘.

Moan, to, than°-chi°, 歎氣.

Moist, sak, 濕.

Monday, °li-pa°-ih, 禮拜一.

Money, *small*, °siau kauh-°ts, 小角子, °siau yang-dien, 小洋鈿.

Month, a, ih kuh nyoeh, 一個月, *the 1st day of a* —, tshoo ih, 初一, *the beginning of a* —, nyoeh-deu, 月頭, *the middle of a* —, nyoeh-pen°, 月半, *the end of a* —, nyoeh-ti, 月底, *last* —, zien-nyoeh, 前月, zien-kuh-nyoeh, 前個月, *next* —, °'au nyoeh, 下月, °'au kuh nyoeh, 下個月, *every* —, °me nyoeh, 每月, nyoeh-nyoeh, 月月.

Moon, ih kuh nyoeh, 一個月, nyoeh-liang, 月亮.

More, too, 多, too-°tien, 多點, *how much* —, °oo-hwaung, 何況, — *than*, 'veh-°ba, 勿罷.

Moreover, °ping-°tshia, 並且, r-°tshia, 而且, hwaung-°tshia, 況且.

Morning, °tsau-zung-deu, 早晨頭, °zaung-pen° nyih, 上半日.

Mosquito, a, ih kuh mung-°ts, 一個蚊子.

Most, °ting, 頂, tsoe, 最, juh, 極, da°-ke°, 大概.

Mostly, da°-ke°, 大概.

Mother, nyang, 娘, moo-tshing, 母親, *my* —, ka (kya)-°moo, 家母, *your* —, ling°-daung, 令堂.

Mound, *a grave* —, ih kuh vung-san, 一個墳山.

Mountain, a, ih zoo san, 一座山.

Mouth, a, ih kuh °kheu, 一個口, ih tsang °ts, 一張嘴.

Move, to, °doong, 動.

Mow, a, ih °m, 一畝.

Much, too, 多, too-hau°, 多化, *how* ——? °kyi-hau, 幾化? *how* —— *is it* (*price*)? sa° ka-°dien, 啥價錢? sa° ‘aung-dzing, 啥行情?

Muddy, wung, 混.

My, °ngoo-kuh, 我個.

N

Name, ming-z°, 名字, ming-deu, 名頭, *your honorable* ——, kwe° sing°, 貴姓, tsung sing, 尊姓, *my humble* ——, bi°-sing°, 敝姓, *please give your* —— (*style*), °tshing kyau° the°-foo, 請教台甫, *my* —— *is?* tshau-z°, 草字, *what is your* ——? ming-deu kyau°-sa°? 名頭叫啥?

Narrate, to, kau°-soo, 告訴.

Narrow, ‘ah, 狹.

Native, a, ih kuh °pung-di°-nyung, 一個本地人.

Near, °jung, 近, siang-°jung, 相近.

Nearly, tsho-’veh-too, 差勿多, mau, 毛, —— *three miles*, man san li, 毛三里.

Near-sighted, °jung-°z-°ngan, 近視眼.

Necessary, pih iau° yoong° kuh, 必要用個, —— *or important*, iau°-°kyung-kuh, 要緊個.

Necessity, iau°-°kyung, 要緊.

Needle, tsung, 針, *thread a* ——, tshen °yung sien°, 穿引線.

Neighbor, ling-°so, 鄰舍.

New, sing, 新, sing-fah, 新法.

New Year’s day, nyien tshoo ih, 年初一.

News, sing°-sih, 信息, sing-vung, 新聞.

Newspaper, ih tsang sing-vung-°ts, 一張新聞紙.

Next, (*juxtaposition*), kah-pih, 隔壁.

Night, ya°, 夜, *at* ——, ya°-deu, 夜頭, ya°-°li, 夜裏.

Nine, °kyeu, 九.

Nineteen, zeh-°kyeu, 十九.

Ninety, °kyeu-seh, 九十.

No, ’veh, 勿, m-sa°, 無啥 (*in answer to question*), —— *one*, m-sa°-nyung, 無啥人, —— *matter*, ’veh nge°-sa°, 勿礙啥, —— *matter who*, ’veh lung°

sa° nyung, 勿論啥人, —— *matter what*, 'veh lung° sa°, 勿論啥, dzoe bien° sa°, 隨便啥, 'veh kyui sa°, 勿拘啥.

Noise, °hyang-sung, 響聲, sung iung, 聲音.

Noon, nyih-tsoong, 日中.

North, pok, 北, pok-pien, 北邊.

North-east, toong-pok, 東北, —— *west*, si-pok, 西北.

Nose, a, ih kuh bih-deu, 一個鼻頭.

Not, 'veh, 勿, —— *any*, m-meh 無末, —— *yet*, 'veh zung, 勿曾, *still* —— *yet*, wan 'veh zung, 還勿曾, —— *only*, 'veh dan°-°z, 勿但是 'veh-dan°, 勿但, 'veh ba, 勿罷, —— *at all*, ih ngan 'veh, 一顏勿, —— *inclined*, 'veh-kau-hyung°, 勿高興, —— *very*, 'veh da°, 勿大.

Nourish, to, °yang, 養, sang-°yang, 生養.

Now, yien°-°dze, 現在.

Nun, a, ih kuh nyi-koo, 一個尼姑.

Nurse, to, su-°tsang, 輸長.

O

Object, an, ih kuh meh-z°, 一個物事.

Obtain, tuh-dzak, 得着.

Of, (*sign of possession*), kuh, 個, —— *course*, z°-zen, 自然.

Offend, to, tuh-dzoe°, 得罪.

Office, an, ih kan sia°-z°-kan, 一間寫字間.

Often, °hau-°kyi-we, 好幾囘.

Oil, yeu, 油.

Old (*not new*), °jeu, 舊, —— (*not young*), °lau, 老, —— (*antique*) °koo-z-kan, 古時間.

Omnipotent, voo-°soo-peh-nung, 無所不能.

Omnipresent, voo-°soo-peh-°dze, 無所不在.

Omniscient, voo-°soo-peh-ts, 無所不知.

On, la°, 拉, *or* leh-la, 垃拉, (*with* laung *after noun*), —— *the table*, la° de-ts laung°, 拉檯子上, —— *account of*, we°-ts, 爲之, —— *the contrary*, °tau, 倒, —— *the other hand*, °tau, 倒.

Once, ih we, 一囘.

One, ih, 一, *no* ——, m-sa° nyung, 無啥人, —— *cent*, ih fung, 一分, —— *time*, ih we, 一囘, ih thaung, 一 遭.

Only, pih koo°, 不過, dok°-z, 獨是, tsuh-tuh, 只得.

Open, to, khe, 開, *to* —— *school*, khe ‘auh, 開學, *to* —— (*as a book*), hyih-khe-le, 揭開來, *to cut* ——, tshih khe, 切開, tshih khe le, 切開來.

Oppose, to, °tsoo, 阻 °tsoo-taung, 阻擋, *unable to* ——, dih-’veh-dzu, 敵勿住.

Or, ok-tse, 或者.

Orange, ih tsah kyoeh-°ts, 一只橘子.

Originally, °pung-le, 本來.

Other, bih, 別.

Ought, iung-ke, 應該.

Ounce, an, ih °liang, 一兩, *an* —— *of silver*, ih °liang nyung-°ts, 一兩銀子.

Our, nyi°-kuh, 伲個, °ngoo-nyi°-kuh, 我伲個.

Ours, nyi°-kuh, 伲個, °ngoo-nyi°-kuh, 我伲個.

Out, nga°, 外, tsheh, 出, nga°-deu, 外頭, *to go* ——, tsheh-chi°, 出去, *to come* ——, tsheh-le, 出來.

Outside, nga-deu, 外頭.

Over, °zaung, 上.

Own, z°-ka-kuh, 自家個.

P

Package, a, ih bau, 一包.

Pagoda, a, ih zoo° thah, 一座塔.

Pain, thoong, 痛.

Painter, a, ih kuh tshih ziang°, 一個漆匠.

Painting, a, ih fok wo°, 一幅畫.

Pair, ih saung, 一雙, ih te°, 一對, ih foo°, 一副.

Pane, *a* —— *of glass*, ih khwe poo-li, 一塊玻璃.

Paper, °ts-deu, 紙頭, *a sheet of* ——, ih tsang °ts-deu, 一張紙頭.

Pardon, nyau-°so, 饒赦.

Part, *a portion*, ih vung, 一分, *for the most* ——, da°-liak, 大略.

Partition, pih, 壁, *to build a* ——, tshi° pih, 砌壁.

Pass, *to* —— *from the old year to the new*, koo°, 過.

Path, ih diau ka, 一條街, *to mend a* ——, tshi° ka, 砌街.

Pawn, to, taung°, 當, taung°-theh, 當脫.

Pay, to, foo, 付, *to* —— *attention*, yoong° sing, 用心, *to* —— *ceremonial visit*, pa° khak, 拜客, *to* —— *respects to*, pa° maung°, 拜望, maung 望, *to* —— *respects to a new year*, pa° nyien, 拜年.

Payment, *to receive* ——, seu, 收, *to receive* —— *for a lease*, seu-tsoo, 收租.

Peace, bing-oen, 平安.

Peach, a, ih tsak dau-°ts, 一只桃子.

Pear, a, ih tsak sang-li, 一只生梨.

Pen, a, ih °kwen pih, 一管筆.

Pencil, a, ih °kwen khan-pih, 一管鉛筆.

People, pak-sing, 百姓.

Perform, to, tsoo°, 做, *to* —— *a funeral ceremony*, tsoo°-koong-tuh, 做功德, nyan°-kyung, 念經.

Perhaps, khoong-pho°, 恐怕, °ok-tse°, 或者.

Permit, to, °hyui, 許.

Person, ih kuh nyung, 一個人.

Phrase, a, ih kyui° seh wo°, 一句說話.

Pheasant, a, ih tsak °ya-kyi, 一只野鷄.

Picul, a, ih tan°, 一担.

Piece, a, ih khwe°, 一塊, *a whole* —— (*dry goods*), ih phih, 一疋, *a ten cent* ——, ih kauh, 一角.

Pig, a, ih tsak ts-loo, 一只猪獹.

Pigeon, a, ih tsak keh-°ts, 一只鴿子.

Pile, *a heap*, ih te, 一對.

Piled, *one on top of another*, dzaung, 幢.

Piles, tsaung, 椿, tsaung-mok, 椿木.

Pity, e-lien, 哀憐, *within the range of* ——, i° tuh-koo°, 意得過, *beyond the range of* ——, i°-'veh-koo°, 意勿過.

Place, di°-faung, 地方, dzang-hau°, 場化, han-deu, �頭, *what* ——? sa° di°-faung, 啥地方?

Place, to, °pa, 擺, faung°, 放, *to be* ——*d in an embarrassing position*, nan-we-dzing, 難爲情.

Plane, a, ih tsak bau°, 一只刨.

Plaster, to, fung, 粉.

Plate, a, ih tsak bung-°ts, 一只盆子.

Play, to, beh-siang, 孛相.

Please, °tshing, 請.

Point, tsien deu, 尖頭, *at the* —— *of*, °kyi oo, 幾乎.

Point, to, °tien, 點, °ts-°tien, 指點.

Politeness, khak-chi°, 客氣.

Poor, joong, 窮, joong-°khoo, 窮苦.

Post office, sing-jok, 信局, su-sing°-°kwen, 書信館, yeu-tsung°-jok, 郵政局.

Pot, *a tea* ——, ih po dzo-'oo, 一把茶壺.

Powder, *gun*, °hoo-yak, 火藥.

Power, *authority*, joen-ping, 權柄, ——, *might*, lih-liang°, 力量, ——, *ability*, nung-koen, 能幹, ——, *strength*, chi°-lih, 氣力.

Pray, to, jeu, 求.

Prayer, °tau-kau°, 禱告.

Preach, to, kaung-su, 講書.

Precious, °pau-pe°, 寶貝.

Prepare, to, yui°-be°, 預備.

Present, to, soong°, 送.

Pretty, tshui°, 趣, °hau-khoen°, 好看.

Price, ka°-dien, 價錢 'aung-dzing, 行情, *what is the* ——? sa° ka°-dien, 啥價錢? sa° 'aung-dzing, 啥行情? *to settle the* ——,°kaung-ding°, 講定.

Priest, *a Buddhist*, ih kuh oo-zaung°, 一個和尙, *a Taoist* ——, ih kuh dau°-°z, 一個道士.

Proclamation, ih tsang kau°-°z, 一張告示, *to put forth a* ——, tsheh kau°-°z, 出告示.

Profit, iuh-tshu°, 益處, °hau-tshu°, 好處, *to make a* ——, dzan, 賺, ——*s in business*, dzan-deu, 賺頭.

Promise, iung°-°hyui, 應許.

Propriety, kwe-°kyui, 規矩.

Prosecute, to, —— *at law*, °tang kwen-s, 打官司.

Protect, °pau-‘oo°, 保護, °pau-yeu°, 保佑.

Provide, to, yui°-be°, 預備.

Pupil, ih kuh ‘auh-sang-°ts, 一個學生子.

Purposely, °yeu-i°, 有意, koo-i°, 故意.

Q

Quantity, *a small* ——, tien, 點.

Quarrel, to, siang-mo, 相罵.

Quarter, *a* —— *of an hour*, ih khuh, 一刻.

Queue, ih diau bien-°ts, 一條辮子.

Quickly, ‘au-sau, 豪燥, khwa°-khwa°, 快快.

Quiet, *to sit* ——, °zoo-ding°, 坐定.

Quilt, a, ih diau °bi-deu, 一條被頭.

R

Railroad, *a* —— *carriage*, ih boo °hoo-tsho, 一部火車.

Rain, °yui, 雨.

Rain, to, lauh-°yui, 落雨.

Rat, a, ih tsak °lau-°ts, 一只老鼠, °lau-dzoong, 老蟲.

Raw, sang, 生.

Read, to, dok, 讀.

Receipt, seu-phiau°, 收票, seu-diau, 收條.

Receive, to, zeu, 受, *to* —— *payment*, seu, *to* —— *payment for a lease*, seu-tsoo, 收租, *to* —— *a guest*, tsih-khak, 接客.

Recently, °jung-le, 近來.

Reckon, to, soen°, 算.

Recognize, nyung°-tuh, 認得.

Recreation, *to take* ——, beh-siang, 孛相.

Red, ‘oong, 紅.

Regret, to, au-lau, 懊佬, nan-we-dzing, 難爲情.

Reject, the°, 退, the°-theh, 退脫.

Relative (family), tshing-kyoen°, 親眷.

Relax, *to* —— *the mind*, san°-sing, 散心.

Rely, *to* —— *upon*, khau°, 靠, khau°-thauh, 靠托, thauh, 托.

Remember, to, kyi°, 記, kyi°-tuh, 記得.

Remove, *to* —— *a residence*, pen, 搬, pen-dzang, 搬場.

Rent, to, tsoo, 租, tsia°, 借.

Repair, to, sieu, 修, sieu-tsauh, 修作.

Repairs, sieu-°li, 修理.

Repent, to, hwe°-°ke, 悔改.

Reply, we-wo°, 回話, we-sing, 回信, we-deu, 回頭.

Rest, to, hyih, 歇, hyih-sih, 歇息.

Return, to, °tsen-le, 轉來, °tsen-chi°, 轉去, kyui-le, 歸來, kyui-chi°, 歸去.

Revile, to, mo°, 罵, *to* —— *one another*, siang-mo°, 相罵.

Rice, *hulled*, °mi, 米, *growing* ——, °dau, 稻, *cooked* ——, van°, 飯, *to buy* ——, dih °mi, 糴米.

Rich, *to become* ——, fah-dze, 發財.

Ricksha, a, ih boo toong-yang-tsho, 一部東洋車, ih boo waung-pau-tsho, 一部黃包車, *a* —— *coolie*, tsho foo, 車夫.

Ride, ji, 騎, *to* —— *a horse*, ji °mo, 騎馬, *to* —— *in a vehicle*, °zoo-tsho-°ts, 坐車子, *to* —— *in a sedan chair*, °zoo-jau°-°ts, 坐轎子.

Right (*direction*), yeu°, 右, —— *hand*, yeu° °seu, 右手, —— *side*, yeu° pien, 右邊.

Ripe, zok, 熟.

Rise, *to* —— *up*, lok-°chi-le, 踛起果, *to* —— *as the tide*, tsang°, 漲.

River, a, ih diau kaung, 一條江.

Road, a, ih diau loo°, 一條路.

Robber, a, ih kuh °jang-°dau, 一個強盜.

Roll, to, °kwung, 滾, °kwung-'au°-chi°, 滾下去.

Room, a, ih kan, 一間, *guest* ——, khak-vaung-kan, 客房間, *bed* ——, vaung-kan, 房間, *shroff's* ——, tsang°-vaung-kan, 帳房間, *dining* ——, chuh-van°-kan, 吃飯間.

Root, kung, 根.

Rope, a, ih diau zung, 一條繩.

Rough, mau, 毛.

Round, yoen, 圓.

Row, *classifier of things*, da°, 埭, *a* —— *of trees*, ih da° zu, 一埭樹.

Rumours, yau-yien, 謡言, *to start a* ——, zau-yau-yien, 造謠言.

Run, *to* ——, bau, 跑, *to* —— (*as water*), lieu, 流, *to* —— *about*, bau-le-bau-chi, 跑來 跑去.

Russia, Ngoo-kok, 俄國.

Russian, ngoo-kok-nyung, 俄國人.

S

Safe, °‘wung-taung, 穩當.

Sail, a, ih sen° boong, 一扇蓬.

Sail, to, ‘ang zen, 行船, khe zen, 開船.

Sake, *for the* —— *of*, we°, 爲, we°-ts, 爲之.

Salary, sok-sieu, 束修, sing-foong, 薪俸, sing-°soe, 薪水.

Salt (noun) yien, 鹽, (adj.), ‘an, 鹹.

Same, ih yang°, 一樣, siang-doong, 相同.

Satin, doen°-°ts, 緞子.

Saturday, °li-pa°-lok, 禮拜六.

Saucer, a, ih tsak dzo bung-°ts, 一只茶盆子.

Save, to, kyeu°, 救, *to* —— *life*, kyeu°-ming°, 救命, *to* —— *time*, °sang-koong-foo, 省功夫, *to* —— *money*, °sang, 省, °sang doong-dien, 省銅錢, tsoo° nyung-ka, 做人家.

Saw, a, ih °po ke°-°ts, 一把鋸子, ka°, 解, zih, 截.

Say, to, wo°, 話, —— *to him*, te° yi wo°, 對伊話, kau° soo° yi, 告訴伊, *nothing to* ——, m-sa° wo°-deu, 無啥話頭.

Scald, to, thaung°, 烫.

Scales, *balance*, thien-bing, 天平.

Scholar, ih kuh ‘auh-sang-°ts, 一個學生子, *a learned man*, dok-su-nyung, 讀書人.

School, a, ih kuh ‘auh-daung, 一個學堂, *to open* ——, khe-‘auh, 開學, *to* *dismiss* ——, faung-‘auh, 放學.

Scissors, *a pair of*, ih po tsien-tau, 一把剪子.

Scorch, to, hyuin, 燻, tsiau, 焦.

Screen, a, ih sen° bing-foong, 一扇屏風.

Sea, °he, 海.

Seal, *to* —— *a letter*, foong, 封.

Season, a, kyi°, 季, *the four* ——*s*, s°-kyi°, 四季.

Seat, a, zoo°-we°, 坐位, *please take a* ——, °tshing °zoo, 請坐.

Second, the, di° nyi°, 第二.

Secretly, ‘en°-‘en-°li, 暗暗裏, theu-ben°-ts, 偷伴之.

Secure, °‘wung-taung°, 穩當, bing-oen, 平安.

Sedan, *a* —— *chair*, ih °ting jau°-°ts, 一頂轎子, *a coolie*, jau°-pan, 轎班, jau°-foo, 轎夫.

See, to, khoen, 看, khoen-kyien°, 看見.

Seek, to, zing, 尋.

Seize, to, tsauh, 捉, nau, 拿.

Self, z°-ka, 自家.

Sell, to, ma°, 賣, ma°-theh, 賣脫.

Send, to, soong, 送, *to* —— *a person*, tsha, 差, *to* —— *a letter*, kyi°, 寄.

Sentence, a, ih kyui° seh-wo°, 一句說話.

Separate, to, fung, 分, fung-khe, 分開, li-khe, 離開, fung-bih, 分別.

Servant, a, ih kuh yoong°-nyung, 一個用人.

Settle, *to* —— *the price*, °kaung-ding°, 講定.

Seven, tshih, 七.

Seventy, tshih-seh, 七十.

Sew, to, ling, 紉.

Shall, iau°, 要, pih-iau°, 必要.

Shallow, °tshien, 淺.

Shameful, than-°tshoong, 攤寵.

Shanghai, °Zaung-°he, 上海.

Sharp, khwa°, 快.

Sharpen, to, moo, 磨.

She, yi, 伊.

Sheep, yang, 羊.

Sheet, a, ih diau °bi-tan, 一條被單, *a —— of paper*, ih tsang °ts-deu, 一張紙頭.

Ship, zen, 船.

Shirting, *a piece of*, ih phih yang-poo°, 一疋洋布.

Shoes, *a pair of*, ih saung ‘a-°ts, 一雙鞋子.

Shoot, *to —— with a gun*, faung°, 放, *to —— birds*, °tang tiau, 打鳥.

Shop, a, ih ban tien°, 一爿店, *a tea ——*, ih ban dzo-kwen°, 一爿茶館.

Shore, ngoen°, 岸, *to go on ——*, °zaung ngoen, 上岸.

Short, °toen, 短, *a —— time*, ih hyih koong-foo, 一歇功夫.

Should, khau-°i, 可以, iung-ke, 應該.

Shroff, a, seu yang-dien kuh, 收洋鈿個, *a ——'s room*, ih kan tsang°-vaung-kan, 一間帳房間.

Shut, to, kwan, 關.

Sick, °yeu bing°, 有病.

Side, pien, 邊, pien-deu, 邊頭, baung-pien, 旁邊, *right ——*, yeu° pien, 右邊, *left ——*, tsi°-pien, 左邊.

Sign, a, kyi°-‘au°, 記號, ‘au°, 號.

Silk, s, 絲, dzeu, 綢.

Silver, nyung-°ts, 銀子.

Sin, °dzoe, 罪, °dzoe-nyih, 罪孽.

Since, kyi-zen, 既然, °i-°‘eu, 以後, *—— it is so*, kyi-zeu zeh-ke°, 既然實蓋, *—— then*, di°-kuh °i-°‘eu, 第個以後.

Single, tan, 單, dok, 獨.

Sink, to, dzung-°‘au-chi°, 沉下去.

Sister, *older*, ah-°tsi, 阿姊, *younger ——*, °tsi-me°, 姊妹, me°-me°, 妹妹.

Sit, to, °zoo, 坐, *to —— down*, °zoo °zoo, 坐坐, *to —— quiet*, °zoo-ding, 坐定.

Six, lok, 六.

Sixty, lok-seh, 六十.

Size, doo°-°siau, 大小.

Skin, bi, 皮.

Sky, thien, 天.

Slack, *water*, bing-°s, 平水.

Slander, to, wo°-°liau, 話獠, hwe°-°paung, 毀謗, wo°-°wa, 話壞.

Sleep, to, khwung°, 睏.

Slippery, wah, 滑.

Slow, man°, 慢, —*ly*, man°-man°-nung, 慢慢能, *to walk* —, man°-man°-nung-°tseu, 慢慢能走.

Small, °siau, 小, *very* —, ih ngan-ngan doo°, 一顏顏大, *a* — *quantity of*, tien, 點, °yeu-°yien, 有限, — *money*, °siau kauh-°ts, 小角子, °siau yang-dien, 小洋鈿.

Smash, to, se°, 碎, °tang-se°, 打碎, khau-se°, 敲碎.

Smoke, ien, 烟, *to* — *meat*, hyuin, 燻, *to* — *tobacco*, chuh-ien, 吃烟.

Smooth, kwaung, 光.

Snake, ih diau-zo, 一條蛇.

Snow, sih, 雪, lauh sih, 落雪.

So, zeh-ke, 實蓋, — *that*, °i-ts°, 以至, *about* —, tsho-'veh-too, 差勿多.

Soap, bi-zau°, 皮皂.

Socks, *a pair of*, ih saung mah, 一雙襪.

Soft, °nyoen, 軟.

Soldier, a, ih kuh ping-ting, 一個兵丁.

Some, °yeu kuh, 有個, °kyi-kuh, 幾個.

Somebody, °yeu nyung, 有人.

Somehow, dzoe-bien° na°-nung, 隨便那能.

Sometimes, dzang-z, 常時, °yeu kuh z-°eu, 有個時候.

Son, ih kuh nyi-°ts, 一個兒子, ih kuh 'eu-°ts, 一個兒子, *your* —, ling°-laung, 令郎, *my* —, siau-noen, 小囝.

Soochow, Soo-tseu, 蘇州.

Soon, °tsau, 早, 'veh too ih-hyih, 勿多一歇.

Sorrow, ieu-dzeu, 憂愁.

Sort, ih yang, 一樣, ih le, 一類.

Sound, sung-iung, 聲音.

Soup, thaung, 湯.

South, nen, 南, —— *east*, toong-nen, 東南, —— *west*, si-nen, 西南.

Southern, nen-pien, 南邊.

Sparrow, ih tsak moo-tshiak, 一只麻雀, ih tsak moo-tshiang, 一只麻將.

Speak, to, wo°, 話, bak-wo°, 白話.

Spectacles, *a pair of* ——, ih foo° °ngan-kyung°, 一副眼鏡.

Split, to, phih, 劈.

Spoil, to, wa°, 壞, wa°-theh, 壞脫.

Spoon, ih °po tshau, 一把鈔.

Spring, tshung, 春, tshung-kyi°, 春季.

Square, faung, 方.

Squirrel, ih tsak soong-su° (tshu), 一只松鼠.

Stairs, voo-thi, 扶梯.

Stamp (postage), nyung-deu, 人頭, or yeu-phiau, 郵票.

Stand, to, lih, 立, —— *still*, lih-ding°, 立定, —— *up*, lih-chi-le, 立起來.

Star, ih kuh sing, 一個星.

Start, *to commence*, khe° °seu, 開手, *to* —— *on a journey*, °doong-sung, 動身, *to* —— *a boat*, khe° zen, 開船, *to* —— *a rumour*, zau yau-yien, 造謠言, *to* —— *a fire*, sang-°hoo, 生火.

Stay, to, tung-la°, 等拉, dzu, 住, *to* —— *with a person*, be, 陪.

Steal, to, theu, 偷.

Steam, *a* —— *boat*, ih tsak °hoo-lung-zen, 一只火輪船.

Step, a, ih boo°, 一步.

Stick, a, ih kung °baung, 一根棒.

Still, *yet*, wan, 還, dzung-jeu°, 仍舊, —— *more*, kung°-°ka, 更加, yoeh-°ka, 越加, —— (*not yet*), wan-'veh-zun, 還勿曾.

Sting, to, ting, 叮.

Stitch, to, ling 紉, *to take a* ——, ling-ih-tsung, 紉一針.

Stockings, *a pair of* ——, ih saung mah, 一雙襪.

Stone, a, ih khwe° zak-deu, 一塊石頭, *a* —— *mason*, ih kuh zak-ziang°, 一個石匠.

Stool, a, ih tsak ngeh-°ts, 一只杌子.

Stop, to, ding, 停, —— *a minute*, ding-ih-ding, 停一停.

Story, *classifier for stories of a house*, dzung, 層.

Stove, a, ih tsak °hoo-loo, 一只火爐, *a cooking* —— (*foreign*), ih tsak thih-tsau, 一只鐵竈, *a cooking* —— (*Chinese*), ih tsak tsau-deu, 一只竈頭.

Street, ih diau ka, 一條街.

Strike, to, °tang, 打, khau, 敲, *to* —— *against*, bang°-dzak, 碰着, *to* —— *a match*, wak, 劃, *to injure by* ——*ing*, °tang-wa°, 打壞.

String, to (*as cash*), tshen, 穿.

Study, a, ih kan su-vaung, 一間書房, dok, 讀, dok su, 讀書.

Such, zek-ke, 實蓋.

Suddenly, hweh-zen, 忽然.

Suffer, to, °zeu-°khoo, 受苦, °zeu-nan°, 受難, *to* —— *an injury*, °zeu-'e°, 受害, *to* —— *a defeat*, °tang-su, 打輸, °tang-ba°-tsang°, 打敗仗, °tang-ba° 打敗.

Sufficient, keu°-z°, 殼事, keu°-z°-tse, 殼事哉, °yeu-tse, 有哉.

Sugar, daung, 糖.

Summer, 'au°, 夏, 'au°-kyi, 夏季.

Sun, nyih-deu, 日頭.

Sunday, °li-pa°-nyih, 禮拜日.

Supper, ya°-van°, 夜飯.

Suppose, °khoong-pho, 恐怕.

Suppose, to, or *to think*, tau-nyung-ts, 倒認之.

Surprised, *to be*, hyi-ji, 希奇.

Swallow, a, ih tsak ien°-°ts, 一只燕子.

Sweet, dien, 甜.

Sword, a, ih °po tau, 一把刀.

T

Table, a, ih tsak de-°ts, 一只檯子, *a dining* ——, chuh-van° de-°ts, 吃飯檯子, *a* —— *boy*, ih kuh si°-tse°, 一個西崽.

Tablet, *a Chinese ink* ——, ih kuh nyien-°ts, 一個硯池, ih kuh nyien-de, 一個硯台.

Tailor, ih kuh ze-voong, 一個裁縫.

Take, to, tan, 担, nau, 拿, *to* —— (*by force*), tshiang, 搶, tshiang-doeh, 搶奪, *to* —— *away*, tan-chi, 担去, nau-chi, 拿去, *to* —— *off* (*remove*), nau-theh, 拿脫, *to* —— *off* (*clothes*), thoeh, 脫, thoeh-thoeh, 脫脫, *to* —— *off* (*hat*), dzu, 除, *to* —— *hold of*, nyah, 捏, *to* —— *with one*, ta°-chi, 帶去, *to* —— *care*, °taung-sing, 當心, °siau-sing, 小心, *to* —— *great care*, too° °taung-sing, 多當心, to —— a wife, °thau nyang-°ts, 討娘子.

Talk, to, wo°, 話, bak-wo°, 白話, *to* —— *to*, te° (yi) wo°, 對(伊)話.

Tall, dzang, 長.

Taoist, *a* —— *priest*, dau°-°z, 道士, *a* —— *idol or god*, ih tsung zung-dau, 一尊神道.

Tea, dzo, 茶, *a box of* ——, ih siang dzo-yih, 一箱茶葉, *a* —— *shop*, ih ban dzo-kwen, 一爿茶館, ih po° dzo-°oo, 一把茶壺.

Teach, to, kau°, 教, *a* ——*er*, ih kuh sien-sang, 一個先生.

Tell, to, kau°-soo°, 告訴.

Temperature, °lang-nyih, 冷熱.

Temple, ih zoo° miau, 一座廟.

Ten, zeh, 十, *a* —— *cent piece*, ih kauh, 一角.

Texture, tshoo-si°, 粗細.

Than, °pi, 比, *more* ——, ’veh °ba, 勿罷.

Thank, to, zia, 謝.

That, i-kuh, 伊個.

Thee, noong°, 儂.

Their, *theirs*, yi-la°-kuh, 伊拉個.

Them, yi-la°, 伊拉.

Then, nan-meh, 難末.

There, leh-la, 垃拉, i-deu, 伊頭, i-khwe°, 伊塊, —— *is*, yeu, 有.

Therefore, °soo-i, 所以, keh-lau, 蓋佬.

These, di-kuh, 第個.

They, yi-la°, 伊拉.

Thick, (*not thin*), °‘eu, 厚.

Thickness, °‘eu-bok, 厚薄.

Thief, ih kuh zuh, 一個賊.

Thin, bok, 薄, —— (*in reference to person*) seu, 瘦.

Thine, noong°-kuh, 儂個.

Thing (*concrete*), ih kuh meh-z°, 一個物事, —— (*an affair*), z°-°thi, 事體, ——*s of every sort*, yaug°-yang°, 樣樣.

Think, to, °siang, 想.

Thirty, san-seh, 三十.

This, di°-kuh, 第個.

Those, i-kuh, 伊個.

Thou, noong°, 儂.

Though, soe-zen, 雖然.

Thought, i°-s°, 意思.

Thousand, ih tshien, 一千.

Thread, a, sien, 線, *to* —— *a needle*, tshen °yung-sien°, 穿引線.

Three, san, 三.

Through, koo, 過.

Throw, to, tieu, 丟.

Thursday, °li-pa°-s°, 禮拜四.

Thus, zeh-ke°, 實蓋, zeh-ke°-nung, 實蓋能.

Thy, noong°-kuh, 儂個.

Tide, dzau, 潮, dzau-°s, 潮水, ——*flowing in*, tsang°-°s, 漲水, ——*flowing out*, lauh-°s, 落水.

Tie, to, vok, 縛, *to* —— (*a small parcel*), tsah, 紮, *to* —— *up*, paung, 綁, to ——*firmly*, vok lau, 縛牢, vok lau dzu°, 縛牢住.

Tiger, ih tsak °lau-°hoo, 一只老虎.

Timber, *a pile of* ——, ih te mok-deu, 一堆木頭.

Time, z-'eu°, 時候, zung-kwaung, 晨光, koong-foo, 功夫, *what —?*, °kyi °tien-tsoong, 幾點鐘, *a long* ——, dzang-°yoen, 長遠, dzang-°yoen-tse, 長遠哉, ta-z-tse, 多時哉.

Tin, sih, 錫.

Tired, sa-doo, 弛瘏.

To, tau°, 到, *say* —— *him*, te yi wo°, 對伊話, *give* (*it*) —— *me*, peh ngoo, 撥我, —— *and fro*, le-le chi°-chi°, 來來去去, —— *no purpose*, bak-bak-li, 白白裏.

Tobacco, ien, 烟.

To-day, kyung-tsau, 今朝.

Toe, a, ih tsak kyak-tsih-deu, 一只脚指頭.

Together, da ka, 大家, ih dau, 一淘, ih doong, 一同.

To-morrow, ming-tsau, 明朝.

Tongue, zeh-deu, 舌頭.

To-night, kyung-ya°, 今夜.

Too, thuh, 忒.

Tools, *a set of*, ih foo ka°-sang, 一副傢生.

Touch, to, mok, 摸.

Towards, tau°, 到.

Towel, ih diau °seu-kyung, 一條手巾.

Town, dzung, 城.

Travel, to, ‘ang, 行.

Treat, °de, 待, *to* —— *rudely*, de°-man°, 待慢.

Tree, a, ih khoo zu°, 一棵樹.

Tricky, diau°-bi, 調皮.

Trousers, khoo°-°ts, 褲子.

True, tsung, 眞,°lau-zeh, 老實.

Truly, zeh-dze, 實在.

Trunk, a, ih tsak siang-°ts, 一只箱子.

Trust, to, khau°, 靠, thauh, 託, *worthy to be* ——*ed*, khau°-tuh-dzu, 靠得住, *unworthy to be* ——*ed*, khau°-’veh-dzu, 靠勿住.

Try, to, s°-s°-khoen, 試試看.

Tub, doong, 桶.

Tubular, *classifier for* —— *things*, kwen, 管.

Tuesday, °li-pa°-nyi°, 禮拜二.

Turn, to, tsen, 轉, zien-°tsen-le, 旋轉來, *to* —— *over, fan*, 翻, fan °tsen-le, 翻轉來, *to* —— *around*, zien, 旋, zien °tsen le, 旋轉來.

Twelve, zeh-nyi°, 十二.

Twenty, nyan°, 廿.

Twice, °liang-we, 兩回, °liang-thaung, 兩 趟.

Two, nyi°, 二 °liang, 兩.

U

Ugly, pho°, 怕, pho°-le, 怕來.

Umbrella, an, ih po° san°, 一把傘.

Unable, ’veh nung-keu, 勿能殼.

Under, ti-°‘au, 底下.

Understand, to, °toong, 懂, ming-bak, 明白, °hyau-tuh, 曉得.

Universal, °phoo-thien-°‘au, 普天下, ‘eh-thien-°‘au, 合天下.

Unmarried, an —— woman, °siau-tsia, 小姐.

Unripe, sang, 生.

Unroll, to, than-khe-le, 攤開來.

Unstable, °doong °lau °doong, 動佬動.

Until, dzuh-tau°, 直到, °tung-tau°, 等到.

Up, °zaung, 上.

Upon, la° laung°, 拉上.

Upset, °tang-fan, 打翻.

Us, °ngoo-nyi°, 我伲, nyi°, 伲.

Use, to, yoong°, 用.

Useful, °yeu yoong°-deu, 有用頭.

Useless, bak-bak-li, 白白裏.

V

Vain, *in* ——, bak-bak-li, 白白裏.

Value, (*price*), ka°-dien, 價錢.

Variegated (*colours*), °ng-ngan-lok-suh, 五顏六色.

Vegetables, tshe°, 菜, —— (*served on table*), °siau-tshe°, 小菜.

Vegetation (*general*), hwo-°tshau-zu°-mok, 花草樹木.

Venerable, °lau, 老.

Very, ’man, 蠻, tsoe, 最, °ting, 頂.

Victory, *to gain a* ——, °tang-sung°-tsang, 打勝仗, °tang-yung, 打贏.

Visit, to, maung°, 望, pa° maung°, 拜望, *to return a* ——, we pa°, 回拜, wan pa°, 還拜, *to pay ceremonial* ——, pa° khak, 拜客.

Visitor, a, ih we khak-nyung, 一位客人.

W

Wages, koong-dien, 工錢.

Wait, to, °tung, 等, —— *a minute*, °tung-ih-°tung, 等一等, hyih-ih-liyih, 歇一歇, °tung-ih-hyih, 等一歇.

Walk, to, °tseu, 走, °tseu-loo°, 走路, *to* —— *slowly*, man°-man°-ts-tseu°, 慢慢之走.

Wall, ziang, 墻, *build a* ——, tshi°, 砌, tshi° ziang, 砌墻.

Want, to, iau°, 要.

Warm, °noen-nyih, 暖熱.

Wash, to, zing, 淨, *to* —— *the face*, kha mien°, 揩面.

Washbasin, *or bowl, a*, ih tsak mien°-bung, 一只面盆.

Washerman, zing°-i-zaung-kuh, 淨衣裳 個, da°-i-zaung-kuh, 汏衣裳個.

Washstand, ih tsak kha-mien° de-°ts, 一只揩而檯子.

Waste, to, saung, 喪, fi, 費, fi-theh, 費脫.

Watch, a, ih tsak piau, 一只錶.

Water, °s, 水, *a bucket of* ——, ih doong °s, 一桶水, *boiling* ——, khe °s, 開水, *hot* ——, nyih °s, 熱水, *cold* ——, °lang °s, 冷水, *a* —— *buffalo*, ih tsak °s-nyeu, 一只水牛.

Way, loo, 路.

We, °ngoo-nyi°, 我伲, nyi°, 伲.

Wear, to, tsak, 着, *to* —— *a hat*, ta° mau-°ts, 戴帽子.

Weasel, ih tsak waung-laung, 一只黃狼.

Wednesday, °li-pa°-san, 禮拜三.

Week, a, ih °li-pa°, 一禮拜.

Weigh, to, tshung, 稱.

Weight, chung-dzoong, 輕重.

Welcome, to, (*guest*), nyung-tsih, 迎接.

Well a, ih °kheu °tsing, 一口井, hau, 好.

West, the, si, 西, si-pien, 西邊.

Wet, sak, 濕.

What, sa°, 啥, sa°-kuh, 啥個, na°-nung, 那能, —— *is the matter?* sa°-z°-°thi, 啥事體? —— *is the price?* sa° ka°-dien, 啥價錢? sa° 'aung-dzing, 啥行情? —— *is your honorable name?* tsung-sing° da°-ming, 尊姓大

名？—— *is your honorable age?* kwe°-kang too-°sau, 貴庚多少？°kyi-hau° kwe°-kang, 幾化貴庚？

Whatever, *whatsoever*, 'veh lung° sa°, 勿論啥, dzoe-bien° sa°, 随便啥, 'veh kyui-sa°, 勿拘啥, —— *time you please*, dzoe bien° kyi-z, 隨便幾時.

Wheat, mak, 麥.

Wheelbarrow, a, ih boo tsho-°ts, 一部車子, °siau-tsho, 小車.

When, °kyi-z, 幾時, sa° z-'eu°, 啥時候.

Whence, 'a-li, 那裏, sa°-di°-faung, 啥地方, sa° dzang-hau°, 啥場化, sa° °'oo-daung°, 啥戶蕩.

Which, °'a-li, 那裏, °soo, 所.

Whichever, dzoe-bien°, 隨便.

White, bak, 白.

Who, sa° nyung? 啥人, (*relative*), °soo, 所.

Whole, *the* —— *of a thing*, ih tshih, 一切.

Whosoever, van-i°, 凡係.

Why, we°-sa, 爲啥, we°-sa°-°lau, 爲啥佬.

Wicked, auh, 惡.

Wide, khweh, 闊.

Wife, *to marry a* ——, °thau-nyang-°ts, 討娘子, *a husband and* ——, ih te° foo-tshi, 一對夫妻.

Will, the, °tsu-°i, 主意, ——, *auxiliary*, iau°, 要, tsiang-iau°, 將要.

Willing, *to be*, °khung, 肯.

Wind, foong, 風.

Window, a, ih sen° tshaung, 一扇窗.

Wine, °tsieu, 酒, *a* —— *shop*, ih ban °tsieu-°tien, 一爿酒店.

Winter, toong, 冬.

Wipe, to, kha, 揩.

Wise, tshoong-ming, 聰明.

Wish, to, iau°, 要.

With, tah, 搭, doong, 同, ih dau, 一淘.

Wolf, ih tsak za-laung, 一只豺狼.

Woman, °nyui-nyung, 女人, *unmarried* ——, °siau-tsia, 小姐.

Wonder, to, hyi-ji, 希奇.

Wood, mok-deu, 木頭.

Word, seh-wo°, 說話, wo°-deu, 話頭.

Work, koong-foo, 功夫, sang-weh, 生活, *to commence* ——, °doong-°seu, 動手, khe-kong, 開工, tsoo sang-weh, 做生活.

Worship, to, pa°, 拜.

Wound, to, °tang-saung, 打傷, *to be* ——*ed*, °zeu-saung, 受傷.

Write, to, °sia, 寫.

Y

Ye, na°, 倻.

Year, a, ih nyien, 一年, *half a* ——, pen-nyien, 半年, *this* ——, kyung-nyien, 今年, *last* ——, °jeu nyien, 舊年, *next* ——, khe-nyien, 開年, ming-nyien, 明年, le-nyien, 來年, *New* ——, sing-nyien, 新年, *New* ——*'s day*, nyien tshoo ih, 年初一, *every* ——, nyien-nyien, 年年, °'me-nyien, 每年, *the end of the* ——, nyien-ya°, 年夜, nyien-°ti, 年底, *at the beginning of the* ——, nyieu deu laung, 年頭上, *to pass from the old* —— *to the new*, koo-nyien, 過年.

Yellow, waung, 黃.

Yes, °z-kuh, 是個.

Yesterday, zau° nyih, 昨日, *day before* ——, koo°-nyih-°ts, 過日子, zien-nyih-°ts, 前日子, i-nyih-°ts, 伊日子.

Yet, dzung-jeu, 仍舊, *not* ——, 'veh zung, 勿曾, *still not* ——, wan 'veh zung 還勿曾.

You, noong°, 儂, (pl.), na°, 倻.

Your, *yours*, noong-kuh, 儂個, (pl.), na°-kuh, 倻個.

Printed by Libri Plureos GmbH in Hamburg,
Germany